The Morganza, 1967

The Morganza, 1967
Life in a Legendary Reform School

WITHDRAWN

David E. Stuart

UNIVERSITY OF NEW MEXICO PRESS | ALBUQUERQUE

13   12   11   10   09   1   2   3   4   5

LIBRARY OF CONGRESS CATALOGING-IN-PUBLICATION DATA

Stuart, David E.

  The Morganza, 1967 : life in a legendary reform school / David E. Stuart.

    p. cm.

  ISBN 978-0-8263-4641-4 (pbk. : alk. paper)

1. Reformatories—Pennsylvania—Canonsburg.

2. Youth workers—Pennsylvania—Canonsburg.

I. Title.

HV9105.P22M677 2009

365'.42—dc22

                              2009012648

All photos © Cynthia M. Stuart

Book design and type composition by Melissa Tandysh

Composed in 11.5/14.25 Dante MT Std   •   Display type is 321impact

]|[

For the Stuart girls—

descendants of the South Philadelphia half of my family

Mary Stuart Spangler

(and her daughter Erica)

Madge Stuart Pelz

Janet Stuart Lake

(deceased, and survived by her daughters Elizabeth and Rebecca)

Chrissa Stuart Osborn

]|[

Contents

ACKNOWLEDGMENTS / AUTHOR'S NOTE
xi

CHAPTER 1.
We Have a Job Opening . . .
1

CHAPTER 2.
Students *Will* Be Rehabilitated
3

CHAPTER 3.
Let's Break Him In
7

CHAPTER 4.
The Tower
16

CHAPTER 5.
Rabbit
23

CHAPTER 6.
A Day Off
30

CHAPTER 7.
Where's the Graveyard?
34

CHAPTER 8.

I'm *Black*!

43

CHAPTER 9.

Not Behind the White Fence

50

CHAPTER 10.

Mr. Davenport, We Have to Talk

57

CHAPTER 11.

Sorry About the Fork Thing

64

CHAPTER 12.

Nefertiti

71

CHAPTER 13.

What We Have Here Is a Failure to Communicate

76

CHAPTER 14.

Jelly Baby

87

CHAPTER 15.

We Got Duppies Up on 2

93

CHAPTER 16.

The Price of Identity

101

CHAPTER 17.

Daddy

109

CHAPTER 18.

Billy, I Have Something to Tell You . . .

118

CHAPTER 19.

Dammit! It's Rabbit Again . . .

131

CHAPTER 20.

Cat Missing

139

CHAPTER 21.

Happy Halloween, 1967

149

CHAPTER 22.

Who? Who?

158

CHAPTER 23.

Her Majesty's Dance

171

CHAPTER 24.

I'll Take Extra Shifts

179

CHAPTER 25.

The Changing of the Guard

190

CHAPTER 26.

Punish Me! *Punish* Me!

196

CHAPTER 27.

Sanna's White . . . It Gonna Open for You

202

CHAPTER 28.

We Lost *Four*?

212

CHAPTER 29.

It's an Inside Joke

217

EPILOGUE

221

Acknowledgments/Author's Note

My thanks to Elise McHugh, Christie Chisholm, Anne Egger, and Dawn Davis of Albuquerque, who read and made suggestions to improve this memoir.

I write my books at the Flying Star Café on Central Avenue / Route 66, in Albuquerque. It's a great place, and the staff there is very writer friendly. My special thanks to counter workers Mazen, Jess, Jadira, Mikey, Paul, Jaime, Matt, Jonathan, Bernadette, and Dave; bus staff Efraín, Carlos, and Nilka; and managers Leo, Jesse, and Roger.

In this book, as in *The Guaymas Chronicles* I wrote a few years ago, I have novelized parts of this narrative to protect the identities of the youths who were once "students," as well as many of the staff members portrayed. The liberties taken allow me to both simplify events at the Morganza, tell a crisper story, and reduce the confusion created by the different versions of narratives that seemed to dominate. There was always an "official" version, as well as student and staff versions. Here, I have simply written *my* version, with all its limitations of perspective.

Still, I hope the personal stories found herein will in some small way stir reflection on lives—heroes, villains, victims—seldom written about.

David Stuart
Flying Star Café
Albuquerque
March 2, 2008

chapter 1

We Have a Job Opening . . .

"**G**oddammit! Where are you taking me?" squeaked the balding man from his wheelchair.

"Shut the fuck up—you ain't people. You mutha-fuckin' Honkey. We tired of your 'there you go actin' like a nigger again' uppity cracker-ass voice."

The cripple turned to Crazy Kamensky—the only white guy in the group of reform-school students who surrounded him, and begged, his voice ending in a tortured shriek, "I've never called anyone names. *Never!*"

Sinbad smiled and nodded at Sugarbear, who slapped the man hard. His skinny neck twisted. The cripple attempted to protect his face with an upstretched arm. "Then Sugarbear laughed and smacked him again, hard upside his head," as the boy known as Rabbit later explained. "Kamensky helped push him into the billiard room, crying like a baby. Then they busted the window and threw him out."

"*Out?*"

"Yeah . . . out the window, wheelchair and all." Rabbit's ordinarily unresponsive eyes glistened as he continued, "He bounced . . . his head hit first. Made the same kind of crack that a roach does when you stomp on it just right." Rabbit batted his long eyelashes and furtively caressed his crotch. The hairs on the back of my neck stood up as if ready to beat a hasty retreat.

I left Rabbit to his creepy crotch polishing, caught Palco in the downstairs kitchen, and asked about the incident. He scoffed. "I had the day off, Mr. College Boy. If I'd been here it wouldnta' happened. There are two different stories, one written up by those liberal pussies in charge up there on the Hill. In the official report it was an accident, but Charlie, the janitor, told me different. His version is the one I buy. Worse yet, the two doofuses who took the fall for it weren't even the ringleaders."

Palco rattled the huge key ring he carried on his belt as he spoke. "Those maggots threw Trezise out the third story onto the bricks. I didn't like the little crip any more than the boys did—they never should have hired him—but it pissed me off anyway. They turned the chair upside down. He went down headfirst. *Splat!*" Palco spit a fetid stream of tobacco juice onto the steaming tray of fresh meatloaf cooling next to us marked "6–2," for "Cottage 6, Floor 2," my assigned cottage and floor, and home of the boys who'd either killed, or not killed, Trezise.

"Jesus, Palco—the kids have got to eat that!" I winced.

"Yep. That's the idea, College Boy," he grinned and aimed another stream of tobacco at the meatloaf. It left a dark stain on the crust of the meat.

Chapter 2

Students Will Be Rehabilitated

I first reported for "temporary status" work on July 1, 1967, at 2:30 p.m. My father had died nine days earlier. He suffered an infarct on June 19, his forty-seventh birthday, and perished three days later.

A widow at forty-five, my mother was devastated. She had always hoped—even convinced herself—that the old man would, before he died, settle down, fall in love with her a second time, and quit working eighty-hour weeks. Her faith was both monumental and, it now seemed, magical.

She got precisely one-third of her dream. Once dead, he worked far fewer hours. It would take her years to deal with the other two thirds. His tombstone, high on a breezy West Virginia hill, would read, when later erected, "Faith is the substance of things hoped for . . . and the proof of things not seen." This seemed more an epitaph for her than for my father, who was a scientist.

I never knew him well enough to know what he actually hoped for, and neither his nor my mother's faith had so far delivered proof of anything of substance. But other folks, especially those who worked for him, found him delightful, as they were irritatingly fond of commenting. They probably imagined he was the same person with me. It was an ordinary enough assumption; catch was, behind closed doors the old man just wasn't comfortable.

He was turbulent, tormented, and had just lost a desperate long-term campaign to hide his paranoid tendencies, deep insecurities, and raw, sweat-soaked fear. He would self-medicate with cigarettes, old-fashioned glasses filled with Maker's Mark and industrial-strength painkillers.

I reckon he was one of the most frightened sons of bitches I ever knew. I feel deeply sorry for him now—living in his skin must have been painful and exhausting—but the day I stepped into the Morganza to report for work, I was twenty-two and still angry with him. I knew that I should have been mourning him, but I was too surprised by his death to react to anything beyond the stunning realization that he'd no longer be on my case. Oddly, to me our turbulent relationship had become normal, in a twisted sort of way.

Somewhere along the line, I'd transformed from a sweet little boy into your basic pain in the ass: edgy, sometimes irascible, a totally bent sense of humor, and wary—"hyper-vigilant," a shrink had once called it. Some days I was damn near as tormented as the old man had been. Maybe his problems were genetic after all, in spite of my mother's whispered explanations of "He was different before the war," or "I think his mother's deafness had a negative effect on him . . . a bonding issue."

My mom went on to become a clinical psychologist—probably to understand him. Or, perhaps, even to understand her epic talent for refusing to accept the reality of him.

But, whatever the formal diagnostics, the family's tense, offbeat dynamics had inadvertently prepared me for my first job—"youth development counselor"—in the Youth Development Center at Canonsburg, Pennsylvania.

Of course, this was a recent euphemism. Regionally, everyone knew the place as The Morganza. A facility of the Commonwealth of Pennsylvania's Department of Justice, the Morganza was a reform school that housed most of Allegheny County's nastiest younger-than-twenty-one rejects. For every crime scene roped off in the Pittsburgh area, the Morganza's overseers recalculated their likely bed count.

The place had started off as The Refuge, a farm for orphaned boys in the nineteenth century. Among its oldest buildings were several stone barns. Part of its 250 acres was heavily wooded—that type of spindly, vine-choked hardwood forest that recarpeted huge expanses of the East Coast after late Colonial-era clear-cutting destroyed virgin forests as the Indians once knew them.

Toward the end of the nineteenth century, the facility expanded to several cottages and a boy's barrack. Its first renaming in the late 1880s was as the Pennsylvania Training School for Feeble-Minded Children. During both the panics of the 1890s and again in the 1930s, the need for make-work projects, combined with inner-city migrations and economic desperation, brought the farm into the full size and abundance of its regional infamy. A few kids were worked to death. A few, they say, were beaten to death. Others were mysteries no one talked about.

The staff back then was often recruited from among "retired" or defrocked cops. Raised on tommy gun-style robberies and a harness bull's "breaking heads sends clear messages" mentality, the Morganza had developed an aura as dark as a gothic novel, even before the socially unlikely 1960s transformed its staff into "professionals" and its inmates into "students."

Since my job opening had been, uh, "unexpected," it was not surprising that most of the staff had already become disgusted with the "Students *will* be rehabilitated with gentle demeanor and respect" style of rehabilitation and longed for the harness bulls to come back. Perhaps that's why Palco, an obese, profane, "Don't sass me" throwback, had managed to survive the '60s liberal reforms and was kept on as a chief of security.

Palco, who stood about six feet tall, was blocky and muscular, with a belly that had already turned to fat. Like many middle-aged men in denial, he wore his pants two sizes too small, making his beer gut even more prominent. But, unlike most men, he also had a fat, flabby ass. He needed to face reality and wear a women's girdle and go lighter on the Grecian formula he obviously combed, with limited success, into his receding hairline.

He wasn't allowed to carry a gun, at least not openly, so his trademark key ring, attached to his belt by a long trucker's steel chain, was his weapon of choice when a student got out of line. Several of Cottage 6's "residents" sported what looked suspiciously like key-scarred left cheeks. Even Sinbad—the grinning six-foot-five black ringleader of Floor 2, foreswore eye contact with Palco . . . who had ruled it rude for students to gaze directly upon him. If Palco had been a dog, he'd have spent half his waking hours defiantly peeing on other dogs' curbstones, just to make a point . . . and Sinbad desperately wanted to return the favor.

Sinbad was much more complicated than Palco. A tall, lanky nineteen-year-old café au lait-skinned black, he had an IQ of 108 and was proportioned like a ballet dancer, a lithe-muscled, young Othello, graceful, fluid, even articulate. His long oval face was elegant—his huge eyes, soft. Wide lips, high cheekbones, and a radiant smile made him look angelic, especially when he was high on the methadone he took daily. As the methadone levels faded, another Sinbad would emerge from behind the smile's mask.

The unmedicated Sinbad was mean, angry, cold, and utterly remorseless. That Sinbad had been the one who first accused Trezise of "dissing" his disciples, then ordered one of those disciples, Sugarbear, to push him through the window. That Sinbad was the same one who had allegedly razored off his fourteen-year-old white girlfriend's nipples because she refused to turn tricks for him up on Wylie Avenue in Pittsburgh. "I needed smack," he had explained to the court-appointed social worker, "and she wouldn't *do* for me when I axed her—a womens got to do for her man."

"So why did you strangle her?"

"Bitch kept screamin' . . ."

chapter 3

Let's Break Him In

I usually worked the three to midnight shift. Shifts overlapped an hour on each end in order to attend to the rituals—headcounts, case reports, incident write-ups, and the ever perilous shower time. As a counselor trainee I read lots of files . . .

We had about sixty students in Cottage 6, including the big, ground-floor dormitory room attached to one end of the building. Nearly three hundred guys on the whole "farm," plus a never-discussed number of girls in the secretive Young Women's Unit across the hill.

My cottage informally functioned as the maximum security unit. A surprising number of our "students" were in for armed robbery, rape, and/or murder.

Sugarbear was one of them—a burly, medium-complected black kid from Pittsburgh's Wylie Avenue in the Hill District; he had a seductively cherubic face and cute dimples. He specialized in both rape and murder—in no particular order, of course. In July of 1967 he was seventeen and had already been convicted of six of these particular felonies. Two other cases had been dropped for lack of witnesses. Sugarbear was generally lethargic during the day but became alert and restless each night, in symbiotic rhythm with Sinbad's methadone cycle. His file was a textbook study in abnormal psychology. He openly bragged about killing eight women. "It makes me feel happy when the old bitches scream . . . I get all tingly inside," he'd told one psych caseworker in an interview the year before. Though convicted of only six murders, his left shoulder sported eight dotted bars, tattooed with pen, ink, and spit. The end of each bar was punctuated with a miniature cross, like a baroque exclamation mark.

Sugarbear had an IQ of about seventy. He was raised by a foster grandmother who was now dead but described as strict and God-fearing by a neighbor. Sugarbear was the only member of his extended genetic family, male or female, not already doing thirty-to-life some-where in Pennsylvania's adult prison system. He was built like Mike Tyson and reveled in the role of Sinbad's enforcer. He'd idolized Sinbad ever since he was twelve and had watched his mentor strangle that fourteen-year-old girl. Afterward Sugarbear had his first sex with her corpse—payment for the "halfie" (half of a dime bag of heroin) he'd purse-snatched from a hooker for Sinbad. Six rape and murders later, Sugarbear had finally "made it," in his words, by being sent to the Morganza, where he could be with his only friend. "I'm Sinbad's fam-ily," he warned me on day two. "Don' chu be lookin' nasty at him." He'd grinned, his dimples deepening, as he stared unblinkingly at me, trying to make an impression. I stared back, smiling even more broadly. "You are a hoot, Sugarbear!"

]|[

I'd taken the job because it was the first offer out of college, and it was close to home in West Virginia, where my freshly widowed mother was broke.

I wasn't just some normal "I guess we are middle class" college boy from small-town America. I was the daily survivor of a brilliant but wondrously screwed-up family where primitive cunning was served with dessert. Where being locked in the basement for a week was "a warning," and where, at an IQ of about 140, I was the dummy of the group.

My greatest fear at the Morganza wasn't that I'd be beat on, cut on, or locked up . . . but that, coming from such craziness, I'd be bored. Sugarbear unknowingly gave me a gift—now that I'd have to watch my back, there would be normal turbulence and interest value in this assignment after all.

As I smiled at Sugarbear's warning, it wasn't a mind game . . .

I was pleasantly relieved. Sugarbear, unused to my reaction at his threat, blinked. I turned away and headed for the third-floor pool room. It was time for "activity hour."

Inside the pool room I waited for Mr. Davenport, my evening partner, to usher in the students. Mr. Davenport to me, and just "Dav" to the inmates, was a short, wiry, well-spoken black man. His demeanor was calm but determined and observant—he moved easily, like a railroad brakeman who neither rushed nor missed anything critical. Ever. His balding pate offset by a well-trimmed mustache, he was, I'd been told, a churchgoing deacon who lived near Little Washington, as Washington, Pennsylvania, was then called.

He warned me when I pulled my Rambler onto the grassy knoll behind the cottage at the beginning of my shift, "Rabbit snitched to me that Sinbad's crewe is going to break you in soon."

"What does that mean, exactly?"

"Physical violence, or some other stunt to let you know who is boss." Dav laughed, but there was a hint of seriousness underneath. I expected it to happen in the pool room, so I held a 21-ounce cue in hand as my charges filed in with Mr. Dav, smirking and doing their stylized Wylie Avenue dip and slide pimp strut.

Had they done such a walk on the street fifteen miles away in Southern Pennsylvania's tough, ethnically mixed coalfields, or in one of the even tougher Pittsburgh area's Polish steel towns like Donora, they'd have been kicked to death to the rhythmic taps of steel-toed brogans worn by boys whose hard-drinking daddies had raised them to hate "fairies." But to these black city boys, the carefully choreographed Wylie Avenue strut, enhanced by silk stockings drawn tightly over their pomade-busted hairdos, horizontal comb sticking out like chopsticks in a Japanese geisha's coiffed hair, was their signature of both tough and cool.

Sinbad strutted in last, Sugarbear just ahead of him and already tensed to smack me upside the head at Sinbad's first long-lashed wink. So I winked first. A wave of surprise rippled across Sinbad's Othello-perfect face before he broke eye contact and abruptly stepped out into the hallway, where Mr. Dav was calling him to come downstairs and help set the tables.

The boys may have feared Palco and loathed most of the social workers, but they actually respected Dav. Had any of them been fortunate enough to have had him as a father, they probably wouldn't have made it to the Morganza in the first place. A few of the boys, especially those with no memory of a father, had figured this out, and they followed Dav around like ducklings.

Mr. Dav, I came to discover over the next few months, was a genuine dyed-in-the-wool, work-ethic, take-responsibility-for-your-actions, make-no-excuses, no-bullshit kind of guy. He didn't talk it. He just did it, every twelve-hour shift—five, even six days a week. Dav had family and community obligations, and that meant, at less than three bucks an hour, he needed all the overtime the Morganza would award him.

Mr. Dav was clever enough to hijack Sinbad for table duty, leaving his crewe rudderless, and hopefully sparing me a "breaking in." I supervised a quiet game of eight-ball for a half hour while leaning on my #21 cue, making the students share one 18-ouncer among them.

"Come on, Mr. Stuart, your turn to shoot," Sugarbear prompted, either to assess my skill or to get me to bend over so he could pop me. It didn't matter which . . . never bragging and never letting a potential adversary take one's measure were two fundamental rules of survival among males in Appalachia. "No thanks," I replied.

The third rule was "Never fight a man with your bare hands unless you have to." True, this rule didn't meet the romantic standards of the West's Cowboy Code, but it was effective in a Darwinian way, in that it substantially raised one's statistical chances of surviving a Friday night brawl in some VFW Hall dance in any of Appalachia's coalfield settlements.

The boys from Wylie Avenue and Pittsburgh's Hill District thought they were tough. But most of the crimes they had committed in order to be awarded "two hots and a cot" at the Morganza had been perpetrated, like hyenas, on the already-wounded and weak—teenage girls, old ladies, the homeless, a hapless cripple or two.

I didn't get "broken in" that night, nor the next night. As the first few weeks went by, I even began to relax and got to know some of the nicer boys, the ones I soon discovered didn't belong at the Morganza.

There was Curtis, the big, chubby black kid who'd gone into a liquor store with a friend's uncle when the uncle suddenly shot the clerk in the face for a case of Iron City beer. Curtis, soft-spoken, was the only kid in the place whose mother never missed visiting day. A big woman who worked as a scrubbing maid in the Penn West Utility's grand, marble-tiled lobby on a wide Pittsburgh thoroughfare, she struck me as a strong mom. According to her, he'd never hurt anyone; had earned mostly Bs and Cs until ninth grade, when he'd made the ill-advised beer run; and had helped care for a younger sister with Down's syndrome at home when his mother went to work. There was no mention of a father in Curtis's file, but he had been born in Birmingham, Alabama—his mom must have been among the countless black "northward migration" folks after World War II.

Another kid who didn't belong was Billy. He was a short, sturdy, country white boy from up in Beaver County, north of Pittsburgh. He had an IQ of between sixty and sixty-five, dark, wavy hair, and a surprisingly cute, fresh face that revealed none of his mental limitations. He looked like wide-eyed Ricky Nelson as a dark-haired kid on *Ozzie and Harriett*, before his later rock-and-roll transformation into a second-rate Elvis.

For that reason I was suspicious that his charted IQ test was lower than it should be. He didn't talk much. Full sentences weren't his style. No matter the question I'd pose, "Nope"; "P'raps"; "Dunno" were typical responses. He worked hard at the Morganza—since he was not eligible for even the remedial middle school classes, he first had been defaulted into an auto-shop program. When he couldn't figure out how parts of a car went together, he had been further consigned to the old-fashioned paint stall, where a surprising number of Little Washington and Allegheny County race cars were refurbished on the cheap after crowd-pleasing dirt track wrecks. At polishing and painting he proved to be a one-trick genius.

It had been a combination of hard work and folly that brought him to the Morganza in the first place. He'd been hand-cutting brush for three days on some farmer's wood lot for a supposed payoff of $10. But when payday came, the farmer had insisted he accept a keg of stale beer instead of cash. The farmer told him he could take it to Beaver Falls and return it to the distributor for a $12 refund. Billy accepted the beer. The farmer then drove away, according to the court file. Billy rolled the barrel away, not sure how far it was to town. The farmer had failed to mention that it was eleven miles.

About an hour later, Billy passed the farmer's barn, still rolling the keg. The sight of that barn and a browsing pony out front apparently sparked Billy's chimpanzee-like brain. In a flush of inventive genius, he "borrowed" rope from a hook in the barn, strapped the keg across the pony's back, gave him a piece of candy, and led him down the dirt country road, a hackamore over his head.

It was decent problem-solving for a thirteen-year-old kid with an IQ in the sixties, but it didn't take into account that Beaver County still had a nineteenth-century horse-stealing law on the books . . . not to mention another special statute for stealing farm equipment—the rope. Then there was the unhappy irony that the local magistrate was a nephew of the farmer who'd paid Billy in stale beer. The result was a long sentence for horse-rustling, upheld by a county judge, who was also related to the farmer. That meant a minimum of twenty years hard time before he would be eligible for parole. Billy got another mandatory five added on for borrowing more than a dollar's value of rope. The day he turned twenty-one, his gift would be a pair of hand-cuffs and an escorted ride straight to Pittsburgh's Western Penitentiary, where he'd spend another twenty-some years . . . if he survived the killers in its general population.

Everything about Billy's case made me angry. Thirteen years old. No prior rap sheet. A twenty-nine-year-old mom who was two-thirds of the way to deaf-dumb and whose IQ had never been measured. She took in wash for a living. I met her once, when Billy's frustrated, fresh-out-of-college public defender brought her to see him. She may have been the most bewildered woman I ever met. She was still pretty in a two-year-old, childlike way, and she cried when the young lawyer finally had to drag her from the glass-paned visiting room.

As Billy's mom was ushered out, he cried, too. According to Dav, it was the first time anyone had seen him do that. "Don't take him back to the floor," Dav urged me.

"How about a candy bar down in the kitchen, Billy?" I asked. He nodded and wiped the tears away with his sleeve. Downstairs, I took him into the snack pantry, logged the issued "Hershey w/ almond—Bill T.—fam. vst." and sat him down at the rear table the black kitchen ladies used.

"You OK?" I asked. His face scrunched like a squeezed sponge. "She don't know how's to do for herself . . . she weak in the haid."

Jesus, a retarded thirteen-year-old with an IQ well south of seventy sweating his mom's mental incapacity? I thought to myself. "Who cares for her, Billy?" I asked. He looked confused. I rephrased, "I mean, who *does* for Momma?"

"I does." He smiled. "I wanna go home with her."

"No one else at home?"

He shook his head, sniffled, and began leaking again. "None *now*—she tole me they come and took little sister."

"Why?"

He shrugged. "She couldn't 'member." He unwound into tears again and, not knowing how to handle it, I requisitioned a Clark Bar. When Billy finally calmed down, I took him back upstairs and locked him in his room for safekeeping. If the black guys from the Hill caught him crying it would turn into a scene akin to sharks circling a cluster of baitfish.

Davenport, looking concerned, was waiting downstairs. "Where's Billy?"

"Locked him up . . . 'mild acting out' after a home visit, perhaps?"

Dav smiled. "That works. I'll order a tray sent up later."

"Tell me, Mr. Davenport," I whispered. "What do you know about him?"

"Sweet kid. Never bothers anybody. Makes 35¢ an hour in the paint stall—about $40 a month—sends every penny home to Momma through some preacher up in Beaver County . . . who cashes the check for her. I spoke with the preacher once on the phone when Billy first came. The kid has never done anything mean to anyone."

"So what do you think? . . . Can we write a petition for a new hearing?"

"Won't do you any good, I fear; those whites up there go to church, but they aren't Christian." I was nodding when Dav paused. "Look, you're new here—I don't know why I said it the way I did, but I didn't mean any offense on the 'white' thing."

"None taken. From looking at his file last week, I drew the same conclusion, but I'm not the 'pro' here. I'm green."

Dav studied me for a moment, then grinned. "I never wrote a court petition before—I just stick to the 'dailies'; the college people up on the Hill control the fancy stuff. I'm a $2.85 an hour man."

"Really? Why am I making more? You're the pro."

Dav shook his head. "I never realized you guys from behind the Cotton Curtain might think like that. The college boys who usually cycle through here are white, snotty, and go into senior management within a year." *What's the Cotton Curtain?* I wondered, but didn't ask. Instead I probed career tracks, just in case.

"They move into management here, at the Morganza?"

"Oh, Lord no—they go back to Harrisburg or to Philadelphia and take fat desk jobs at five bucks an hour managing some tutti-frutti social service program."

"All from Pennsylvania?"

"Most—it's usually political. A few are from Ohio and Jersey, but you are the first from below the Mason-Dixon line."

"Ah, so you don't like West Virginia."

"Never been there . . . and what's more, it's never going to happen. Virginia. West Virginia. Maryland. It's all the same down there behind that Cotton Curtain. I've never crossed it . . . and I'm not going to. Whatever they do down there, it's not safe for blacks—no laws; white sheets, long ropes, night-riders. The Klan."

It was odd hearing Dav define "home" that way, but I chose not to argue with him. I'd heard whispers about Klan rallies in central and southern West Virginia. The historical irony was that West "By God" Virginia had seceded from Virginia in 1862–63 over the slavery issue, then joined the Union. From behind the Cotton Curtain (which West Virginians were mostly unaware of) we thought of the Mason-Dixon Line as the Pennsylvania state line where, on the other side, one could walk into a bar, sit down, and buy hard liquor legally.

In contrast, due largely to rabid Bible Belt influences, West Virginia was a dry state. One could buy a watered-down 3.2 beer in a "bar," but wine and hard liquor came from a State Store, or, more usually, were homemade and drunk from a Mason jar. We occasionally heard rumors of Klan and cross-burnings in southern Pennsylvania while sitting on a car bumper sipping from those Mason jars. But it was never my reality, like it was Dav's. The Cotton Curtain may as well have been the Great Wall of China.

As the four o'clock Sunday dinner crowd began to file in, Dav asked, "You really thinking about writing a petition for Billy?"

I nodded. "Why not? I'll have to do some homework—find a model of a successful one up in the Hill's legal files."

"I want to know how to do it, too, Mr. Stuart. I want to be a $3.85 an hour man."

"OK. How about you keep me from getting killed and I'll share the mysteries of legal petitions as I uncover them?"

As Dav and I shook on it, Palco barreled in. "You two datin' now?" Dav rolled his eyes and looked heavenward. Me, I answered Palco, "Yep. You got a problem with it?" Palco, fingering his key ring, stared me down for ten full seconds. "That's the *one* smart-ass comment you get, College Boy!"

"It's 'Mr. Stuart,'" I retorted. Palco's eyes went as cold and empty as Sinbad's when his methadone levels were low. I was going to say more, but Davenport nudged me with his elbow. I let it go. Palco didn't. "You've just made a very special friend, you little weasel."

I returned the favor by flipping him off and bidding him a "tasty" meal. Davenport worried his forehead into deep, wavy creases and gently steered me to the head of the line.

Palco usually ate voraciously, but that evening, when he wasn't staring me down, he sniffed frequently at his food, looking dyspeptic, and ate little.

chapter 4

The Tower

No one knew how trainee assignments were made up on the Hill, but almost anything, "Daily Cottage," "Recreation," even "Field Trip," beat "The Tower."

The "Tower" was a glass-windowed sleeping garret, equipped with phone, cell toilet, cot, easy chair, and electric coffee maker.

The Tower's window looked down into the large dormitory wing that held twenty-seven cots . . . and that appeared to have once served as a gym-floored exercise hall. Overcrowding had dictated the ad hoc makeover. Students, students, students—what to do with them as they flowed in seasonally, like fetid tides.

As summer heated up in Pittsburgh and Philly, the angry and the insane among the under-twenty-one set acted out; the juvenile courts went into high gear, and the dormitory below the Tower overflowed with both prey and predator. The frightened "Virgins," as the new arrivals were called, clawed for the center cots, while smug predators filled out the edges.

July's late-afternoon heat penetrated every pore of the outdated brick and plaster structure. Thus, the dormitory stunk to high heaven, and the smells overtook me as I climbed the stairs to start my watch in the Tower and locked myself into the garret. Some of the dominant smells were mold and variations on the normal range of gym-locker pestilence one would expect when more than two dozen teenaged males are crowded into any circumscribed space. But others were more ominous. The Virgins had their particular smell. Most of them arrived already on a precarious psychological edge. Most had, in fact, lost their highly prized "cool."

The weak, of course, already knew they would become prey. Some had been dealing with that since their first at-home ass-kicking as infants. True, others didn't learn they were destined to be victims until after grade school. I envied those—it's a lot of work to hide the "at-home" bruises in school. But unlike them, I'd never killed a classmate or maimed someone weaker than me in order to offload life's residual anger. So, by the afternoon they were processed for the dormitory, the anxiety-provoked weaker Virgins had become human stink pumps emitting the scents of anxiety and fear, similar to a skunk's.

The dominant predators, like cold-blooded lizards, simply didn't sweat. Sweating was a body signal that got one killed or mutilated by another predator. *If one is successful enough at being a predator to make it to the Morganza*, I asked myself as I settled into the Tower's armchair with a cup of coffee, *does that mean Darwinian forces have already eliminated the violent sweaters from the population pool?*

I pondered that question while I checked the schoolroom clock perched high on the Tower's grimy wall. When the second hand swept past six, Davenport and Palco would usher in the Morganza's newly arrived Virgins below. At the director's orders, I was told, this was officially labeled the "admission interview." No wonder the staff was frustrated by liberalism gone gaga. Unofficially, the admission interview below reminded me of a *National Geographic* spread of wild-eyed wildebeests encircled by lions.

Palco, though charged by the Commonwealth to act as a guardian first and a disciplinarian second, sided with the lions circling their prey. He shouted, rattled his huge key ring in the small, frightened kids' faces, and, apparently recognizing one of his own kind amid the Virgins, winked conspiratorially at an oversized, mixed-race badass so fresh from his sentencing hearing that he still wore the tie and patch of stage makeup where his lawyer had tried to mask his gang tattoos in front of the judge. As I watched him, I wondered if *National Geographic* would ever get around to doing a photo essay on "Street Gangs," our version of tribal society.

Veteran public defenders up in Allegheny County tried to do their jobs by putting violent capital crime offenders into dress shirts and ties. In contrast, the kids up on nickel-and-dime charges usually went to court in their street clothes. Net result: Slicked-up guys who'd raped and cut an old lady rarely got longer sentences on their first conviction than the pathetic kids who'd stolen a six pack of beer or a carton of cigarettes in some hick town of twenty-five hundred. This result, I came to understand, was the byproduct of a system that could not judicially distinguish those addicted to depravity from the harmless but impetuous.

While Palco rattled his keys, barked orders, and flexed his well-pumped muscles, Davenport spoke softly but firmly to the students, often guiding them where he wanted them with a subtle, propelling hand-on-shoulder maneuver, saying, "You are there." If he met resistance, he followed through with a second, firmer, "*You* are *there*." If the kid went with the flow, his voice and touch would go even softer.

In that first twenty minutes Palco got his rocks off reterrifying fifteen already-terrified kids while making unspoken pacts with several potential jackals. Later that particular night he would identify one of the jackals as "That dude who just came in from the Hill is one bad son-of-a-bitch," his voice tinged with grudging respect, while dismissing the weak ones with, "But I wouldn't give you a penny for the rest of those sissy punks." Punk, to those of you fortunate enough not to be familiar with prison culture, originally meant "bottom man" during male-on-male sex.

In just twenty minutes, Davenport would have assessed where each kid stood on a real-world, dominant-submissive scale, the relative fear and anxiety level of each, and each one's human capacity to react to others. "Go with firm, fair, and friendly, Mr. Stuart," he'd tell me, "Unless one of them declares war on you."

"And in that case, Mr. Davenport?" I'd asked.

"Since I'll be there if that happens, I'll try to shout advice while I peel one or two of them off you. That's a one-time service, by the way." He grinned.

"Not paid to save Lilly White College Boys' asses more than once, huh?" I responded.

"Not for $2.85 an hour." He chuckled.

When the new miscreants in the dorm below me were finally on their cots, empty beds were filled by a few of the more docile, regular students who were having cellmate trouble. Most of the Morganza's cottage-level staff were opposed to the "Two students per sleeping room are now necessary as a consequence of our recently increasing admissions rate from juvenile court," announced just several months before I started work. This directive came from the highly educated and elocutionally impeccable but hopelessly, unrealistically liberal, Ph.D.-holding, politically connected, black, female director of the Morganza, who viewed the students as "under my aegis." Predictably, the whole arrangement of "selecting dorm-mates" became an instant comedy of the absurd.

Pair two alpha male predators and one of them could wind up dead, or mutilated, in the night. Pair an alpha male and a nearly-as-dangerous camp follower, and voila! One got a witch's brew like room-mates Sinbad and Sugarbear. Put all the weak kids in pairs and you had too many leftover alpha males to distribute. It was not only a study in the absurd . . . it was, in my view, a time bomb for society at large.

What to do with the stone-cold predators while keeping "incidents"—i.e., murdered, raped, or mangled students—to a minimum dominated every calculation among the well-educated but street-naïve staff on the Hill, who carefully reviewed case files and psychological evaluations and dictated often silly dorm pairings. The true atavistic psychos wound up, like Crazy Kamensky, in the last few "single suites." The Sinbads wound up with their Sugarbears and the screwed up but usually docile students who were victims of physical or sexual abuse often wound up paired with wannabe sugar daddies in for being sexual abusers.

That's what happened to pale, creepy, long-lashed catamite Rabbit. Just thirteen, though he looked considerably younger, he was in the middle of what the other students termed "an ugly divorce" with his roommate. Thus, against Davenport's advice, Rabbit and several other high-profile "problem" kids were put into the dormitory that night to fill the final beds.

Beds had to be filled so that whoever was on watch in the Tower would know instantly which of the numbered cots below had gone empty. This was my third turn in the Tower, so I already knew that trouble came during the blink of an eye and had no audible, easily detectible warning sign.

Unfortunately, the students could see me when I was at the window.

The Commonwealth, like most states, was lavish with construction but stingy with facilities upkeep. Silvered glass was simply out of the question. That meant, look away from the glass and one student was gone. Step away from the window for a quick piss and two more could vanish.

Since there was really nowhere to go, a daring new arrival's choices were to rush headlong into the dormitory foyer for an unexpected date with Palco's keys, hide under his—or the next guy's—cot, or already be on top of another student, either beating or sodomizing him.

So Tower duty required both vigilance and good bladder control. Due to my childhood, I rated a ten on the vigilance scale and, unlike one of my "short-term" predecessors whom Palco had described to me, I wasn't the type to be caught jacking off by my relief officer while watching one hapless kid service two others at the same time.

Part of Tower duty's stress came from the frequent taunts from the new alpha males below, who were anxious to both gain control and to show their classmates just how tough they were. One yelled up at me . . .

"Hey, sweetie. You can come down here and suck my dick. We won't tell, will we, fellas?" *Murmur . . . giggle . . . murmur.*

Then Palco: "Shut the fuck up in there or I'm going to 'sweetie' you in the ass with a number twelve boot!"

Ten minutes later, another had shouted, "Hey, you up there. Yeah you, motha' fucka' . . . quit staring down heah' at my Johnson . . . I don't like faggot cops." *Titter, titter.* Palco, silent, had either snuck off duty or was registering quiet approval.

The two fifteen-minute breaks before dawn were supposed to be sacred. Thus, when Dav came upstairs late to relieve me at eleven, he asked, "You OK?"

"Sure. Why?"

"Just checking. I'm late and most of the inexperienced staff yell back at the kids."

"I'm not *that* inexperienced, but I sure could use some fresh air—the stink from down there rises through the air vent." He nodded and I dashed down the Tower's staircase, grabbed a cheese sandwich left for me by the day-shift housemother, Mrs. Moxon, and walked outside to sit on the grassy hill behind the cottage. Desperate for fresh air and starlight, I had eleven minutes to myself.

Cottage 6.

After the break, I let myself in with the passkey and reclimbed the stairs. By the time I was inside the garret again, there were three locked doors between me and clean air.

Davenport, who had been notating files while I was on break, handed me the stack, announced, "I'll be back at two a.m.," and departed.

Officially, the files were confidential. Practically speaking, the only folks who made regular entries into them and had extended contact with the students were people like me and Davenport, or occasionally one of the schoolteachers. Most of the files' formal "diagnostics" were created by social worker or psych tech interviews conducted in the administration building up on the Hill.

It was easy for many of the students to mask huge facets of their underlying personality and behavior for forty-five minutes to an hour. Sinbad's file, for example, was replete with sidebar notes about his "intelligence," "charm," "increasing self-awareness," etc. These were usually written by twentysomething college girl social workers who, though well-meaning, simply didn't understand the real-world differences between sociopath and psychopath . . . and street-common blends of the two.

Me, I knew this stuff, just from growing up. There wasn't any diagnostic clearer than the sick, churning feeling I'd get in my gut when my old man went into psycho mode. If I tried to engage him emotionally or logically, his essence would simply vanish, only to smugly reappear later in another psychological space. That, his breathtaking mood swings, and his boundless energy when engaged in mind games were all clinical tests as solid as anyone could get from most formal psych workups. The young social workers who fought to interview pretty Sinbad should have been evaluating him with their guts instead of their eyes when they wrote progress reports on him.

On a good day with sufficient methadone circulating and a cute, attentive white social worker to smooth him out, Sinbad was merely sociopathic. Sooner or later, I hoped, one of them would catch him on an off day and discover that while they'd been studying his beautiful, full-lipped face, he'd been fantasizing about just how exciting it would be to razor off another white chick's nipples and bask in the thrill of her screams.

Chapter 5

Rabbit

I groaned when I saw Rabbit file into the dorm below me. Every day, I discovered by the end of my first week on the job, was a day that demanded special Rabbit entries into the daily logs. The kid was a sick daytime TV soap opera in which he played both the male and female lead roles, and also served as director.

Everything Rabbit did displayed impressive theatrical talent. When he took off his day clothes to change into flip-flops and green scrub-like sleeping trousers, it was a dance worthy of Anne Corio or Gypsy Rose Lee.

When he showered, it was more like a choreographed scene from a Hollywood swim production than a shower. And when he was going through one of his regular tortured acts, he was the best Hamlet I'd ever seen. Like virtually every other male staff member, I hated dealing with him. At every shower ritual he dropped the soap, batted his eyelashes, and flamboyantly stuck out his ass as he bent to pick it up. He cleverly passed notes to the black alpha males, ass-teasing them into dorm dates. And, no matter how closely we watched him, he opened the next act of his show by consummating those dates with stunning regularity, first gloating, then rushing headlong into the final act, based on his own signaturestyle epic victim role.

The rhythm of Rabbit's dramas was tediously predictable—to everyone except the members of the psych staff up on the Hill who neither had to suffer through the disruptions he orchestrated with his Kabuki-style acting out, nor write up the endless reports. They only saw him after he was "rescued" and in fragile mode, and they would rush to comfort him. It drove me nuts.

So I watched him like a hawk from the Tower, which turned out to be a mistake. At one, when Dav, below, stepped out to take his fifteen-minute break, I was still upstairs, focusing closely on Rabbit. All of a sudden a new kid on the other side of the room started hollering, "I ain't unlockin' my ass for nobodies. No mens gonna fuck me." One of the other veterans had slipped out of his cot and on top of the new kid.

"'No mens gonna fuck me' . . . 'no mens gonna fuck me.' . . . Where you from, *country* boy?" mimicked someone else.

I paused, unhappy with the fact that Palco was oblivious to the chaos down there. If I could hear it above and through the window, his ears should have been bleeding from the volume. I picked up the phone and dialed, reaching Palco out in the foyer. "Number sixteen, Palco . . . Vet from twenty-one on a Virgin in sixteen."

"OK . . . I'll break it up. Go back to sleep," grunted Palco.

"Yeah, like I'd interrupted you or something. You live for this stuff. Have fun."

"I don't like your ass, Weasel; don't forget it!" he snarled, slamming his phone into the cradle. Soon I heard him slam his keys on the block wall as he made his entrance. "Franzi . . . you little cocksucker. Get off of the new kid." *Whack* . . . Franzi grunted loud enough for it to carry through the glass; as Palco's keys knocked him out cold, he fell off of the newbie on cot number sixteen . . . who would ever after be known as "Country."

Several of the new predators stirred as Palco drug Franzi, one-handed, across the polished wood floor, leaving a slippery blood trail in his wake. One of them tried to grab Palco's leg as he passed. Not wise.

Palco stopped, dropped Franzi, turned, and damn near took the guy's nose off with his key ring. I heard Rabbit giggle.

I watched Palco strain as he dragged both miscreants out into the foyer. I phoned the front desk where Dav usually ate a candy bar and made log entries during breaks.

"Mr. Davenport . . . it's Stuart speaking. Palco nailed two kids in the dorm and dragged them out. No one on the floor . . ."

"I'm on it." Click. Moments later, Dav strode onto the floor, calm and commanding. "It's bedtime . . . no more games . . . we will have you up at six a.m. Number sixteen, *you* move your cot over *here* next to my desk . . . come on. Yes . . . now! That's good . . . OK. Listen up . . . we've got fifteen minutes if any of you need to pee—one at a time. Just call out your number. When that fifteen minutes is up, it's back to bed."

I stood at the window, ready to tap on the glass if anyone made a move on Davenport. Everyone settled down except for Palco, who cursed continually at his two stunned guys until the one night nurse available made it over from the women's unit across the farm. That brought an ambulance to the Hill behind the cottage. Its revolving red dome light flickered eerily into the Tower's high rear window.

It was then, at 1:59 a.m., when Davenport left the floor to relieve me for my second break, that Rabbit made his move. By the time Dav stepped into the Tower garret, Rabbit was already noisily taking it in the ass from a huge, colorfully tattooed homie.

"Ooh! Ooh! Eeek! He's *hurting* me!" moaned Rabbit. "Shut up, bitch!" and a hard *smack* was the response from the boy on top of him. I looked around frantically for Palco, who had been on the floor less than a minute ago. "Where the hell is Palco now?" I yelled to Davenport as he picked up the phone behind me with an exasperated sigh.

Palco didn't answer the phone, either, and Rabbit's familiar seductive script line, "Ooh! Ooh!" transformed from his ritualized crooning into a series of surprised squeaks, followed by a half-real, half-staged crying tantrum.

"Lord . . . here we go again," groaned Davenport. "The last time Palco disappeared, two of the new ones ran . . . and robbed a post office the next morning in South Side Pittsburgh." With that, Dav bounded down the stairs. No more starlight and fresh air for me. Regulations or not, I followed him down.

Dav hit the floor at a trot, yet even then managed to sound calm. "Rabbit . . . get dressed. You, Mr. Tattoos, are in a world of trouble."

The tattooed one scrambled back to his own cot and tried make-believe on Dav. "I didn't do nothin'. What are you lookin' at?"

"I am looking at you, and not with favor. Come over here and stand against the wall!"

"Don't be tellin' me . . ."

"Now!"

Tattoos muttered something foul that I couldn't hear, to which

Dav responded, "It's *Sir*! That or *Mr.* Davenport are your only choices! You will *never* use *that* word here again. Never!"

When Palco finally did show up, I already had a dressed but shaking Rabbit in tow and Dav had Mr. Tattoos in a "If you let me steer you, your arm won't break" wrestler's hold. Too disgusted to even look at Palco, Dav proceeded to march Tattoos past him to the closet-sized six-by-seven solitary cell that opened onto the dormitory's foyer.

Palco sneered, "I leave for two minutes and you two can't handle it."

"Right," I retorted, "then you won't mind that I'm taking my break after I put Rabbit in your office." Rabbit had started to squirm so I didn't wait for a response. Instead, I marched him past Palco and down the hall, while he batted his lashes at me and crooned, "You're strong, aren't you?" When I didn't respond, his face, sporting a slap-reddened cheek, twisted in rage and he spat odd names at me: "fornicator"; "filthy degenerate"; "beast of Sodom." He sounded like an unhinged Bible Belter. Trying not to laugh, I locked him in the Plexiglas security booth and phoned the nurse again. "Stuart . . . 2:13 a.m. Got another one here in six . . . yes. Rabbit. Possible sexual assault victim. Was struck in the face. Can you come over? He's in the security booth. I'll wait for you out back to let you in."

After ten minutes of waiting, I gave up on the nurse and headed back to the floor to check in with Mr. Davenport. He was agitated. "Tough night . . . these kids are all riled up. Where is Rabbit?"

"I locked him in Palco's security booth and stepped outside to wait for the nurse—figured he had to be examined. I gave up after a few minutes . . ."

Dav broke in: "Mr. Palco, please watch the floor. Mr. Stuart and I are going to check on Rabbit." Dav sounded concerned, but pretty calm, until I turned to lock the dormitory door behind us. That's when he accelerated into a fast trot, his keys out.

I took off and tried to catch up, but he was already in the security booth, its door standing open, when I rounded the corner. "I need a hand!" he yelled. I put it in high gear and blew through the door to find Dav bear-hugging Rabbit's thighs and pushing up to relieve pressure from the long-woven restraint strap hanging from the ceiling and encircling his neck.

Rabbit didn't seem much like himself at that moment. He hung there, his usually pale, sly face red and swollen. The blue veins that once crisscrossed his smooth, pallid skin had popped out on his temples in high relief. Glutted with dark, oxygen-depleted blood, they looked like the gnarled, violet-brown veins of a forty-year-old heroin shooter who'd injected a few too many dime bags of high-octane Afghani smack.

At first glance Rabbit looked rather like an aging side of beef hung in a cold room. Before getting out of college, I'd worked the night shift in West Virginia University hospital's Emergency Room long enough to have seen a lot of stiffs. "Dead," I said to Dav.

"No!" answered Dav, looking down at the dressing scissors I wore in my belt, an echo of emergency room days. "Cut him down! He hyperventilates before he does this. Might still be alive." I cut him down with the round-tip scissors that had once belonged to my old man. "I'll do the lip-lock, Mr. Davenport . . . I'm the one who left him." Dav looked relieved.

We got him on the floor. I turned his head, pushed his swollen, purple tongue to one side, hooked an index finger in his throat to clear the mucus, and puckered up for a lip-lock. I blew air in while Dav did the rhythmic sternum pushes. Two minutes later, Rabbit twitched, his slimy tongue only half as big as it had been when I started. I cranked up the air pressure till I think I shared some already processed cigarette smoke with him and Dav slowed his sternum pushes, going for quality in place of speed.

About the time Rabbit's hands began to twitch, he evacuated his bowels and coughed a huge gob of slobber right into my mouth. I gagged and jerked my head up. "Aw! This sucks," I whined. Dav chuckled. "Don't stop! You're damn good at this."

"Don't tell anyone," I muttered and started puffing again. I was going great till Rabbit convulsed and vomited all down the front of me. Jill Dick, the immense night nurse who, I'd find out later, had been standing behind me for some minutes, finally yanked me off of Rabbit with a huge ham-like arm and cleaned out his mouth. "Freshen up, cutie—I'll take it from here."

I dashed to the men's room around the corner and barfed. I got my shirt off and did a waist-up cleaning, then tried to figure out how to cleanse my mouth and face. When I came out of the bathroom, Jill and Dav were helping the ambulance guys with Rabbit's ankle restraint while they got an IV into him. Rabbit, now full of oxygen and wiped clean by Jill, was back into his Act II, "Ooh, ooh" mode.

As Rabbit passed me on the gurney, he winked at me through one seriously swollen, bloodshot eyeball. "Ooh, you saved me," he cooed.

"Don't get used to it," said Dav matter-of-factly. "Next time you pull this crap, I'm going to wrap myself around your legs and help you get it done." Rabbit turned and batted his eyelashes at Dav just before Dav locked the outer door on him and the ambulance crew.

Jill laughed. "Least he puked on someone else this time—last time he nailed *me* in the face! Here," she said, handing me a fresh bottle of hydrogen peroxide from her bag, "For your mouth."

I slipped back into the toilet and gargled, Palco already bellowing at us from the hallway. "Hey! Hello! You guys having a tea party or some shit? How about some help down here!" Davenport shook his head and turned toward the hallway.

Jill hollered back, "And they say behind my back that *I* got some kinda' dick. Sheeeit! Someday I'm going to sucker punch you . . . you loudmouth sadist . . . you mark my words." With that Jill turned to me. "You give good air, cutie . . . you get lonely some night, you let me know . . . old Jill'll exchange a little air with you." Dav had the good grace to pretend he hadn't heard this repartee. Jill left and I headed for the Tower stairs. It was 3:01 a.m.—three hours, plus several morning Rabbit write-ups, to go.

It turned into a much longer morning than I expected. While I was writing Rabbit reports the following morning, I got interrupted by a suit from up on the Hill. Philly accent. "I need to interview you about Lester Squires."

"Huh?"

"The *Lester Squires* incident. . . . Is one of our *students* being sodomized and then hung by the neck of such little consequence to you that you've already forgotten about it?" I looked him over carefully before responding. He was about five foot four, and his suit sleeve cuffs were an inch and a half too short. Light olive complexion, shoes tied twice—like a city kid who grew up wearing leather work brogans. "Philadelphia, right?"

He stopped talking and nodded. I went on. "Somewhere near South Street by the accent. Jewish and Irish . . . maybe Italian. Degree from Temple University?" His fists curled.

"Yeah! You know me or somethin' . . . or just have a freakin' problem with it?"

"Neither—my grandfather's Twenty-second and Bainbridge. It's your accent."

"No shit! . . . I'm Twenty-fourth, near Laudaine . . . you some kinda' detective?"

I shook my head. "Look. I made a bad mistake by leaving Rabbit . . . uh . . . *Lester*, alone in the security booth while the nurse came. His full file wasn't down here so I didn't have the history. Write it up just like that." He nodded so I threw him a bone. "I'll come up and answer questions any day you need . . . just make it afternoon . . . it's tough getting enough sleep with these twelve-hour 'vacation coverage' shifts."

"Yeah. OK. So you aren't going to dispute that it wasn't the best call?"

"Nope . . . not as long as the record states that the full file had not been available down here since I began work about three weeks ago . . . hospital says he's doing well. Expected back in two days."

"Yeah. Well, we do have the file up there—Squires is incident-prone. Well, I'm gone. There will be an interview report for you to sign tomorrow." I nodded and kept on writing . . .

chapter 6

A Day Off

It was 9:20 a.m. when I clocked out and cranked up the gray '62 Rambler Classic I'd bought for $650 from Shorty Anderson out on Stewartstown Road in Morgantown just three weeks and three days before.

No one in hearing range, I yelled, "I hate the Tower duty . . ." from the Rambler's open window and backed away from the cottage.

When I reached the immense Victorian house on East Beau Street in Little Washington where I rented a fourth-story attic apartment, there was a message for me: "Given incident last night and a fifteen-and-a-half-hour duty shift, you are awarded a day off this evening in lieu of overtime. DLC."

"Hand-delivered at nine o'clock," cooed the old bat who knocked at my studio door after I climbed the four flights of rickety outside stairs that rose up from the backyard.

"Was someone else *killed* at the Morganza?" she went on. She shivered, possibly hoping for the worst.

"No."

"Oh. Hmm. Well, you know they *kill* them out there. There is a graveyard on the hill. I saw it as a girl."

"Really? I hadn't heard that," I said as she scuttled away. I sighed and closed the door.

The big house had been, a neighbor said, inherited by two

spinster sisters from their father. They'd converted it into a boarding/apartment house.

Neither worked, went out often, or did anything public, except to go to church together about three times a week. Inside their own world each sister lived in opposite halves of the downstairs, sharing only the big kitchen at the rear of the ground floor.

I rarely heard them speak to one another—maybe they simply didn't need to. Elder sister rented one small downstairs studio and the four small apartments on floor two. The other managed floor three (three apartments) and my studio perched nearly forty feet above the street.

The studio measured about three hundred square feet. Carved out of space under the original attic's eaves, it had a single bed and one swayback armchair. In spite of the antique rose pattern, its faded, hand-sewn chintz curtains had probably ceased to brighten the tiny dormer windows at least forty years ago. The big upsides were an old, freestanding pedestal sink that had been installed under one dormer window and a glass-paned door that admitted light and let out onto the narrow wooden stairs to the backyard. I'd pulled my old man's gray-green WWII army footlocker in front of the pedestal so I could stand on it and piss in the sink rather than walk down a flight and a half of stairs to the nearest bathroom.

In short, my perch atop the old house, at fifty bucks a month, was cheap, private, and gave me a convenient place to piss. Such unrefined behavior was quite unlikely to risk my nonexistent social life; I hadn't been laid since I last visited Mexico City, my home away from home, in '66, and I had no reasonable expectations of getting any lovin' in Pennsylvania.

I was hopelessly in the thrall of a Mexican girl named María, to whom I was engaged . . . she was young, dark, big-eyed, beautiful, and smelled of limes mixed with corn oil. To top it off she was also smart and funny. In spite of her father's and eldest brother's justified, but somewhat overdone, vigilance, we, as Big Jill had put it, had managed to "swap air." Only twice, I admit. But it was good, healthy air. The kind of air that makes you laugh . . . then revel in the warm afterglow for days. Most folks, I supposed, called that "love." But the whole experience was so distinct from my own experiential definition of "love" that I thought of my feelings for her as a state of joy.

I'd met a few cute local chicks around in Little Washington while doing the bars—my only excuse for a life—between shifts. But southwestern Pennsylvania's gritty working-class culture simply didn't motivate girls who could offer you joy into becoming regulars in the local tavern scene.

The chicks I'd met might give you head, might even "swap air," but the capacity for joy had long since been wrung out of them. Most, married at eighteen or nineteen, started doing the taverns, then their husbands' buddies, in their mid to late twenties. While some of them considered fraternizing with single men as an acceptable antidote to boredom, a bad marriage, and disputes with their too numerous children, I simply wasn't interested.

For me, a woman meant the possibility of joy; sex was a distant second as an attractant. That attitude occasionally made for tavern troubles.

One night in The Spot, Little Washington's best late-night "white" bar (blacks and whites still did not drink together in '67), a very nice-looking dark blonde hit on me. "They say you work up at the Morganza . . . buy me a beer?"

"Yes . . . and sure. Tell Jack what you want." Jack, the bartender, was already pulling the cap off two frosty bottles of Iron City. She was tallish—maybe five foot eight, stacked, and looked great in her mint-green miniskirt with matching panties.

"I'm Ileen . . . and you?"

"David."

"You're not local, are you, David?"

"No."

"Want to get a booth . . . and talk?"

"You married, Ileen?"

"Not so's you'd notice it." She smiled, shoving a boob toward the shot glass I'd just instinctively lifted off the counter, out of harm's way.

"Thanks, Ileen. I'm just going to finish this drink and head home. Got another twelve-hour shift tomorrow."

"Shall I follow you?"

"No. Got to get some shut-eye." She looked hurt.

"I got nice boobs . . . what's your problem?"

"The 'sort-of married.'" She turned back to the bartender.

"Hmmph . . . Jack, you shoulda' told me he doesn't get off on women. I'm outta' here!"

Ileen left in a rejected huff. Fifteen minutes later Jack leaned toward me on the other side of the counter. "Well, now, since Ileen doesn't interest you, we could have a couple of drinks after I close up here and see if we click. Whatta' you say?"

"I like girls, Jack, just not married ones."

"No need to be snotty about it," snarled Jack, who promptly snatched my fresh beer and threw it in the trash.

Face it, I told myself as I headed home, *I just don't belong in this world. The town's only bustling late-night club and in less than a month I'm cut off and both genders are pissed at me.*

I drove back to my eagle's nest on Little Washington's east side and climbed the stairs, stepped onto the old man's footlocker, pissed into the sink, and stared at the faded wallpaper until I worked up enough energy to step down, undress, and put Herb Alpert's Tijuana Brass on my portable record player. Craving joy and Mexico, I spun "The Lonely Bull" again and again till the first streaks of dawn filtered through the grime-streaked dormer over the sink. I slept, then dreamed of joy, warm kisses, and the lush brown skin of a dark-eyed girl in Mexico City. She laughed afterward . . .

chapter 7

Where's the Graveyard?

The next day, Saturday, I had another long shift in the Tower. Before work, I ate a bowl of chili and beans at a small diner about four blocks from the eagle's nest—one of the few restaurants where blacks and whites mixed. As I was eating I saw one of my supervisors, Mr. Reddy. Black and a snappy dresser, he had been rather unapproachable, barking orders at the trainees. I gave him a pro forma wave and, to my surprise, he waved back and came over.

"Heard there was another incident with Rabbit last night. Dav said you handled it pretty well. So what are you doing in here? This place is very *neighborhood*?"

"I like the chili. By the way, my landlady keeps asking about a graveyard on the farm. Where is it?"

"It's on the hill behind Willow. No one goes up there these days. It used to be kept up. But it's left over from another age and no one has bothered with it in years."

"How long have you been at the Morganza, Mr. Reddy?" I asked. Several nearby heads, black and white, turned to listen in.

"Since I left the military. I was on the tail end of Korea. Came home after two hitches and took a job on the farm. Moved up to a day shift supervisor five years ago. Well, I've got to get back to the cottage." He straightened his tie, checked the crease in his pants, paid his $1.27 bill with a big, juicy twenty, and left.

I drove out to the farm at two, my dress shirt and tie hanging on a window hook in the Rambler's backseat. Curious, I headed up the steep slope behind Willow Cottage to check out the alleged graveyard.

The Morganza's planted farmlands spread out below me, offering a bucolic scene typical of both southwestern Pennsylvania and northern West Virginia; spreading oaks, stately maples, tall tulip trees, and a few spindly pines all crowded together on the crests of surrounding hills. In the three narrow, creek-fed valleys—"runs" we called them—that joined below me, neat rows of corn marched away into the narrow flatlands that led to Canonsburg.

The lush, natural green of the Morganza's hillside vistas were interrupted only by two tall smokestacks from the farm's coal-fired heating plant, an abandoned hilltop coal tipple about two miles away to the west, an airplane beacon on a summit to the northwest, and some very ugly high-voltage towers that carried juice down to the Allegheny Power Company in West Virginia.

To the southwest, Canonsburg clung to a tight cluster of hills that rose up from the winding banks of wide Chartiers Creek. The creek defined the Morganza's southeastern boundary. Unlike much of the old second-growth forest, which had reinvigorated the region's vistas when coal replaced wood in the 1880s and '90s, the Morganza's hilly slopes supported several small wood lots that had not been cut in more than a century. The oaks and maples were mature and well-spaced. Abundant student labor had kept those small stands from being choked by the ubiquitous creeper vines that strangled most roadsides and woods across a wide swatch of the northeast.

I topped the hill's crest, which opened up into a subtle copse, and found the overgrown graveyard enclosed by a white wooden fence. There were, as best I could tell, about six or eight seasons of uncut weeds and invasive bushes that prospered among the flat concrete markers.

Two small WWI-era eroded concrete crosses were the only upright survivors. I could still read several of the names: Ana Boyd (no dates); George Heintzleman (no dates); Sarah Gray (no dates). Most of the others dated between 1880 and 1920, a *de facto* testament to America's "good old days" when, despite popular mythology, poor, stupid, handicapped, or merely inconvenient children were disposed of "to protect themselves and society."

In short, except for the Morganza's current official name, dandified as The Youth Development Center at Canonsburg, nothing important had changed from the era when the Morganza had been The Pennsylvania Training School for Feeble-Minded Children. Nineteen-sixty-seven's kids may have been a bit meaner and demographically blacker than when the Scots-Irish, Dutch, and Pennsylvania German names had originally been engraved on the markers in front of me, but the Morganza students' averaged IQ had probably held rock-steady at somewhere in the high seventies for more than a century.

Contemplating the throwaway child phenomenon, I lit a smoke, opened a tepid Coca-Cola, and sat on one of the flat grave markers like Quakers use, daydreaming about joy . . . and Mexico. When I'd first arrived in Mexico City at age nineteen, it had been a cultural shock— Spanish, which I'd never heard before; bright colors; foods, like avocado, that I didn't know existed; beautiful, dark-eyed women; and a national passion for the pursuit of joy to balance out the more somber realities of daily travails.

Unlike the kids under the grave markers, I wasn't a throwaway . . . in fact, my problem was the reverse. I was trapped by a culture and a family that sucked at my essence, just like a fat trucker in a roadside eatery sucks at the end bone of his pork chop, trying to tease out the last of its marrow. Every time I tried to be happy, someone around me sucked in response—whether to suck out my momentary joy or merely to eliminate it. I was never sure which.

I hadn't yet been sucked dry, but I was becoming desperate for something, anything, good to happen. As tough as he was to deal with, I missed the old man and his craziness—in an unhealthy sort of way. My relationship with him had operated on two entirely separate levels. The first was intellectual. By age ten I was grading his medical students' anatomy exams for pocket money. That didn't earn his open approval . . . he never complimented me on anything . . . but it must have been acceptable, since he never did more than go "Humph" when I'd hand him the exams—which he carefully regraded.

On the second level—the emotional one—he was like a cold, angry wind that clawed endlessly at me, eroding my sense of self. For me, that had become normal.

Thus, when Mr. Reddy complimented me in the diner at lunch, it was unfamiliar dialogue . . . somehow even more embarrassing than the bartender Jack hitting on me in front of the other patrons. Competence was a core issue. *My family says I'm not competent. Reddy . . . and several of my profs in college say I am. Christ. Who's right?* I wondered. Personally, I had no idea.

My whole life had been divided into discrete moments. Some were connected by meaningful dots, others, totally disconnected, formed no pattern I could identify. "Bad"; "angry"; "You screwed up" all had familiar patterns. Thus, they were knowns; comforting and controllable in an offbeat way. "Love"; "joy"; "dreams"; "accomplishments" were disconnected incidents of mere chance. Like amazing accidents, these were unknowable and unexplainable; therefore the good stuff was neither controllable nor repeatable.

Had it also been like that for the forgotten kids buried where I now sat down to smoke? Was "throwaway" or "captured" as different from one another as they seemed on the surface? Or was the essential dynamic that drove kids off society's cliffs really about "controllable" and "uncontrollable" and learning the meaning of joy? In other words, just what did "life, liberty and the pursuit of happiness" really mean in a society where a huge sector of it, by mere accident of birth, had already struck out on several of the formula's basic elements?

"You think too much!" insisted a voice nearby. I jumped. "*Whooh!* You scared the shit out of me."

"That's what you get for doing your thinking out loud," smiled Big Jill, huffing up the hill. She settled her wide frame down on the ground next to me. "I come up here a lot. I wonder who they were. I imagine them as they were. Even talk to them . . . especially Ella and Emma over there . . . don't really know why. Want to help me clean off the graves tomorrow?"

"I have Sunday and Monday off. Got to go home to Morgantown, to see my mom. But I can bring back some hedge shears and help out Wednesday or Thursday."

"We've got tools here on the farm. It'll be a big job . . . they don't do it anymore since they changed policy to prohibit unskilled work details for 'students'—it's almost as if they *want* the weeds to take over, so that *my* kids here disappear."

"Or perhaps they'd rather have the students sit in the lockups than to actually give them fresh air and something to do," I countered. "Meet you here at two next Thursday?" She nodded and left. I watched her make her way back toward the girls' unit, the black beads of a rosary hanging partway out a side pocket in her nurse's uniform.

I stepped over to take a look at the flat, concrete grave markers she'd pointed to: "Ella Douglass, died November 2, 1897, at age 18" and "Emma Ginton, died November 2, 1897, at age 19." I passed back through the broken-down white rail fence that enclosed the graveyard, wondering who Ella and Emma had been, and why they had both died on the *same* day seventy years before.

That evening as Dav and I got the boys ready for dinner, I asked him, "Are students allowed to volunteer for a farm work project?"

"Depends, Mr. Stuart. What . . . and who . . . do you have in mind?"

"Billy. Clean up the graveyard up on the hill. I need to interview him for the petition, someplace comfortable . . . familiar. I was thinking a project would help him open up to me. When I try to talk to him in here he's very watchful . . . worried."

"I think that'd be OK. Shall I ask my mentor, Williams?"

"What does Williams do here?"

"He's senior staff. Knows the Hill and all its rules inside and out."

"I'd appreciate that." After dinner I climbed the steps up to the Tower. The Virgins no longer Virgins with a few nights at the Morganza under their belt, and Rabbit cooing futilely in a cell trying to lure another new roommate, it was a quiet night.

At 6:15 a.m. I cranked up the Rambler to pull away from Cottage 6 and head south toward the "Cotton Curtain."

"Don't get hurt down there," Dav advised, dead serious, as I rolled down the windows to blow out the hot summer air.

]|[

Route 19 neatly divided Canonsburg in two. I turned south, crossed Chartiers Creek, and took that route to Morgantown. It was a pretty morning . . . hot but not yet ruined by the humid haze so common on summer afternoons. This is a region of lush, rolling farmland, wooded hills, and small towns, a number of which were founded as frontier outposts between 1780 and 1820 when the country was still young, densely forested, and American Indians west of the Monongahela River far outnumbered whites. Until the 1820s, small, scattered herds of woodland bison roamed the forests between the district's great rivers—the Allegheny, Monongahela, and the Ohio. Wolves survived in the wild till about the Civil War.

My mother's people had been deeply rooted in these parts since the French and Indian wars of the mid 1700s. My ancestors included the Densmores, Vandergrifts, Sarvers, Rylands, Wheatons, and Goldboros. The Vandergrifts and Densmores eventually had spread as far north as Oil City, Pennsylvania, where my great-great-great grandmother, née Sophia Sarver, later Vandergrift (granddaughter of John Hart, who had signed the declaration of Independence in Philadelphia), had been born in 1804.

The Wheaton-Vandergrift branches of my family spread as far south as Point Pleasant, West Virginia, where the Kanawah joins the Ohio River. Many were "river men," riverboat captains, first mates, or ship builders; some worked in the Homestead, Pennsylvania, rolling mills; others were farmers. Later came a few teachers, industrialists, and engineers.

The Vandergrifts came from Hoorn, Holland, in the 1640s. Jacobus Vandergrift had sailed his own ship, licensed to the Dutch East India Company, to New Amsterdam (now New York City), sold it, and started a new life, seeding the "river man" traditions. His great-great grandson William had been the first to build a riverboat and sail it down the Allegheny. At that time Pittsburg was still Fort Pitt and hadn't yet morphed into the modern Pittsburgh.

One of Sophia Sarver's sons, Captain J. J. Vandergrift, was first a riverboat captain; later he founded the Allegheny and Ohio pipeline company, transporting oil out of Oil City, and even later founded Apollo Iron and Steel, giving his name to Vandergrift, Pennsylvania, about twenty-five miles northeast of Canonsburg. He was a quintessential American—a mix of Dutch, English, and who knows what else. He believed in hard work, industry . . . and making money.

In the early 1800s, the lowland Scots Densmore strain added to the genetic brew, yielding descendants who worked with even more terrifying intensity, saved money as if they somehow knew the Depression would come a century later, and were every bit as proud and hardheaded as had been any of Rome's legendary centurions.

Some of them, like those centurions, were ground down by the realities of their era and their occupations: Boats were "lost" on the Ohio and the Mississippi. In the 1860s some were fired on and taken as prizes by the Confederacy; eventually others would be requisitioned during WWI. Then there were the realities of ordinary nineteenth-century life: Death and iffy medicine. Babies born dead. Drowned men, who left young wives with yet unborn children. Yellow fever in New Orleans. Measles, mumps, heart attacks, cancer, consumption (TB), ordinary infections, and all-too-common work accidents.

When my father died so young in 1967, most people would have classified it as a tragedy. But for three centuries before, such events were simply part of everyday life. It was like the Morganza, where the realities of poverty, crime, broken families, and "feeblemindedness" had inexorably pulled generations of children onto the farm, only to finally meet denial in the post-WWII twentieth century.

How did that history morph into "Our students will be rehabilitated with education and respect?" I wondered. This notion, like so much else during the "American Century," represented a stunning leap in the magical power of expectation over reality.

Born in 1945, like others of my generation, I grew up with that legacy of "expectation trumps reality"—an idea that had become easy to sell as a subclause in the social contract we usually call "The American Dream," but damned hard to implement in the real world. For good, or ill, winning World War II had cemented that subclause in the modern American psyche. But that belief system would neither change the fact that my old man was dead three days after his forty-seventh birthday nor that Billy, doing thirty-to-life in the Morganza for the beer barrel and pony fiasco, still had an IQ of sixty to sixty-five. My father was dead. And stupid is stupid. Neither are negotiable conditions.

About the time I crossed the railroad tracks in Point Marion, Pennsylvania, I'd decided that what was wrong at the Morganza was also what was wrong with America. The reality that fate—or God—can be forced to grant only good days, good times, growth, prosperity, perfection, and *more* of everything totally ignored the reality of America's rise to greatness. That reality had been based on huge sacrifices: blacks forced to work for free; babies dead in childbirth; farm boys lying dead on Missionary Ridge; millions of other early deaths; and, above all, massive applications of thrift, hard work, and common sense.

Billy, Jill's rosary, and that damn graveyard at the Morganza had all put me into one of my reflective moods.

][(

Mom and Morgantown hadn't changed in the ten days since I'd been home. M-Town was still a hilly, pleasant university town toughing it out through a hot, studentless summer, and mom was still toughing out the loss of the man she loved in that determined, twentieth-century "Expectations over Reality" sort of way. I suspected she was mourning him twice—both for the loss of the man he was . . . and the man he wasn't. Me, I didn't really know how to help her, so, like the week before, I put her in the Rambler and drove around for hours.

She was in a driving and wandering mode, as if she imagined she'd somehow get lucky and find him walking alone out on a quiet country road. I took her north, crossing the bridge that spanned Cheat Lake's narrows, and pulled the Rambler into second gear to climb the steep grade up Cheat Mountain to Cooper's Rocks State Park. There the views of the river gorge were spectacular—at about three thousand feet in elevation, the mountain was the highest point in that part of West Virginia. From it she could see several of the places where she had summered with cousins and second cousins as a girl in the late 1920s. "I spent summers with my Goldsboro cousins in Fairchance," she told me, a faraway look in her eyes.

I took her to dinner at a small checkered-tablecloth Italian place about a mile from our hillside house and watched her pick at a large salad. I bagged it for her and took her home. She was still in her impenetrable daze, and I was running out of things to do. I fixed her a cup of tea, washed the dishes, hugged her, and finally told her, "I need to go back to Little Washington, Mom."

"How long is that, John?"

"The drive's an hour and a half . . . and I'm *David*, Mom."

"Oh, I'm sorry—I knew that! Where's your brother? Why isn't John here?"

"He's in the army, Mom. He went back to Fort Sam Houston the day after Dad's funeral. He only got a forty-eight-hour family emergency leave."

"Oh . . . yes . . . I knew that, too, didn't I?"

"Yeah. It's OK, Mom. I'll see you in a week. It'll be my first payday. Can you make it on cash till then?" She nodded and stared off into the distance. "I'll be all right by the time you visit again, John. Can we take another drive?" I gave her a hug and settled her in the living room with her cup of tea. I was at the door when she spoke again. "I like being alone. Always have . . ."

I closed the door behind me, tried to shake off the osmosis of her desperation, and drove back to Little Washington.

chapter 8

I'm Black!

I decided to work a double shift—twenty hours straight—when one of Mr. Reddy's dayshift guys didn't show on Monday morning. An extra seventy bucks would pay for an entire month's rent, smokes, and laundry. Even better, it gave me less time to think about my mom—or to ponder my dad's death, which I'd still not faced.

My first day shift started out just fine. In fact, the day shift had it easy: Make hungry teenagers eat breakfast, grab their outdoor shoes from hall-end lockers, then head to either the farm's high school or off to the vo-tech shops. By eight thirty, it was just Mrs. Moxon, Mr. Reddy, me, and five students.

With three in punitive isolation in their rooms, that left chubby Curtis and Golightly, who were scheduled for lengthy, on-site evals whenever a social worker arrived. Golightly was the tall, light-skinned black kid who looked so much like Andrew Young that some of his brethren ragged him every time "Andy" showed up on the evening news. "Hey, Golightly, there go your brother. You sure you's daddy is Golightly?" From his angry reaction, Golightly wasn't sure.

Crazy Kamensky, our Polish head case, was certain of his race. The problem with that was that no one else agreed with him. He had a date with some high-powered imported shrink who was going to try new meds. Ordinarily a kid like Kamensky would have been driven up to

Pittsburgh for such a consult, but Crazy Kamensky was just too crazy to risk that.

Kamensky was always moody, unpredictable, and extremely volatile. He had a decent IQ of about eighty-five, wore a constant scrunched-up frown, and had odd, fat lips. He was tall, large, and powerful. The most interesting thing about him from Dav's perspective was his penchant for explosive violence. From the perspective of the social workers on the Hill, it was that he "had the emotional maturity and disposition of a six-year-old bully."

But from my perspective, it was that he honestly, passionately, expressively believed he was black. I reckoned he was unable to bear the reality of who he really was—a totally screwed kid whose parents had left him in front of a bar and walked away one night when he was four or five. So, with no sense of who he'd once been, he became black to avoid retribution from the black orphanage population, then was rewarded for it by them.

But whatever the reason for his conviction, you simply could not tell Kamensky that he was white. That approach created the kind of dissonance that even Sinbad didn't want to take on. When I asked Sinbad one evening why he laid off of Kamensky, he'd grinned. "Gotta cut some slack to a dude fucked up enough to want to be called a spade."

"Why do you think that is, Sinbad?" I pressed.

"He's white trash—got nothin'. Bein' black is a huge step up."

"But he's *not* black?"

"Don't *look* black, but *is* black," the ever-present Sugarbear said, grinning.

Thus, Kamensky was permitted to be black, mostly because the cottage's young black overlords had approved the bizarre identity switch . . . and why not? Kamensky, at about 205 pounds and six foot one, was built like a college tailback and did what he was told, even if it was pushing a guy in a wheelchair through a third-story window or beating the snot out of other white guys who gave Sinbad and Sugarbear trouble.

Hell, when I closed my eyes, Kamensky even *sounded* black. Dav agreed that he did, too. "His Wylie Avenue dip and strut is perfect, too," said Dav. "I hate that exaggerated, stereotypical behavior, but hatin' it's not going to stop it."

To Dav's credit, he firmly and consistently tried to curb stereotypical role-playing, both black and white. To Kamensky's credit, Dav, indeed none of us, had any effect on him whatsoever.

"I'm *black* . . . don' you got eyes? Ah's *black*! Born *black*. I'm a *spade* from up on the Hill."

"OK," I'd answered on day two of my Morganza gig. "But I didn't ask you what you were . . . I don't much care."

"Well, I'm'a tellin' you jes' so's you know. You new ones gets it all backward sometimes . . . makes me *angry*."

I should have thought to tell that to the natty-suited shrink from Forbes Avenue who checked into an interview room and pulled out a fancy leather-cased pad while Reddy and I went to get Kamensky.

With Kamensky the protocol was always, "Two male staff. No exceptions!"—even for the evening shift's every-other-day, four-minutes-by-the-clock shower. Kamensky was a time bomb whose own detonator clock ticked to no knowable rhythm.

When Mr. Reddy and I took him out of isolation, where we'd held him till the shrink arrived, he was pissed off at the world, strutting like a pimp, and hissing racial insults at us through his puffed lips. You lily-white, punk-assed *cracker*!" If the unmistakably black Mr. Reddy was surprised this slur was directed at him, he sure didn't let on.

In a way I admired Reddy; in public he was gracious beyond reproach even when the kids stared him down, and he never, ever broke into a sweat. Even in the middle of July, when everyone else had dripped and wiped endlessly, his meticulous sartorial splendor had remained unsullied by so much as one tiny bead of offending perspiration. He was the only man I'd ever known who never blew the fresh crease on a dress shirt and never stuck to his trousers when it was ninety-two degrees inside.

God had intended him, I imagined, to become the maître d' to the front foyer of Hades, so that incoming guests wouldn't become alarmed and put up a fuss. From Reddy's presence—cool, smiling, and nicely creased—one would never guess what might await them once seated near those mythical fires. I imagined him as a major character in one of Dante Alighieri's books—the complex majordomo who embodied that all-important but unknowable line that divided redemption from damnation.

Reddy and I ushered Kamensky in to see the shrink. Kamensky

bit his inner lips to keep them puffed up and swollen to respectable, black man specs . . . something he did so obsessively that he no longer drank the morning orange juice because of the pain its acids induced.

"Here is student Kamensky," Mr. Reddy said coolly to the shrink. "One of us can stay . . ."

"No thanks. Routine . . . I can handle this." Kamensky sneered while indulging his compulsion to chomp down on his reddening lower lip meat till it bled. The shrink waved us out with his reading glasses without ever looking up. "Nice suit!" whistled Reddy once we were out in the hallway. "Italian wool. Must have cost one-fifty."

"Forbes Avenue consulting shrinks don't work cheap . . . why do you think he's here?"

"Probably a snotty friend of Her Majesty's."

"Who?" I asked.

"That's our director."

Twenty minutes later, Reddy and I were both seated in the dining hall updating charts, me sweating, Reddy not, when a searing crash and the sound of splitting wood reverberated from somewhere in the rear corridor.

"Kamensky?" I exclaimed.

"Perhaps. Why don't *you* go and check it out," said Reddy, flashing me his widest, used-car-dealer smile and straightening his tie. Mrs. Moxon coughed from the doorway. "Perhaps you'd *both* better go. I just phoned security."

Mrs. Moxon, officially the housemother, seemed to have much more juice than her job description implied. And it wasn't due to her physical presence. In nondescript black shoes and an apron worn over faded print dresses, she was a dowdy, smallish lump of a woman. She was, I later decided, defined by mission, rather than appearance—and that gave her authentic, moral authority. When Reddy hesitated at her announcement, she stared him down and clarified, "You should probably know that Kamensky refused his meds this morning." That got Reddy out of his chair.

"That *punk* needs to be sent to Camp Hill. I swear I'm gonna . . ." Reddy didn't shut up till we turned the corner and encountered the spectacle: Kamensky, sprawled on the hallway floor, dazed and bleeding copiously from a huge gash over one eyebrow.

Inside the meeting room, the shrink slumped eerily in his chair. "You take the doctor," ordered Reddy. I dashed past and checked the pulse in his neck. Strong, but a bit fast. I stepped in front of him and gently raised his head. One side of the doc's face sported a huge, red, well-defined knuckle print just under his left cheekbone. Kamensky had apparently decked him, then broken through the locked door.

I shouted for Mrs. Moxon. "Bring a cold washcloth and smelling salts!" Reddy yelled. "We'll need a pressure wrap and gauze for his head!" For a short, squat, middle-aged lady, Mrs. Moxon was quick and efficient. I held a cool towel to the doctor's face, leaned him back to get some fresh blood into his noggin, then waved the salts under his nose. He jerked and coughed right on cue.

For once we didn't need to put restraints on Kamensky. His pupils were still unfocused as he gazed up from the floor looking surprised. His lips had puffed up to the size of a pig's snout, giving him a remarkably grotesque look.

The shrink, finally on his feet and squawking like a parrot on speed, kept repeating, "He's crazy. He's crazy! He thinks he's black! Did you hear me . . . he thinks he's *black*. Crazy. Says he's black. Black. Crazy . . . *black*!" Reddy and his perfect creases finally snapped; I thought his gold tooth would fly out of his mouth.

"Yeah, doc, I *think* I'm black, too. Does that make *me* crazy? No, doc, I *am* black. Crazy is head-butting a goddamn door that I've got to write an F . . . F . . . F . . . ing report on . . . and another on *you*, who waved us out. Being alone with Kamensky is nuts. *That's* nuts, doc . . . no one here gives a damn about what Kamensky *thinks* he is. But *I* give a *damn* about having to write reports!"

At that the shrink turned toward me, stunned. I smiled. "We're all nuts here. . . . Go put ice on that cheek before it swells more. Mrs. Moxon over there is holding a bag for you."

Still muttering to himself about Kamensky's blackness, the Forbes Avenue shrink staggered out the door. Mr. Reddy, now in the front office, alternated between writing furiously and watching the wall clock. On the upside, he didn't utter another word all afternoon.

Mrs. Moxon and I wrapped up the ordinary shift business, checking in students as they trickled back from school around three thirty. She clocked out at five. I clocked in for the second time then checked on Mr. Reddy. The front office was already vacant . . . just a note to me from Reddy on top of the "in progress" incident report: "Stuart. Order. Finish this tonight! R."

Davenport stuck his head in as I tucked the incident report under my arm. "Anything interesting happen today?"

I laughed and recounted the incident. Dav shook his head. "Did Reddy leave the report for you half-finished?" I nodded. "Well, sounds like everyone is in character."

I nodded again. "By the way, did you find out if Billy can work on the graveyard with me?"

"Yes he can. It's not ordinary manual labor. But take two, so there are no questions."

"OK. I'll take Curtis. He goes to chapel on Sundays."

Dav smiled. "There you go! Where did they take Kamensky?"

"Pittsburgh General, for openers. Allegheny Ambulance. That was three hours ago. We should get a call."

"I'll phone Allegheny. Can you take today's recreation group over to the pool?"

Every day in summer we rotated groups of eight into the brick swimming pool building about 250 yards away. When alone the trick was to assign an alpha male to the front, like a lead dog, and bring up the rear, keeping the kid most likely to run right in front of you. The "maybes" in front of him in a row of three and the "not-so-likelys" in the front file behind the day's designated lead dog.

Sugarbear led. Country—the "No mens gonna fuck me in the ass" kid—was within arm's reach of me. Once inside the pool, it was easy. A security assistant and lifeguard were on duty till seven, four groups of eight, four at a time maximum, and there were six staff for thirty-two students. Workable.

I cornered Curtis, who regularly read the Children's Bible while others watched TV, when he pulled himself onto the tile after his first cannonball dive. "Curtis, my man! How about going up to the graveyard with me on Thursday? Got to clean up those graves from fifty years ago. It's the Christian thing to do."

"But Chaplain says we aren't allowed up there—no desecratin'."

"I'll check with him again, Curtis, but Mr. Dav is good with it. It'll go in your progress file." Curtis, born near Birmingham, Alabama, studied me for a few moments.

"I'll do it for baby Jesus! You can write it up if you want to."

I nodded. "I'll come get you on Thursday at two thirty. Billy will go with us." I shooed Curtis back into line so he wouldn't lose his turn. Getting out one's aggressions by cannon-balling was a harmless, and therefore encouraged, diversion.

At dinner I recruited Billy, using his mother as bait. "Three dollars cash money for Momma! Thursday, two thirty."

"I'll forget." He frowned.

"I'll come get you at the HUB [vo-tech shops] at 2:35."

He smiled. "Will I get candy?" I nodded. That sealed the deal. Done, I wrote myself a note to mention this to Father Ralph.

Needs varied among the students: For some, every act cultivated dominance; others wanted "good time" to shorten sentences. For Billy it was "Momma." For Curtis, it was baby Jesus. Both wound up incarcerated for different versions of a teenaged beer run. Neither belonged in the Morganza. The fact that they were confined in here with the likes of Sugarbear, Sinbad, and Kamensky had already started to rankle me deeply. Liberal bullshit or not, the Commonwealth of Pennsylvania's juvenile justice system—of which I was now a part—was killing some of these kids an inch at a time.

chapter 9

Not Behind the White Fence

As the rhythm of daily routine gradually lulled me into a sense of normalcy, I became less vigilant and more relaxed.

It was an ordinary, hot summer Tuesday in early August—still short-staffed in our cottage, I was to work from noon to six the next morning. The farm's dank brick cottages, offset by stone accents and disingenuously innocent-looking white timber trim, made the whole Morganza look deceptively like just another of the classic, well-worn, late nineteenth-century college campuses that dotted Pennsylvania in alarming profundity.

I wondered what the eighteenth-century Colonel Morgan, whose family had already founded the original fortified blockhouse and cluster of farmhouses later known as "Morganza, Pennsylvania" by the time of the 1740s French and Indian wars, would have thought of the current use of his family's farm holdings.

Within an hour of arriving for my shift, I was summoned to the Morganza's administration building. I wasn't certain but guessed, correctly, that it had something to do with my excursion with Curtis and Billy to the graveyard.

Rendered in a perverse interpretation of Dutch and Colonial styles mixed with early art deco, the imposing, green copper-spired brick building was damn near big enough to serve as the capitol of a "we got a small population" state like Montana or one of the Dakotas. That it was the "nerve and policy" center (in the words of the same liberal, politically connected director) of a reformatory farm housing several hundred teenagers, yet required about a hundred bureaucratic staff in the admin building itself, explained everything anyone needed to know about Pennsylvania's breathtaking tax rates but obstructive, decision-averse bureaucracy.

As a child, I'd started school in West Chester, Pennsylvania. As a grade-school student I could get a free Kleenex if my nose was runny, a counselor if I was in a funk, a bandage if I fell . . . but a teacher who could answer your philosophical questions like "Why does two plus two equal four?" Kiss your curiosity good-bye.

The Morganza was no different. There we obsessed about daily details, investing massively in "testing," "evaluating," "diagnosing," "exploring policy vectors" (whatever that meant), and candy bars. But *do* something tangible that wasn't on a prevetted list elicited an "Oh, no. We aren't going *there*, Mr. Stuart."

I answered, "I thought it would be nice" in response to the first question I was asked by a very hostile senior assistant to the director. She was *Mizzz* Champlin, only about five years older than I, very white, very nasal, very Main Line Bryn Mawr, and, by West Virginia standards, a stone-cold bitch. Her high, aquiline nose twitched as her nasal passages puffed up in preparation.

"*Ordinary* staff are *not* permitted behind the white fence . . . and, judging from the records I have here in front of me, you are, uh, how shall I put it . . . *quite* ordinary . . . you have no business in *policy* matters, Stuart. So tell me *again* why you did it."

"Again, I thought it would be nice to clean up the graves . . . a *respectful* thing to do. The chaplain approved. Mr. Davenport and others were consulted, and Ms. Dicks, the evening nurse, actually suggested it."

"I see . . . well, then, quit *thinking* . . . you aren't very good at it, are you?"

"Why the nastiness?" I asked, sounding dead calm but irritated about three full layers of psyche beneath the only façade this Main Line chick would ever have access to. "We cleaned off a dozen graves. Two students, two staff . . . no cost to the farm."

"Activities like this are *bid* projects! A project like this must be *bid*. Then reviewed by accounting. Then by legal. Then by the public relations officer. Then me. *Then* the director. And, finally, Harrisburg. . . . I am writing you up for this infraction and recommending loss of a day's pay. Have you *any* final questions?"

Yeah, I had a lot of questions for this loser—and some statements, too, most of which would've gotten me fired. So I held back. "Why did Emma Ginton and Ella Douglass both die on November 2, 1897? One was eighteen; the other nineteen."

She blinked. "What do you mean?"

I enunciated clearly for her sake. "Why did *two* young women die on the *same* damn day in 1897—were they *murdered*? Did they *fight*? Were they *pregnant*? *Raped*? And why isn't anyone allowed behind the fence? What is this place hiding?"

Her eyes widened. "Is this your way of directing the subject away from your performance situation?"

"No. Write up whatever fantasy suits you. The question is, what is that graveyard doing up there and why does it press buttons to clean it up?"

"Now I *am* angry," she said.

"Good! So find out why Emma and Ella died on the same day."

She picked up the phone. "No—that's not what I mean, Stuart. Our meeting is over. I'm calling security."

"You mean Palco? Tell him to kiss my ass." I smiled and walked out through the bursar's office and its fancily painted antique "Gibraltar" safe. I exited the reception area, passing under the Hill's fifteen-foot-tall, elaborate iron doorway and sidelights. As I crossed the steps in front, Palco arrived, breathless with excitement.

"Why did you drive, Palco?" I asked, "It's just four hundred yards."

"Emergency. What are *you* doing here, Weasel?"

"Oh, just discussing the philosophy of management with the director's assistant."

"Ah, Jesus! It's *you* she called about."

"Yeah. I got my ass roasted for cleaning up the graves on the Hill."

"Huh? Why do they give a shit about that?" I shrugged. "Get in, Weasel, while I'm still in a good mood. I'm taking you back to work." I followed him out. "So what is *Mizzz* Champlin like?" Palco asked, his voice raspy with innuendo.

"Delightful! When I asked her for a date, she told me she liked mature guys. 'Big teddy bears' is I think how she phrased it."

"Not into scrawny Weasels like you, eh?" gloated Palco.

"Nah . . . that and West Virginia. She's a true-blue Pennsylvania gal." With any luck, Palco would soon find an excuse to discuss my "performance issues" with Champlin and hit on her. Palco snickered. "But hey, a guy can fantasize!" I continued.

"So either she's pissed over the graveyard or pissed because you hit on her, eh?"

"Yeah. But said graveyard. Something about 'ordinary' staff not permitted behind the white fence."

"That's nuts. She needs a good fucking is all." The pain in the ass part of me did an inner high five.

Two days later I was summoned back to the Hill for a hearing on my "performance issues and judgment." The sleek, twitchy-eyed chief counsel for the farm, along with the personnel director and five overstuffed assistant pooh-bahs, formed a hearing committee. Everything about the chief counsel shouted, "I'm spoiled, vain, and insecure": his professionally manicured nails, Italian suit, designer glasses, meticulous haircut, and own monogram engraved on everything he wore. Like an inbred show dog, he was pampered, well-groomed, and hyper-tense—but had "good conformation." I imagined him on the judging stand at the Westminster dog show as some old bat lifted his upper lips to check his teeth. Thereafter, I just called him Lawdawg.

Since I was still in my first six months, personnel policies made it clear that I didn't get an appeal or any time to prepare.

"Tell us again why you did this without authorization," twittered Lawdawg.

"That's a misstatement. I consulted four senior staff and received approval from all. We cleaned up about a dozen graves—there are more we didn't get to. Some markers are missing. Then the chaplain conducted a short service." Lawdawg put his hand up to indicate the answer was sufficient, then went on.

"Who was there?"

"Me, Nurse Dicks, and two students."

"Their names?"

"Why?"

"Their *names!*"

"Curtis and Billy," I answered. He turned to an assistant—"Take care of it"—then turned back to fix his gaze on me. "Now . . . as for your assault on Mizzz Champlin . . ."

"*Assault*? Asking a question is not an 'assault.'" He put his palm up to interrupt me again, but I ignored him. "Champlin said such projects had to go out for bid. Have to be approved all the way to Harrisburg. I paid $3 into each student's work account out of my own pocket then gave each a candy bar." I slapped a Franklin 50¢ piece onto the table, along with a document.

"What's that?" he snapped.

"An official Commonwealth 'Incidental Projects' bid form. I've bid $6.40. You owe me a dime."

"You can't tender a bid . . . you are an employee," he goggled. "Besides, there is no RFP." Everyone stared at everyone else, smirking.

"The Request for Proposals is attached to the bid. Read it—Father Ralph made the request. State law provides for small scope of work letters for 'incidental projects' under $50, providing only that a regular employee may not be a payee. I'm neither a regular employee nor the payee." The top law dog turned bright red.

"And your assault on Miss Champlin?"

"I asked her why two female wards of the Morganza, one aged eighteen, the other nineteen, died on the same day of November of eighteen and ninety-seven and were buried on that hill. Instead of answering, she picked up the phone and called Palco. So I left, met Palco at the front door, and he drove me down to the cottage."

"And . . . ?"

"And I've been researching newspaper files in Little Washington and in Pittsburgh to answer my question. I intend to find out about those girls." It went quiet. Everyone checked out everyone else again, but this time they weren't smirking. He put his palm up for the third time. "Well, that's all for today. . . . We have your statement and are hereby adjourned."

][[

Several days later I received a typed letter from personnel: "Docked one day's pay for improper procedure while in a six-month training capacity." It was office stamped but not signed. I would have shrugged it off if it hadn't been for the fact that Curtis and Billy's work accounts were each docked the $3. They also each owed the farm a candy bar and were rejected for the one day of "good time" and a reduction in sentence the chaplain had submitted for each. *The pricks didn't even have the nuts to sign it*, I noted.

And Father Ralph was not a happy man when I took the chapel-going students to mass on Sunday. "David . . . I filled out the form as you suggested . . . so how did Curtis and Billy get into trouble over this?"

"I don't know, Father. It has to do with Champlin in the director's office and questions about, or even interest in, the graveyard."

As a consequence, the ordinarily good-natured Chaplain who, Dav told me, had won two Bronze Stars at Anzio during WWII, tried to raise hell with Mizzz Champlin and the director. Predictably, he was dumped on, more genteelly of course, by bitch Champlin and never even got a meeting with the director, so he raised the issue with the archdiocese in Pittsburgh. Several days later, according to one of our cottage student snitches, the bishop of Pittsburgh called the farm.

The results were surprisingly swift and effective. Mizzz Champlin suddenly—and "coincidentally," some insisted—accepted a "better assignment" in Harrisburg, and everyone in the copper-spired administration building went into "I know nothing" mode, just like Sergeant Schultz in the *Hogan's Heroes* TV series. The unsigned reprimand disappeared from my personnel file as quickly as it had been inserted. My pay was not docked, and Curtis and Billy's $3 reappeared. Father Ralph even got some unexpected paint and roof repair to the small stuccoed chapel that sat at one edge of the campus. Palco, of course, seemed temporarily deflated—on two counts, I assumed. First, I didn't get into big trouble; second, he didn't get into Champlin's pants.

Dav was impressed. "Damn! I should have been raised Catholic! Paper has been disappearing so fast around here that it makes my head spin. By the way—can we get together on Billy's petition? Off campus would be good."

We made a lunch and paperwork deal for the following week at an Italian place in Little Washington. For a few days, I invested every spare moment in that petition. When we finally met, Dav wanted to write the "Progress in Rehabilitation" summary. He handed it to me a week later on my way to the Tower. "I got some help on the editing from our reverend. Let me know what you think, Mr. Stuart."

"I'm still not the pro, but I think it's *very* good!" I told him when he came to give me a break later that night. "I'd like to get it submitted soon."

"Yes. Billy's mom isn't doing well, according to their preacher up in Beaver Falls. He wants to bring her down here again on Visitor's Day and meet with us. Shall I arrange your schedule so that it works out?"

"Sure, Mr. Davenport. It's all the same to me as long as I get a day and a half between now and then to go see my mom. I'm going home when I get off in the morning."

]|[

The next day, Mom was still dazed but had progressed to occasional crying fits that made me very sad. If I'd been one of the shrinks from the Morganza, I might have charted it as a "positive sign of working through grief issues." But I wasn't a shrink. I was just her son—so I kept myself busy, doing what I could for her.

I put money into her checking account, helped her clean house, bought groceries hoping that she'd eat, and gave her permission to get rid of "Ed's things."

"Sure, but there is no hurry, Mom. Why not move downstairs into my bedroom? Get a change of scenery?" We drove around again. I got a few hours' sleep and hit the road for Little Washington around five. I wanted to submit Billy's new hearing petition to his sentencing court, which first had to go through the Commonwealth's departments of Youth and Family Services, then Justice.

Obviously the Commonwealth's intention with such a multi-pronged procedure was to delay and discourage appeals, but I hoped my work would get ten to twenty bureaucrats head-tripping over a barrel of beer, a borrowed pony, and a dollar's worth of rope. If successful it might shorten the time Billy was incarcerated on the inside, stewing over the reality that his mom couldn't make it alone on the outside.

In an abundance of bureaucratic exuberance, I at last filed Billy's petition for case review and a new hearing everywhere. When I began the project I convinced myself I had to do it because "the system" had failed Billy—a '60s thing. But once the petition was actually in the mail, I began to see my persistence for what it was, as though somehow the petition for Billy might free my mother, too.

Chapter 10

Mr. Davenport, We Have to Talk

By mid-August I had enough seniority among the in-training staff to draw mostly three to eleven shifts. I really liked the change because I could get an extra shift or fill in hours till midnight as the regular staff's vacation season continued.

The afternoon shifts also gave me time to rummage through the *Washington County Observer*'s newspaper files on the Morganza. Precious little turned up. After the 1880s it was the same story with the *Pittsburgh Post*. If there was info to be had on Emma and Ella, it was probably buried in Harrisburg or in one of the Hill's locked basement file rooms.

Striking out on the newspaper files, I settled for striking up conversations in restaurants and gas stations. Everyone in Little Washington and Canonsburg, it seemed, spoke of the Morganza either in hushed tones or not at all. In fact, the more questions I asked, the fewer answers I got.

][(

Western Pennsylvania in August flat-out sucked. Two months into the 88–78 phenomenon, eighty-eight degrees Fahrenheit at seventy-eight percent humidity, the thick bricks and plaster walls of the Morganza's cottages could have doubled as very effective warming ovens. The walls were hot to the touch. I was hot. The students were tired, hot, and cranky. Roasting in his clerical garb, Father Ralph regularly verged on ungodly.

I'd been reading Melville's *Moby Dick* again on breaks. At that season I needed to feel the spray of the sea—my eagle's nest studio on Beau Street demanded it. Besides, Melville had done one heck of a job depicting pathologically obsessive stubbornness and abiding, atavistic rage. If you are going to work in a reform school with teenaged capital crime types, Melville is at least as important in understanding the action around you as your college text in abnormal psychology.

Given the unremitting heat, it was inevitable that someone would snap out. The question was not if, but who, when, and where. Most of us, I think, believed it would be Kamensky. I imagined him breaching, blowing a huge spout of spit from his pain-puffed lips, then hitting the water, and taking Cottage 6 down with him as he sounded.

But it was not Kamensky, or another student, who first breached and spouted. Seems Lawdawg was hearing from half a dozen tentacles of the Commonwealth's clinging bureaucratic octopus, and Billy was the recurring subject: His tainted trial, and the so-called Justice System up in Beaver County, had rankled a number among the "I'm rich and connected, so I can feel poor Billy's pain as a substitute for my own social guilt" set. "Trust fund commies" we called 'em down in West Virginia. And God bless 'em, they *were*, according to Lawdawg, righteously pissed off over a kid doing life for borrowing a farmer's pony then being sentenced by the complaintant's relative, who was also the presiding judge.

On the downside, Lawdawg was equally righteous in his own pique, which I discovered when he summoned me to his office. "This makes it look like *we* are involved in this mess!" he squeaked nasally, both palms up.

"Aren't we?" I asked calmly, my hands folded in my lap. "After all, the debate in this building is whether we hammer these kids as underage cons or try to rehabilitate them. The juvenile court system doesn't even have the sense to separate the violent kids from the nonviolent." In response, Lawdawg looked down at his monogrammed Oyster Rolex and said nothing. I elaborated. "Don't we act as legal *in loco parentis*—court-designated guardians, as it were." Whoosh! An unexpected spout of Melvillian rage damn near blew a hole through his office's twelve-foot-high ceiling.

"Get out! . . . And *stay out* of this building. Director's orders."

"Why? We are overcrowded and this kid simply doesn't belong here."

"Because the director and I say so. Because a court says he stays *here* and because what we do, policy-wise, is none of your business. Out!" He stood, red-faced and shaking a finger at me.

"I am sorry," I said. "His mom needs him."

"*We* decide such things up *here*. As a trainee, you don't decide *any-thing*! Out! *Now*!" He was spouting steam again when I left.

"Mr. Davenport, we have to talk," I whispered back at the cottage.

"Yes. Williams warned me about backlash from the petition." Ten minutes later, we got some scarce privacy. I briefed Dav. He shook his head. "They don't like outside scrutiny on the Hill . . . and Her Majesty, the director, some say, is terrified when politics spread hither and thither."

"What's 'hither and thither' mean?"

"Whites. Crackers. Catholics. Unions. Jews—the politically dangerous."

"Jeez! Why doesn't she just add 'Indians' and put on a white sheet?"

Dav grinned. "*You* can tell her that if you want to, but I won't know you anymore. Besides, there really are gun-toting crackers up in Beaver County. It's not easy directing a unit like this. Nobody's happy. Everyone wants to lay society's problems on us. The director's problem is that *we* didn't raise these kids. She absolutely believes in rehabilita-tion. But *we* don't get to sit on the juries, so they send us a witch's brew of everything from Kamensky to Country. We're just the local bank—we get society's deposits, but almost no one out there owns up to their dirty money."

"Hmm. . . . Should I talk to the director?"

"You serious?"

"Yeah. I want Billy to get a chance. Maybe I am looking at this too one-sidedly. Perhaps she'd support it if I explained."

"Damn . . . you are as crazy as Kamensky. Uh, sorry, Mr. Stuart . . . that didn't come out quite right."

"Well, you have a point. Kamensky's convinced he's black, but he's not. I'm convinced ordinary people can make a difference . . .

and maybe they—or I—can't. But I want to talk to 'Her Majesty' just in case."

Dav's eyes widened. "You're serious, aren't you?" I nodded. "OK. I'll talk to Williams. He gets along with her." Dav paused. "Is this part of what being white is all about?"

"Huh?"

"I mean, half of our people go marching. Organize. Get most every black minister in the country on board . . . *then* we get to face Bull Connor's nightsticks, dogs, and fire hoses . . . knowing that some of us will get jailed and beat up . . . maybe lynched . . . just to get a message on a newsreel in the off-chance we can get an itty-bitty piece of grudging, piss-ant change. You, now . . . you want to talk to a woman who probably hates you. You don't *care* about that. You don't have to care."

"Wow, that's profound! You need to write that up and publish it."

Dav rolled his eyes. "You don't need to kiss my butt, Mr. Stuart . . . I already told you I'd ask Williams."

"No offense, Mr. Davenport . . . but you *are* profound. Believing you aren't . . . is that part of what 'black' is all about?" Immediately, I regretted what I'd said—it was rude and out of line.

Dav pursed his lips in thought. His lower lip's dark dot of misplaced mustache puckered out . . . as if he intended to respond . . . but, as was so often the case, Palco inconveniently intruded.

"How about some backup down here . . . I gotta do rounds!" Part of Palco's job was to check in and get a "census" from each cottage after the students came home from school.

"Black or white," I muttered, "Palco is a pain in the . . ."

"I can hear you, Weasel!" growled Palco.

)|(

After dinner I drew recreation duty. Same old, same old . . . it was pool up in the billiard room. I took eight of them upstairs at a time for thirty minutes then exchanged them for another eight down in the TV room.

Group one was peaceful. Rabbit flirted with Country, who panicked and withdrew, stiff-legged, to the other side of the table, "locking" his ass again, I assumed.

We worked very hard to prevent sexual incidents . . . and usually succeeded. But guarding every student twenty-four–seven just wasn't possible with the staff we had. That's one big reason we locked students into their rooms each night around nine. Dav told me it worked darned near perfectly in the era when it was more staff and one kid per room.

Now, with two per room and occasional dormitory/Tower stints, it was a lot harder, so we watched Country carefully. He had a charted IQ of sixty-eight, flaccid, protruding lips, and was basically sweet and stunningly credulous.

What Country did not seem to understand was that Rabbit was a classic "bottom man." Rabbit was, if not watched, a willing victim . . . the Venus flytrap . . . but not the dominant partner in the actual sexual encounter. Still, I worried about Country. He was from the rural South and probably didn't know much more than I did about aberrant sex—most of what I'd learned had been from the emergency room in Morgantown. Some of it was, frankly, more than I wanted to know. But it proved useful at the Morganza.

Country had been in the north for less than a year. Malleable, stupid, and seeking approval, he'd been in the wrong car at the wrong time. Someone had been shot inside a small Italian grocery on Pittsburgh's north side—shades of Curtis's story. All agreed that Country had waited in the car. But that still made him guilty of armed robbery and attempted murder.

Slam! Bang! One very unsophisticated, somebody-please-love-me, gentle, hardworking black kid wound up in the Morganza . . . and no more belonged than did chubby Curtis or Billy.

The thing Country educated me about was "duppies." Those head-on-backward, zombified, wide-eyed, walking, and very dangerous undead that followers of voodoo had to contend with when certain unspecified things went horribly wrong.

We didn't have duppies in West Virginia. Instead we grew up listening to endless rants about Lucifer, the devil, or the Evil One in his various disguises—utterly uninteresting when compared to a black dude whose head was screwed on backward and who could turn you into a replica just by staring at you through huge, cloudy, wide-lidded eyes . . . and, unlike Lucifer, who was, according to local theologians, a one-off model. There were lots of duppies. "Some of them right here at the Morganza," insisted Country. "I seen one staring at me in the window. They comes outta trees on the Hill."

In the billiard room, Country held forth on duppies while avoiding Rabbit's seductive wiles delivered from the far side of the table. To my surprise, several of the other black kids were not only conversant with the duppy phenomenon but were scared shitless of them.

))((

After talk about duppies, I ushered group two into the billiard room. Orders of the Hill, it included Sinbad, Sugarbear, and Kamensky . . . putting those three together was yet another artifact of bureaucratic street stupidity. I watched Sinbad carefully, ensured that he went first, and declined to shoot pool with him when invited.

About halfway through our thirty minutes a tussle broke out over whose turn it was. Golightly, the tall, handsome "High Yella," as he was known to Kamensky and the other blacks, insisted it was his turn. Scarpetti, a cold, sleepy-eyed Sicilian kid, insisted it was his. I leaned over to intervene . . .

As I did, something hit me in the butt, like a tongue of fire. Sweat foamed out of every pore in my body and a shockwave of pain radiated upward. My ass exploded.

Someone tittered. I straightened up slowly, turned and reached behind me. To my amazement, I discovered a long, two-pronged serving fork from dinner buried deep in my right gluteus muscle.

Sinbad's eyes sparkled as the pleasure of witnessing my pain combined with the evening dose of methadone, remolding his face into a peaceful, smiling anomaly. For a fleeting moment he looked just like one of those angelic, winged cherubs smiling down on baby Jesus and the Madonna from the painted clouds on a medieval church window.

Sugarbear, on the other hand, crouched, ready for action. Kamensky, his healing forehead stitches now puckered like his lips, slipped from behind me, a malevolent grin on his face.

Trying not to faint from the pain, I straightened up, pulled the fork out, and heard myself say rather calmly, if not distinctly, "Dammit, this is inconvenient. I'm going to take this thing back to the kitchen." Kamensky's eyes widened and he stepped away from me. I stared him down. "If any of you act out while I'm gone," I said, pointing at the table, "I'm going to make you swallow one of those balls. Got it?" Amazingly, I still sounded calm.

Everyone nodded; some even gaped. I left. Going down the stairs hurt beyond description, but I reached Dav before I fainted. My ears were buzzing and everything seemed distant. Sometime later I came back into focus in the main floor's isolation cell. I was facedown on a cot and Big Jill was chattering to someone while taping a dressing on my butt.

"I cleaned it out and gave him a hypo of tetracycline. Whooh! That's gotta hurt!"

I interrupted her. "Am I *OK*?"

"Oh, yes, honey. Your butt is as soft as a baby's."

"I was being serious, Jill."

"So was I . . . your cheek is gonna be one huge hematoma for a few days. I'd kiss it to make it better, but we have company. I'll call the house doctor and get you a 'scrip for some pain medication. If you start running a fever, get yourself to the hospital in Little Washington . . . we are sending you home."

"No, I've got to go upstairs. Who's up there with group two?"

"Palco. I'll drive you home."

"I live on the fourth story . . . I won't be able to make it."

"OK, we'll bunk you here in isolation," decided Jill.

It was a long, hot night, and the codeine-laced painkiller didn't arrive from Little Washington until hours later. Big Jill brought it, along with a big bowl of "My spaghetti soup," and changed my butt dressing. "How ya doin', cutie?" she asked when I groaned. "Still hurts, Jill."

"I'll bring the ice bag back. That'll help."

Ice. No ice. Meds. No meds. It didn't really matter. My butt was swollen and on fire. I never developed a fever, but it took nearly a week before I could climb stairs without breaking out in another sweat. As I'd asked, the incident was handled with no comment and no fanfare . . . revenge, it is said, is a dish best served cold. And cold suited me.

Chapter 11

Sorry About the Fork Thing

The mysterious Williams had managed to arrange my audience with Her Majesty as soon as I was recovered. In response to student rumors that Billy would get a new trial, an air of tension rippled through the cottage's halls. Neither Dav nor I had anticipated the possibility that students would hear about Billy's petition . . . but we should have.

The favorite students got sweet after-school work assignments up on the Hill. Some of them could—and did—read everything found on desks—not to mention pinching an occasional desk drawer candy bar, ballpoint pen, or letterhead.

The pens, innocuous everyday tools to the uninitiated, were easily refashioned into weapons. All one needed was a grinding wheel, another piece of pen barrel to attach as a T-shaped push handle, and one had the incarcerated world's primitive equivalent of a stiletto.

Such a sharpened ballpoint could easily be driven through a predator's heart, into his liver . . . or into that soft spot several inches above the belly button, which usually punctures the aorta. This was the kind of carefully priced and secretly traded commodity in our eccentric little world.

Finally realizing from the gossip that I might have some practical value beyond the temporary high he had obtained from watching me sweat and stiffen with a fork sticking out of my ass, Sinbad turned sweet on me. "How you doing, Mr. Stuart? Sorry about the fork thing. I told my crewe that whoever did it was immature . . . it won't happen again."

"Ah. Good. Maybe I shouldn't bother to finish writing it up. It wasn't a big deal, anyway," I replied, rolling my eyes.

That night, I drew group two again for the first time since the fork incident. It was a major stroke of fortune. Dav was off and I had Sinbad and the "forking crewe," as I irreverently called them, all to myself.

Sinbad pimped and strutted as his flock lined up to shoot pool. Golightly tried to sneak behind me, but when Kamensky gave me his best lip-puffed, mad-dog stare, Sinbad intervened. "Be cool, man. We're cool."

I smiled, trying to keep Golightly in my peripheral vision while looking casual, and handed the 18-ounce cue to Sinbad, motioning for him to break. Sugarbear shrugged and joined the others seated on the bench positioned against the opposite wall. Sinbad, wearing a mellow, methadone-induced grin, bent low over the table. I choked up to get a tight grip on the shaft of my #21 cue and snapped the rubber butt out, connecting with the bony bump behind his left ear.

Sinbad grunted, went limp, and sprawled satisfyingly onto the pool table. "Sloppy break," I commented, then turned to Golightly behind me. "Who wants to shoot next?"

Golightly retreated to the bench and Sinbad's crewe suddenly lost interest in table sports. Kamensky's eyes bulged and his lips expanded like those on a blow-up Mickey Mouse balloon.

"Mutha'fuk—Mr. Stuart's snapped."

"Nah. I'm good . . . wanna shoot, Kamensky?"

"Fuck no! I wanna go to my room, man. Don' you come no closer . . . I ain' shittin' you . . . don't you jack me up!"

Everyone suddenly lined up, docile. *Ah, the sound of a deflated bully is sweet,* I cackled to myself.

Sugarbear, still processing, whined, "Ain'chu gonna do nothin' for Sinbad?"

"You're right, Sugarbear," I said, herding him back into line with the tip of my cue. "I'll call Palco." I picked up the security phone and dialed. Palco growled. "Taking group two back to the second floor. Come up here to billiards and check on Sinbad. Banged his head on the pool table. The methadone, I think." I hung up. "There." I nodded at Sugarbear.

"You ain't nice!" he whined.

They moved out, morbidly quiet for once. For some odd reason they jostled one another until Kamensky was nearest me at the back of the line. He covered the back of his head with both arms, bent forward, and crab-scuttled, flinching for the blow that never came.

My partner that evening was Richard, a newbie and the only college boy to be hired after me. He had been on the job about two weeks. He was black, very well spoken, and had been raised by an aunt ("ont," he pronounced it) in Little Washington. She was—or had been—a schoolteacher.

Richard always wore his Howard University tie and pulled on a madras jacket for dinner, no matter how hot it was. He was genteel beyond words. Polite. Organized and hardworking. I don't think it ever crossed his mind that anything had happened, other than "Sinbad lost his balance and banged into the table rail." Had Dav been there, he'd probably have seen through it and been on my case. Palco could have thought anything. Frankly, I didn't care.

Group two in their rooms, Palco went to retrieve Sinbad, who was awake but confused when Palco stepped into the billiard room. Jill arrived and rushed upstairs to check on Sinbad while Richard and I got some activities going in the TV room for those who preferred to play checkers. Golightly, the only one in group two who, oddly, hadn't wanted to be locked in, played chess with Richard while I played checkers with Billy. "I wanna go home. I got to do for Momma," Billy pleaded as he took my last black checker almost effortlessly.

"Can't just yet. Preacher and Momma are going to visit you next week."

"Why are Sinbad's frens talkin' 'bout my trial, Mr. Stuart?"

"Do you remember the details of your trial, Billy?" He shook his head and smiled. Five minutes later he hammered me at checkers again. *How the hell can a kid with an IQ in the sixties do that?* I wondered. It wasn't something the standard IQ scale could explain: "Genius," "Above Normal," "Normal," "Dull Normal," "Idiot," "Cretin" had as little to do with Billy as his sentencing to the Morganza.

Palco came strutting in just before bedtime at nine thirty and tapped my shoulder. To my amazement he didn't call me Weasel. "Stuart, I need to speak with you."

"Let's talk once they're in bed," I suggested. He nodded and headed for the kitchen. "Old Palco has to work hard to keep that gut in good shape," I commented to Richard as we gathered the troops. Richard chuckled.

A half hour later I met Palco, who was lounging alone in the TV room, legs sprawled wide, watching *The Tonight Show* and working his way through the tall stack of baloney and cheese sandwiches Mrs. Moxon had made for all three of us.

"Well," said Palco, "I think someone popped Sinbad, but he doesn't remember anything except leaning over. When did he take his methadone?"

"Off-cycle—just after dinner—twenty to thirty minutes before he hit the cue rack—least I think that's what happened."

"I talked to Kamensky . . ." Palco leered. "Says you 'snapped out.'"

"Yep. He got himself agitated and started chewing on his lower lip. I didn't need a riot so I let him know I'd nail him with a cue if he screwed with me."

"Uh huh. *Riiight.*"

"OK, I snapped out . . . if it makes you feel better."

"It does; gives me faith you aren't one hundred percent Weasel."

"Ah, faith is the substance of things hoped for . . . and the proof of things not seen," I said. Palco rolled his eyes.

"Want to see my report before it's submitted?" he asked me.

"Nah. Is Sinbad going to be OK?" I asked.

"Fucker will never be OK. Damn shame his head's as hard as granite."

"You can't win 'em all, can you?" I commented.

Palco laughed. "I should visit West, how's that go . . . by 'fuckin' heaven,' West Virginia someday. Could find people I like."

"It's 'West, *by God* . . .' Got to remember that or you'll get your ass kicked by some immense simian who wields a chest drill in a dog-hole mine all day and drinks boilermakers all night."

"Jesus—what did you just say? You guys speak a different language down there?"

"Yep . . . ask Davenport . . . we are behind the Cotton Curtain."

"No shit? I didn't know they grew cotton there."

][

Two days later, I met with Her Majesty. She, unlike Senior Assistant

Champlin, gave me a chance to talk. I roasted in a jacket and tie for the meeting and talked softly . . . knowing that the unflattering images of me already created by Lawdawg and others might make it hard on Billy.

"Why did you not consult us about this petition, Mr. Stuart?"

"Your assistant was so nasty . . . as were the legal office folks . . . that I assumed no one would care about this, uh, 'student.'" She paused to process, possibly trying to figure out if I was playing with her, then responded, "Tell me about him." While I did, she made marginal notes in an opened folder, which I assumed was Billy's file. Then she interrupted. "Why *this* student? Are you certain you aren't overidentifying with him . . . ? He's white and rural, like you."

"Fair question. I'm not sure. Unlike Kamensky in our cottage, I know I'm white . . . "

She grinned. "I've heard . . . go on."

"But I'm not true 'rural.' My dad was from Philadelphia. My mom's close family, longtime Pittsburgh and points South—till some moved to Philly's Main Line years ago."

"Where does West Virginia come in?" she asked. I looked up. My turn to pause. "Home territory for my mom—riverboat people. We moved there in the fifties—my father was vice president for the West Virginia University Medical Center when he died two months ago. Ph.D. from Penn. M.D. from Duke." She raised her eyebrows. "My background is complicated, Doctor."

I wasn't sure why she was asking so many questions about my personal life, but she was engaged in the conversation, so I went on. "So, mostly . . . Billy's, I mean William's, case bothers me as an *American*. It's just not right—not American—to have a relative rule in a case where some farmer took advantage of a kid with that kind of IQ, then followed it up by being the architect of ruining his life. . . . So, as an American . . . the petition." She leaned back.

"My assistant was upset by you, and the folks up in Beaver County aren't too happy, either, about all you've stirred up. Why shouldn't I terminate you . . . ?"

"Obviously they are unhappy people . . . or a few of them would be too busy to ruin a kid's life over rope and a borrowed pony. And if it were really America up there, the farmer would have been charged and done time for 'contributing' by paying an underage kid in *beer*."

Her Majesty blinked at me for a while, then leaned forward. "My word! That is so obvious . . . but it has never come up and, I admit, I didn't think of it, either, when I read this file. . . . That issue should have been the basis for an appeal!" She reached for a phone. I stood up.

"Thank you, Doctor. Thank you for your time." She nodded and cradled the handset between her neck and shoulder as I pulled the door behind me.

][[

On Visiting Sunday the preacher came with Billy's momma. She had lost more weight and looked terrible. Billy cried inconsolably. Momma still couldn't remember where baby sister was, but the preacher, a Pennsylvania German Lutheran, knew: "The child is in Human Services foster care in Aliquippa. Why there, I don't know."

"Who initiated the HSD visit?" asked Dav.

"The same member of my congregation who first gave Billy the beer. This whole situation is upsetting and, uh . . . " Looking uncomfortable, the minister glanced at Dav and turned bright red.

Dav nodded. "Well, Reverend, please excuse me, I've got to check on Billy and his momma." The preacher exhaled. When Dav closed the door behind him, the preacher began to stutter. I interrupted.

"It's hot in here, so I'd like to get to the chase . . . are you uncomfortable talking in front of Mr. Davenport?" He nodded in the direction Dav had exited. "I, uh, don't know much about *them* . . . I never know what to say."

"Well, that's misplaced. Mr. Davenport is a more upstanding Christian and a far better human than the farmer who screwed Billy . . . and this is a state institution—race, culture, class, and politics are *all* in play—Billy, Momma, and baby sister are pawns. And you guys up there in Beaver Falls live in a world that's part of the problem rather than part of the solution. The member of your flock who stuck it to Billy is guilty of contributing to the delinquency of a minor—paying a thirteen-year-old in beer is a huge no-no. He's also violated the family's federal civil rights. It's been a long, hot summer . . . and working here has me nearly as edgy as black America. . . . I need your help."

"What do you mean?" he asked as he leaned forward.

"What I mean is that I intend to file *amicus curiae* briefs in both state *and* federal court until your farmer is sitting in the Allegheny big house."

The preacher paled. I gave him a few seconds with the image I'd created. "Is there another alternative?" he asked.

"Sure. *You* can explain the legal . . . and prison . . . situation to your farmer and see if he'll explain it to his cousin, the judge. If not, in a few days I'm going to file with the Commonwealth's Legal Ethics Board. Your judge is going to have to go to Harrisburg or Philly and answer questions that may get him thrown off the bench."

"What good will that do?" He wiped his forehead. "For Billy, I mean."

"It may get them to leave his family alone, *if* we manage to get Billy a new hearing. That is, unless you think a pastoral session with your farmer on Christian charity would help."

"I've already been down that road," he said, shaking his head.

"Will you explain legalities to the farmer?" He nodded. "Bluntly?"

"Yes . . . but I can't talk to the judge."

"Then I will. Do you have a phone number?"

He reached into his suit jacket. "Here, I'll write it on my card. Call me if you make any progress with the judge."

"OK. I'll call him tomorrow and let you know what happens."

]|[

Dav and I ended the evening watching the *CBS Evening News* on the activity room's black-and-white TV. The aftershocks of Detroit's riots still echoed through black ghettos all over the upper Midwest and the Northeast. Dav commented, "I can't wait till this summer is over. Too hot; too ugly. Too crowded in here. It's like the whole world's gone nuts."

"Yeah, Mr. Davenport . . . and from my perspective, not the wisest summer for a white boy from West Virginia to begin working here."

Dav laughed. "Mr. Reddy's right. You are nuts . . . and now even Her Majesty considers you human, which makes you even nuttier."

"What did the director say?"

"The farm is going to file for 'Contributing' on the beer."

Chapter 12

Nefertiti

The students hadn't been sleeping well in the heat. At 10:00 p.m., it was still eighty-one degrees, muggy, and echoes of Visitor's Day had all left their marks. So I requisitioned two candy bars—one for Billy and another for Country, his current roommate. Between the two of them, their IQs added up to about the minimum it took to get admitted to Washington and Jefferson College just a few miles away.

I unlocked their door, handed them each a candy bar, and squeezed a couple of shoulders, then locked them in again.

Most kids had no visitors, so they were angry or depressed. A few, like Kamensky, pretended they didn't care. But most cared a lot. Others, like Billy, had their visits . . . which often reignited the agony of realities they could no longer control.

Often, kids who got no visitors would displace their anger onto weaker—or merely different—kids around them. Such anger often leaked across racial lines. Most of those racial tensions were expressed by name-calling, taunting, and intimidating behavior. Puffing up like a baboon often made the weaker kids slink and get out of an angry reject's way. In general, the black kids liked to rank on, then beat up, the white kids who'd had visitors.

In contrast, the white kids tended to be quieter and less physical but far sneakier—like the time I saw a white boy maneuver a black kid to the back of the serving line at dinner, then sneer, "At least you know your place, *boy*." Too often, Dav and I would have to pry types like these apart. At times this process was akin to chipping paint from a weathered window frame with a dull razor blade.

This whole way of doing things is a disaster, I told myself as I set up for my night watch at the end of the main residence's upstairs hall.

I pulled an armchair into the hall near the head of the stairs, where I could see all the rooms, set up the portable record player I brought from the eagle's nest, and spun a 33 ⅓ of Miles Davis's bootleg, not yet officially released, *Nefertiti*. It had been a gift from a connected friend in Pittsburgh. Miles's horn filled the hallway with the title cut's mournful melody.

"Turn it up, Mr. Stuart!" someone shouted. I cranked up the volume, lit a smoke, and leaned back into the chair to read a recent copy of *Time* that obsessed on America's racial violence, asking, as if no one knew the answer, "Where have we gone wrong?"

I was halfway through the cover piece when the lights flickered, then went out. The scent of acrid smoke drifted into the hallway. Downstairs in the foyer of the dorm, Palco bellowed, "What the fuck?!"

I hollered down the hall, "Sugarbear—you'd better pull the candy wrapper out of the socket, 'cause I'm going to restart the lights in about thirty seconds—that'll fry you and Sinbad when it comes on."

Sinbad's voice answered, "Be cool, Mr. Stuart! We're cool here. Honest!"

"Good! Since we're in love now, do me a favor and make sure Sugarbear's hand is still in the socket when I throw the switch."

"Aw, Mr. Stuart . . ." whined Sugarbear as scattered snickers leaked out from under hallway doors.

"'Aw, hell! You and Kamensky still owe me an apology—a fork in my ass in front of everybody. Keep fishing for the tinfoil and pray that you get it out before I get to the switch." More titters echoed along the hallway as I felt my way downstairs and reset the main breaker. Just as the lights went on, someone shrieked upstairs.

"Sweet Jesus!" yelled Palco. "Can't you handle it up there, Weasel?"

"Relax! That's just Sugarbear being electrocuted, Palco!" I bellowed as I stepped into the security booth, grabbed a flashlight, and flipped the breaker off again as I passed it on my way to the stairs.

"Goddamn!" yelled Palco. I ignored him, climbed the stairs, and leaned back into the chair again. "Don't you care about the scream, Mr. Stuart?" hollered Golightly.

"No. I hope it was Sugarbear frying. I'll report him dead in the morning, so Mr. Reddy gets to write it up."

"You hard, Mr. Stuart!" protested Sugarbear. "Wasn't me screamed. It was Country."

"Country, you OK?"

"Yassuh! But I seen another Duppie at the window. He done looked right at me . . . dem big smoky eyes. Can you read some Bible out they-ah? Duppie, he don' like to hear no Bible." Someone snickered.

Palco got the lights on again, pissing and whining the whole time, so I went downstairs, got a copy of the Bible from activities, returned to my chair, and read Adam and Eve from Genesis.

To my amazement, someone way down the hall shouted through the crack under the door, "I can't hear! I want the story, too." Someone else answered, "Me, too. Grams used to read to me!"

I dragged the armchair halfway down the hall . . . it wasn't easy for them to hear through the Plexiglas-paned wooden doors that secured each room. "Why was she forbidden fruit?" shouted Curtis. "White, likely," answered Golightly. Sinbad butted in, "That's silly, man. That would mean we're all related . . . "

"Well, we are," I said, and asked them, "Did you notice that when you went to the Pittsburgh Zoo last month and looked at those big, hairy orangutans that they all looked exactly alike?"

"Yes," said Golightly. "What's that got to do with anything? I'm not no *ape*."

"No . . . we're not directly descended from apes as we know them, but all of you guys there doing the looking *are* far more genetically alike than the orangutans you're staring at that *look* exactly alike."

"No we isn't!" yelled Kamensky.

"Yes, you is!" I hollered back, then continued, "All living humans are so much alike that it's like sprinkling salt on your meatloaf; all those little grains of white. Then you look real close and notice one speck of black pepper in among hundreds of grains of salt and go, 'Now, how did *that* get in there?' But you don't give a damn, even if you don't like pepper, because it's so much salt that one speck of pepper doesn't change the flavor. That's what humans are like, genetically. Six or seven genes . . . specks of pepper among millions, *millions* of specks of salt— other genes—account for all the differences among us in this cottage."

"You jivin' us, Mr. Stuart?" asked Sinbad.

"Nope. That's what I studied in college. And that's also what the Bible is telling us. We are—though we don't want to hear it—one big family."

"What about *me*?" asked Golightly. "I'm mixed."

"If the speck of pepper weren't black against white, you'd never even know it was there. The only one here who has it right is Kamensky. He's black because he perceives himself as black. The only thing he's missing is the one speck out of millions of specks. That's the skin color speck we all fuss over."

"So why don't they teach us this? Are you sayin' 'black' and 'white' is more about what we imagine than what's so?"

"Exactly."

"See, tole yous I wasn't nuts," pouted Kamensky. "Ahs a spade from the Hill!" I doubt Kamensky was comforted by the howls of laughter. Sinbad shouted, "Quiet! I got a question. So, about the riots and all. H. Rap Brown. Blackstone Nation. Bull Connor and his dogs . . . this is more about who people *think* they are than *what* they really are?"

"Yep. Bible's clear on it. So's science. But most don't want to hear it. Got to have someone to dump on when they feel bad." *That should be a heart shot with some of these characters*, I thought.

"I'm trippin'," said Sinbad. "So you aren't as 'white' as we think you are . . . and I'm not as 'black' as you think I am?"

"You are close enough for an A-."

"Man!"

"Look. I'm done reading to you. I've got charts to work on . . . want *Nefertiti* again or some Coltrane?"

"*Get down*, Mr. Stuart! You got 'Trane?"

"Yeah . . . it's almost one a.m. Settle down. I'll be the DJ, but softer so old Palco doesn't dump one in his pants."

I wrote and spun music till about four. At 6:45 a.m. when we did room checks, I found nearly a dozen kids on the rooms' floors, sleeping against the door cracks so they could hear the music, blankets doubled up as mattresses.

]|[

As July moved into August, the nation's riots abated. Race relations on the farm smoothed out. It cooled down outside for a brief spell, and things at work were becoming easier . . . just the daily, inevitable arguments over things like whether we should watch *Hogan's Heroes* reruns (black guys voting for this one) or *Gilligan's Island*, which was the white kids' preference, but a bit *too* white for the black kids . . . that is, except for the ongoing debate over whether they'd prefer to ball Ginger or Mary Ann.

During such a debate, Kamensky got me to the side, looking troubled. "Am I a head case?"

I paused—this was the most surprising thing Kamensky could have said, and I needed time to think.

"Am I?" he repeated, his brow furrowed.

"Yes. You need some honest-to-God counseling. Want a referral?" He nodded and disappeared before the others noticed him fraternizing with the staff . . . bad for image, I assumed.

chapter 13

What We Have Here
Is a Failure to Communicate

The next morning, a Monday, I called Billy's judge in Beaver Falls before I clocked out. I'd been preparing a complaint against him. Mr. Reddy bitched, "You got balls, Stuart . . . messin' with some judge and dragging the farm into it." Unmoved, I dialed. He listened over my shoulder.

"Hello, Judge. This is Mr. Stuart at Youth Development Center, Canonsburg. I wanted to ask several questions about William Terrell's trial—the horse stealing conviction. Ah . . . yes . . . you can't remember? Lots of cases . . . I understand. Let me give you your county file number. Sure, I'll wait."

Half an hour later I was still sitting there holding the phone when a female voice came on. "Who's holding?"

"Counselor Stuart, YDC, Canonsburg. The judge said he was going to get a trial record."

"He's been in court for half an hour . . . there must be some misunderstanding."

"Then please tell him for me he'd better get his pending family cases out of the way quickly as he'll be removed from the bench in ninety days or so." She gasped. "*Who* is this?" I hung up gently.

"Man, you are beyond nuts!" shrieked Reddy. "Her Majesty isn't going to like this." I just smiled back—I didn't bother to tell Reddy that Her Majesty was quite likely to soon become one of Judge Holpfuz's main problems in life.

I was on duty Monday evening from 8:00 p.m. to eight the next morning and worked feverishly on the Beaver County judicial ethics complaint, napped afterward in my Little Washington eagle's nest, then drove up to Pittsburgh, draft in hand.

I had a friend, a former classmate whose current summer job was in a Pittsburgh law office as a legal assistant. I needed advice on the draft, so I had called her from the farm on a whim and she had promised to help me out. Angela was black, sort of. She had big eyes and a gorgeous mouth, dimples deep enough to absorb after-dinner mints, and the body of a dancer—not surprising since dance had been her minor. But what stoked me most about her was her smile, her brains, and her frankness. Being around her was exciting—she was luminous. She glowed when she spoke . . . even seemed to glow when she smiled. On the downside, she fretted endlessly about her dad . . . and her weight and her hair. She'd inherited her dad's kinked hair genes. That alone stereotyped her into the margins of the black community. I guess our common bond was that we were both trying to find worlds that we could live in without the hard work of never-ending pretense.

Angela always insisted that favors be paid in dinner and a few dances, as was common for platonic dates in the '60s. Unfortunately, if not tragically, sex had always been out of the question. "We are merely friends," she further insisted. But I knew better. Daddy, a surgeon, was both a prude and a bigot. I'd first met his daughter in class at WVU, where she went for one year until Daddy couldn't handle it any longer. "He's afraid I'll reject black culture and try to *pass* . . . or, uh . . . "

"Or what, Ange?" She'd looked away and I never brought it up again. We were both eighteen then—both of us still in denial over social realities. Now we were both twenty-two and all too aware that every place we went was racially tense. If we went to white restaurants, the service was terrible and the whites stared at me in unabashed disapproval. If we went to black places, the black men dissed her openly and mercilessly. After three "nondate" dates in ordinary Pittsburgh neighborhoods, we'd settled on dinner in neutral territory between Pitt and Carnegie Mellon where college student culture softened the boundaries just enough for us to get through a meal without incident.

I ordered a small Porterhouse, with home-fried potatoes and

onions. Ange wrinkled her nose and, as always, ordered a salad. "No dressing, please. Just dice a small piece of chicken into it."

"How do you survive on that stuff, Ange?" I asked. "Don't you ever get hungry?"

"I'm *always* hungry, David . . . but my dad has a thing about fat black women."

"And your mom?"

"She got skinnier and skinnier after the radiation treatment. All he said to me during that period was, 'Everything will be all right—your mother looks just like her old self again.'" She shivered.

"You OK, Ange?"

She shrugged. "It makes me angry."

"So why the salad when you are hungry?"

She glared at me. It was that kind of silent, icy put-down that spoke volumes, as in, "So what if I dance and eat nothing? If you even blink, much less try to analyze my motives, I'll rip your nuts off right here, send them to the kitchen to be sautéed, then make them the first red meat I've eaten in three years." I got the message, smiled, and changed the subject. "OK . . . where are we going to dance tonight?"

The dancing venue always proved the hardest part. Since it was a weeknight and Angela was now in a petulantly rebellious phase, we headed to the new Hurricane Club in the Hill District. It was the flamboyant, but not quite as classy, successor to the legendary, original Hurricane's legacy of black music. Aretha Franklin's "Respect" was playing when we stepped in. Weeknights were DJ nights, so two hours later, Angela made it out only being called a "honkey lover" twice. "I can't stand this," she told me on the way out. "Doesn't the 'honkey' bother you?"

"Nah—beats 'mutha-fu . . .'"

"*Don't*, David! That is *the* worst. Do you get *that* at work?"

"Yep . . . and 'peckerwood' . . . and 'cracker' . . . and 'redneck' . . . and 'lily-white punk-ass' . . . and some really innovative combos . . . and just think, Ange, *this* is being billed as the 'summer of love.'"

"Wish I were in San Francisco again," she said. "Good music, good food. Mellow mix of cultures . . . the sea. Fewer stereotypes . . . I'm going to try for law school somewhere out there."

"Speaking of 'law,' let me know what you think after you've read the draft of my complaint I gave you at dinner. I need advice on Country and Curtis, too."

"Who are they?"

"Two more harmless kids. I simply do not understand why anyone thinks it's smart to throw kids like that in with stone-cold killers. It's a social time bomb."

"I'll ask if I can be assigned pro bono—that way I can look at the files legally—we might even get to see each other more often. Can I get the YDC director's number? Dad knows her."

"Really?"

She smiled, "Of course . . . he's on one of HSD's advisory boards . . . his 'civic duty' thing." She rolled her eyes.

"Why so cynical?"

"He makes me angry. If he knew we were out together he'd have a fit."

"He doesn't even know me, Ange."

"He thinks he does. You're white . . . it makes him crazy . . . and I think he's gone crazy. Mom was white."

"*Was?* From what you said earlier, I thought she got better!"

"She died two years ago. Cancer. Now he's angry at whites."

"I had no idea . . . what does that mean for you, if you're half white?"

"Let's drop it," she said and was abnormally quiet until I dropped her off at her apartment. "When will I see you again?" she asked.

"Later this week—I'm bringing a group to the movies on Thursday . . . when are you going to invite me upstairs?" I teased, knowing it would spark a reaction from her.

"When you get over your fiancée in Mexico."

"You're hard, woman," I said laughing.

She reached for the door handle. "Is she lighter complected than I am?"

"No."

"No? . . . Then prettier?"

"'Bout the same."

"Slenderer?"

"No; a little fuller." Ange grinned.

"Smarter?"

"That's four questions. You are two over the limit."

We were in August's three-week summer break from the farm's high school. Tensions, after a brief hiatus, had once again been running high between the black and white kids at the Morganza.

It got to the point that even the black students were tiring of dumping on the white guys. "Cracker" had been used so often that it had lost its bite.

On the white side of the great divide, the mentally challenged were simply out of clever tricks, like pennying doors shut or drawing crude cartoons of black guys in jailhouse stripes eating watermelons.

Do the racial tensions explain this participant list? I wondered as I read out the names of those the Hill had chosen to go on a field trip to the "cinema" in Pittsburgh, in an effort to remedy the fighting among students.

If one didn't count Kamensky, I was the only white who was going on the trip. As they lined up in the cottage, I couldn't figure out why Sinbad, Sugarbear, and Kamensky had been chosen, along with Curtis, Country, Golightly, and another ten characters who ranged from out-of-control and colorful to meek and invisible.

It started out with all the usual detention rituals. Richard and I watched Palco pat everyone down. One of our newer "admissions" was hiding a shank fashioned from a toothbrush and a razor blade, so his ticket went to another kid on the waiting list.

After pat-downs, we organized the agonizingly slow change into street clothes—"No humiliating students in public" were the orders from up on the Hill. That meant cheap, off-brand dungarees, plaid shirts, and real shoes instead of stamped rubber flip-flops.

"The better to run with," sneered Palco. About twice a month I inadvertently found myself actually agreeing with the fat S.O.B. Each time I agreed with Palco it took me several days to shake off the jitters.

Finally, we got everyone onto the bus. But I wished the high-pay, idiot-laden staff on the Hill had been there to see it . . . like these kids didn't stick out in a crowd! We might just as well have hot-branded a two-inch-high "YDC" on each of their foreheads.

Confined on the moving bus, Richard and I were in control. "My main man, can I have a quarter for Tootsie Rolls when we get there?" or,

The high school at Morganza.

"Richard here's my main man; he's gonna buy me popcorns, ain'tchu, Mr. Richard?"

"Ain't works." Richard shrugged, and whispered to me moments later, "Do we have anything for them?"

"Yeah. Got sixteen dollars credit at the theater for treats . . . and I have three packs of Kools and a box of Snickers for the trip home." Richard seemed surprised. "We're allowed to give them smokes?"

"Yes. Where do you think they get them during the day? We issue two cigarettes or two chewing gums a day. That's why they always have smokes behind their ears around the cottage."

"That's not healthy . . . and why Kools . . . real people don't smoke Kools."

"We aren't dealing with the Winston generation here, Richard," I answered, thinking, *Man alive! Your 'Ontie' must have expended one hell of a lot of effort to protect you from the real world around you.* Out loud I asked, "Haven't you ever heard them say, 'I want Kools, man. I ain' no Marlboro-smokin' honkey cowboy.'" Poor Richard looked shocked. "No! I haven't handled commissary yet . . . they say that *in front* of you?"

"Yep."

He shook his head and folded his thin, madras-clad arms. "That is unacceptable."

"You need to run for Congress, Richard. You are the very last untainted gentleman in America."

"Are you teasing me, David?" He narrowed his eyes at me through his wire-rim glasses.

"No way. I admire you." I laughed. "Don't change . . . I mean it."

)|(

We bussed up Route 19, passing about a mile east of the old South Side cemetery above the Monongahela where four generations of my mom's immediate family were buried. That cemetery, founded in 1870, about the same time the farm was created, was the peaceful "end of life as you lived it" destination for a fair share of what had once been south Pittsburgh's emerging white elite. In troubling contrast, the Morganza coexisted thirty miles away as the not-so-peaceful "end of life as you *knew* it" destination for Pittsburgh's young rejects.

As we crossed the Monongahela, heading toward Downtown, our Pittsburgh students perked up, breathed deep, and inhaled the promise of the Hill District, just as surely as a sailor responds to the first scent of the sea. To them it represented drugs. Women. Freedom. Power. And the thrill of home turf. They joked, shouted at chicks out the windows and touted the Hill's glories.

Twenty minutes later we filed into the venerable New Granada Theater on Centre Avenue for the midday matinee. A number of regular theater patrons recoiled. Some left and others sought more distant seats in reaction to our sixteen students in cheap plaid shirts, Levi's, and state-issue high-top work brogans, sans belts and shoelaces. I wanted to seat everyone in one row, but the Hill's ticket arrangements created yet another major mishap. We'd been split into two rows—eight students in each. Richard and our driver were in front, me at one end of our row behind them, which was in the dead center of the theater. As a tactical layout it was a disaster.

The newsreels came first . . . they focused on the recent race riots—especially Detroit's, which had stunned white America. "Thirty-five dead," the narrator repeated breathlessly, "H. Rap Brown arrested."

Sugarbear booed. I leaned forward and whispered in his ear, "You know, you didn't make peace with me like Sinbad and Kamensky." He gulped and shut up. Then the lobby food treat reel flickered on. "Popcorn and hot dog combo, 80¢." The lights went up; Golightly and Curtis went with Richard to order food.

A few minutes later the lights dimmed again and the feature came on. The titles flickered to life: *Cool Hand Luke*, starring Paul Newman.

"Who dat honkey?" someone in row one asked. *Hmmm . . . What's this about?* I wondered. As if on cue, the screen faded to the scene of a knee-walking Paul Newman's inebriated grin as he laboriously topped a row of parking meters with a long-handled pipe-cutter. Busy pushing Golightly back into his seat, I missed the next scene, which faded to another scene where Newman is being admitted in striped uniform on a prison farm somewhere down in America's own Heart of Darkness. Our students, for once, quit squirming, whispering, even breathing heavily, and gave the cops-and-cons flick their total, wide-eyed attention.

I suffered one of my sinking feelings of impending doom, similar to the night five years before when my old man found a pack of rubbers in my twin brother's wallet and asked, "Just what do you think you are doing with these, young man?" The old man's tone was as cold as one of those Alberta clippers that whips down from Canada now and again, just to freeze "the balls off a brass monkey," as folks at home behind the Cotton Curtain usually phrased it.

I had unwisely answered the old man, "It's not his fault. I was hoping to screw Morgan Bower's daughter." That my twin and I'd been hoping since the beginning of tenth grade when the rubbers were new—and were still hoping to use the same pack of pocket-weary pro-phylactics nearly three years later—meant no more to the old man than did the concept of meanness to Strother Martin, who abruptly interrupted my train of thought up on the screen as he ruefully whacked Paul Newman upside the head, with, "What we have here is a failure to communicate."

One of our kids yelled, "Motherfuck! Jive-ass honkey mutha' fucka'!" I think my pulse hit 130, but it could have been 180. Someone gasped as other ordinary folks in front of us rubbernecked to see what was going on. I began to panic. "We'll talk about it later tonight," I hissed to the kid.

A few minutes later another round of "mutha' this" and "honkey that" erupted when Newman finished digging his own private metaphor of life hole, only to have brother Strother order him to fill it up again. A burly patron growled from the row behind us, *"Shhh!"* Kamensky yelled back, *"Shhh* your own ass!"

About the time Newman finished refilling his hole and had finally got his "head right," the less stable among our students plainly had got their heads wrong. Two nervous teenaged ushers joined us when the "Taking off shirt now, Boss" routine sent a half dozen of the Morganza's finest into full, Wylie Avenue, "I hate pigs" righteous mode. Their choreographed, a cappella "oinking" was, I concede, distracting to the other patrons, who had begun to flee with their kids. We lost two of our wards as a group of patrons exited.

The fourteen remaining in my YDC matinee detachment cheered a few minutes later when Newman went on the run and sent snapshots back to George Kennedy.

Before I knew it we had only ten students left in the two rows. Moments after the silvered, sunglass-wearing deputy they called "No-Eyes" shot Newman in the throat for spite, I tackled Sinbad as he jumped out of his seat and streaked down the side aisle. I didn't slow him down much, especially with Sugarbear running interference for him.

Richard lost a separate attempt to bring Kamensky down, and while both of us were wrestling our agitated bad boys, three other YDC kids behind us exploded like a covey of quail from their center seats, did their Wylie Avenue dance across several rows of ordinary, but stunned, patrons, and disappeared behind the vintage theater's stage. Newman's grinning body rippled eerily as they blew past the screen.

By 2:42 p.m. I had earned the distinction of being the only trainee ever to have lost six in one day. By 5:00 p.m., my distinction had grown— three of those six, Sinbad, Sugarbear, and Kamensky, had commandeered a U.S. Postal Service truck, thoroughly tenderized the driver, then crashed through the doors of a postal substation and robbed the place. By 3:00 a.m., an all-night drug store on Forbes had been "boosted" of its narcotics by Sinbad's little trio, its pharmacist cruelly "jacked up" and in Allegheny General Hospital, contributing to a neurosurgeon's lack of sleep.

By the time I got off duty at 7:00 a.m., Golightly and two others had separately engineered a run of car thefts and grocery store burglaries around the lower Hill. By the time I Jose Cuervoed myself into the semblance of early-morning sleep up in my roasting eagle's nest, four new Paul Newman fans—Sinbad's trio, plus Golightly—were back in custody and out of it on drugs. The two other kids with them had disappeared to God-knows-where.

]|[

I made it to work late that afternoon, both hungover and convinced I'd be fired. I did take flak from Reddy and Palco while I ate a cheese sandwich and waited for one of Her Majesty's finest to come down from the Hill and escort me off campus. Watching me sweat it out, Palco was happy . . . no, that's a misstatement . . . *giddy* and *fulfilled* are more accurate.

It was the only time I ever saw him help Mrs. Moxon make the sandwiches. The sight of a carefully aproned Palco spreading mayo in the kitchen almost made up for the grief he'd dished out at my expense. Still, no one showed up from the Hill.

So, to my amazement, the first real butt-roasting I got was from Angela . . . over the cottage's outside phone . . . and it had nothing to do with the cinema. "You were going to call me *yesterday*. What happened?"

"I lost a bunch of guys in the theater yesterday . . . the movie was *Cool Hand Luke* with Paul Newman."

"Why didn't you call me later?"

"Sorry . . . reports. Then I drank myself to sleep after three of them robbed the post office."

"That was immature."

"Perhaps. Please watch it, and try to picture me there with sixteen students . . . if you are stirred to forgiveness, I'd like to buy you dinner."

She snorted, not sounding the least bit luminous. "We'll see." Click.

I returned to waiting for the YDC ax to fall. Palco chewed gum noisily while retelling old "escape from farm" stories, "Just to cheer you up." He snickered when I suggested he "shove a sock in it." At 4:20 Reckoning itself stepped into the cottage's foyer in the unexpected person of Her Majesty. She looked grim. Reddy suddenly had things to do. Dav took a group over to the pool, and Palco, for once, hauled his fat ass out of a lounge chair, stuffed a half-eaten sandwich into his pocket, and summarily stationed himself in the upstairs hallway.

Her Majesty sighed, "I'm not sure how to put this . . ."

I interrupted. "I'll write up my resignation, if you prefer."

She looked surprised. "Why? It's embarrassing for all of us, but especially for me; I came to apologize." My head spun.

"I *personally* chose that film—I thought it would create a basis for dialogue and demonstrate that whites also suffer from a profoundly flawed judicial system. I hoped it would create some common cause among our diverse students."

"Unfortunately, unless you count Kamensky, I was the only white guy there . . . and *dialogue* is a serious, uh, *understatement*," I commented.

She drew back and gasped. "Oh, no . . . not again!" I thought she might explain, but she simply stiffened and apologized. "I *really* am sorry."

"Apology accepted, but not necessary . . . I'm the one who lost the students and, except for the viewing circumstances, it's a hell of a movie." Reddy walked in and she stood to go.

"I'd prefer that our conversation remain private," she said, and left.

The phone rang again a few minutes later. Palco picked up then bellowed cheerfully, "The Hill . . . for you, Weasel. Hah! Been nice knowing you." Rabbit, lurking, as usual, in the doorway, wagged a finger at me as I went to take the phone call. "Oooh. You are in *trouble*. Naughty, naughty," he said leering. For a moment I considered murdering him, but decided I didn't want to give Palco the role of star witness at my trial.

By the beginning of the night shift, I had the distinction of being the only trainee ever to have lost six in one day, and, as punishment, be invited to a business lunch with the director the next day.

"I'd like us to continue our conversation," she said into the phone. "Will you join me in the executive dining room tomorrow?"

Palco, trying to listen but misunderstanding just why I was hastily writing down the meeting time and place with Her Majesty, was breezily wistful. "Well, Weasel, you can't win 'em all."

chapter 14

Jelly Baby

Summer's heat cranked back up to a new level of oppressive, and America remained committed to its odd cassoulet of ugly racial turmoil mixed with "everything is fine in fairyland."

Everyone, according to news reports, was getting laid out in California as the Summer of Love rolled on . . . apparently oblivious to the reality that elsewhere, there was also a whole lot of screwing going on, but it certainly wasn't the "Yeah, baby, give me more" kind.

Inner cities burned. The Klan robed up, its fat, insecure acolytes furtively holding hands in sultry clearings and cheering their burning crosses as if they were "this little light of mine" beacons in the racial darkness of the Deep South. Predictably, the Klan's backbeat was provided by prominent political conservatives who pissed and whined about "law and order"—which had become a surprisingly rare, real-world commodity as National Guardsmen and U.S. Marshals bayoneted or riot-gunned their way through the hotspots. Finally, those ultraliberals not already on acid began once more to atone for stuff they hadn't actually done to anyone.

In short, one quarter of America was stoned, half were in psychological hiding, and the final quarter seemed intent on taking to the streets and reenacting—as if it were performance art—a flamboyantly revisionist version of Reconstruction's craziest period, which had reigned while U. S. Grant was still president. Meanwhile, I was stuck with the pathetic refereeing of evening TV sessions as our black and white students fought over programming then traded racial barbs.

During one rerun of *Gunsmoke*, Golightly, again "in residence," suddenly went off like a Roman candle. Matt Dillon pistol-whipped a cowboy who'd just gleefully beat the snot out of colorful, mule-riding Festus. The white kids cheered. Golightly protested, "I don't want to watch no more honkey TV. 'Festus' sounds too much like 'Rastus.' It's always a *brother* who gets jacked up!" To consider smelly, unshaven, cracker-like Festus "a brother" was rather overwrought, I thought, but I hesitated. Mistake.

Sinbad, enraged that he was back in custody, smiled that crazy angelic smile of his and deftly poured fuel on the fire. "I want *Soul Train*." On cue his crewe started chanting, "*Soul Train. Soul Train. Soul Train*" louder and louder. That drew Palco into the TV room like a fat maggot hungry for rotting meat.

"Calm down now, Palco," Dav soothed before Palco was able to say a word, but to no avail. "Sinbad, settle your boys or you're going to get a number twelve up your . . ."

"Stuff your boot up'n your own ass!" shouted Sinbad, who was running low on methadone. Palco lost it and lumbered over toward Sinbad, keys out. Predictably, Kamensky and Sugarbear, good vassals that they were, moved in on Palco to protect their boss.

That provided what Dav called the spark that lit up the room. "Chaos here is as easy and as quick as tossing a match into gasoline," Dav told me once. "We've already got the fuel here—anger, frustration, sorrow. It only takes one little spark . . . and poof. You got a riot."

Kamensky got to Palco first. "You fuckin' wit' us just 'cause we BLACK. You WOP!" Snarling, Palco unhooked his key ring and drew back to brain Kamensky. But, too pissed off to notice, he hadn't counted on Sinbad catching him in a chokehold from behind . . . or on Kamensky ripping the keys from his hand and throwing them on the floor.

To my deepest sorrow, Palco's pride was the only thing mortally wounded. But from the way he danced and bellowed over a tiny trickle of blood that might not even have drawn a minor roughing penalty in a Pittsburgh Penguins hockey game, you'd have thought it was a first-degree felony case of "Great Bodily Harm."

By nine, with the help of nearby cottage staff, two state troopers, and Big Jill, who could bear-hug miscreants with the best of the cops, we finally had everyone locked in their rooms. Big Jill stayed and began systematically attending to the minor injuries.

Holding Palco's head to keep him from squirming, she slapped on a small butterfly Band-Aid, mostly to appease him, and tossed him an ice bag. Meanwhile, Dav quietly retreated to the security room and unchambered the goose loads in the old short-barreled Greener shotgun that Palco hid on two hooks under the foot well of his desk. Dav returned with a wink and stuffed the shells into my Wrangler's pocket. "Just in case he decides to go huntin' later tonight."

"Knowin' him it'll be *coon* huntin'," muttered Jill. Dav wrinkled his nose. "This summer's got to end soon. There are *never* any winners in a race war. It is a dehumanizing virus."

"It's a what?" grumbled Palco from the corner of the room.

"He means it's not smart to invite a whore with the clap to a fuck party, Palco—does *that* make it easier for you to understand?" scolded Jill.

"Well, don't blame *me*," interrupted Palco. "Did you hear him call *me* a wop? I've had enough of that."

Dav tried diplomacy. "It's hot. They are facing five years' time added, the federal beef coming up Lord knows when, *and* the evening news is making it worse. Let it go, Mr. Palco."

"What do you mean, 'Let it go'? I'm writing those punks up."

"That will get them more time . . . you'll just have to deal with them for longer," I commented.

Triage over, everyone went back to their usual routines. I went to the desk and pulled out a blank incident report and began recounting events but was interrupted by Jill. "Can you escort Country upstairs? He was hiding during the whole melee." I nodded. She added, "Meet me in the graveyard at your break." I nodded again and went to collect Country, who was still crying.

"You OK?" I asked.

"No'zuh . . . I gonna lose ma' baby."

"Huh?"

"Mizz Jill tole me my baby done gone."

"What baby, Country?"

"Ah's wuz gonna have a little jelly baby . . . ah's wuz happy 'cause ah'd have baby to rock with whilz the others done gone to school." I suddenly felt queasy. I patted him.

He looked up, expectant. Trusting. That wide-eyed look like a ten-week-old puppy's always got me right where it hurt. Even I, Mr. Pain-in-the-Ass, suffered frequently from the trembling urge to wrap my arms around Country, rock him, and assure him that everything would be all right. But confused, I merely stuttered, "I, I don't know much, actually, anything . . . about jelly babies. I'll talk to Mizz Jill and ask her more. OK?" He nodded.

Upstairs, I walked him down the hall past Davenport, who watched Country intently as we passed. Country's current roommate was chubby Curtis. Dav had supported my petition to put them together. I hoped my petition hadn't become a tragic mistake. I had never heard of a "jelly baby," but there were only so many conclusions one could draw, and none of them helped me past my lingering nausea.

Unable to look Curtis in the eye for fear he might be part of this "jelly baby" problem, I locked Country in with him and went over to Dav. "Need information, Mr. Davenport." He nodded. "Ask."

"Not here." Dav jerked a thumb toward the linen cabinet at the head of the stairs and we walked silently over. "What's up, Mr. Stuart?"

"Country. Crying over losing his 'jelly baby' . . . out of my league." Dav's shoulders fell. "That's bad news. *Very* bad. May mean he's been performing fellatio on someone . . . or several. Could mean anal sex. He's so vulnerable that these city boys can dominate him easily. How'd you find out?"

"He told me after Jill told him he had no such baby . . . he wanted something to rock." Dav's face grew tense. "Find out what you can. We need to be very aggressive on the sexual abuse. Got to protect the weak." He turned to leave, then paused and explained in an uncharacteristically soft voice.

"Some days I hate this work . . . a kid like Country doesn't belong here. You'd think the Commonwealth would have figured that out by now."

At 11:00 p.m., Dav stayed to give me a twenty-minute break because I was also going to work the eleven to seven shift before driving to Morgantown. On my break I snuck up to meet Jill at the forbidden cemetery. An orange, heat-swollen quarter-moon hung low in the sky, illuminating puffy clouds that floated above the roofline of Willow Cottage. Cicadas chattered rhythmically among the oaks.

Jill was at Emma's grave, lighting a candle. "Say a prayer for her with me, sweetheart. I'll lead. Our Father, which art in heaven. . . ."

The prayer over, she got down to business. "Country's been servicing Sinbad, who has him believing he's going to have some kind of semen baby from the oral sex . . . a 'jelly baby,' they call it. I'm upset, sweetheart. I take this stuff personally."

"Why?"

"Had a girlfriend like that once. Abused by her stepfather."

"How'd she handle it?" I asked.

"Just between us . . . she ate her way out of it so men would leave her alone. Now don't ask me more. I've already told you too much."

"Jill, he told me that he was sad because he wanted that baby; he wanted something to hold. To rock."

"Promise me you'll take care of him," she said softly, moving toward Ella, the other unknown's grave. I watched as she leaned over and lit a second candle for Ella.

"What can I do for him?" I asked.

"If you file the right papers and get a therapist to agree, you can get him time with a cat every day. Cats are allowed here on the farm."

"Got it," I said, then turned and headed back down the hill. She said something as I was walking back, but whatever it was had been drowned in the noise of the cicadas buzzing in the oaks. I looked back when a third candle flared on the hill behind me.

]|[

"Mr. Davenport," I called when I got back to the cottage. "The culprit, at least one of them, is Sinbad, according to Jill. She suggests we get Country some cat-rocking time."

"OK, I'll leave a note for Mrs. Moxon. She can start the process. We'll need a psych therapist to agree. How's the petition for Billy going?"

"I'll see my paralegal friend up in Pittsburgh this coming Thursday. She's checking it out for me."

"Speaking of your friend, Mr. Stuart, tell Miss Angela that her daddy's not very happy she was seen in the Crawford Grill with a white boy last week." Dav was smiling.

"Do you know everything that happens in Allegheny County?" I asked.

"Yep—and Washington County. I'm a church man. It's not quite a direct line to the Lord, but it's close enough to the gossip mill to know when a member of the black elite is fixin' to go on the warpath. Thought you should know." With that, he pushed his time card into the wall unit, stamped it, and let himself out.

]|[

The drive to Morgantown the next morning seemed longer than usual. It was about nine when I arrived, deposited most of my check at the bank on High Street, then pulled the Rambler into second gear for the steep climb up Falling Run Road.

Mom seemed better. She talked more, mostly about the old man and taking the bus alone to Tyler, Texas, in '43, her grandmother Sophia Vandergrift's hand-sewn wedding dress on her lap, to marry my father before he shipped out to the Pacific. Before that trip, the furthest west she'd ever been was East Liverpool to visit cousins who lived just across the Ohio River. Those cousins, like most of the others, were also descended from a long line of river men.

"Marrying your father was like you going to Mexico, David," she said. "Like you, I needed to go to start my own life."

"You'd do it again?" I asked her.

"Yes . . . at least I think I would. But he was so different after the war. The little boy in him was gone by then. I missed that part of him."

I'd been hearing this line since the old man first started jerking me around at age four or five, but now it sounded different. This time it wasn't so much an excuse as a statement.

I took her to lunch at the Mountainlair, West Virginia University's student union. She'd gone to work part-time at the university's Student Counseling Center. That took some pressure off me since it meant she'd have her own paycheck and be out of the house a good bit. She liked the counseling work and was good at it . . . I guessed it gave her a chance to help others avoid some of the disappointments she'd suffered.

After lunch she was all talked out and wanted to be alone, so I said good-bye, drove back to Little Washington, and slept till I went to work that evening. I had called my cottage from Morgantown and taken a night shift, followed by a day shift, in order to get Thursday evening off for dinner and dancing with Angela.

chapter 15

We Got Duppies Up on 2

onday night was Labor Day, so I received credit for time and a half, but our students were still on edge from the prior night's melee. Its aftershocks shattered every ordinary routine as cobra-like doses of retribution were meted out at a late eight o'clock dinner in the form of clandestine, but intense, under-table foot combat.

Most of the under-table footsie blows were softened by the farm's mandatory rubber flip-flops, but somehow Sugarbear got cut and snapped out. Dav watched my back as I extracted a New York City Puerto Rican named Carlos from Sugarbear's death grip while nearby students cheered them on. Dav snarled in a way I didn't think possible for him.

"Apparently the Lord's Prayer didn't take! . . . We'll do Psalm 23. NOW! Put down your forks." Instinctively, Sugarbear relaxed his hold on Carlos. "He cut me, Mr. Stuart. Honest!"

"Let go, Sugarbear . . . I don't need you to do my job." Sugarbear relaxed and I extracted Carlos, who at the moment looked far more purple than brown. But Carlos's stupor proved to be a sham. As soon as he was free he dove onto Sugarbear again, a toothbrush-handled shank in one hand, cursing in Spanish.

"¡Puto! ¡Degenerado! ¡Nunca te doy mi culo!"

"¡Déjalo, ya!" I shouted and twisted the shank-holding arm behind him. The students watched, wide-eyed, mouthing the words to Psalm

23. Dav leaned forward. ". . . And yea though I walk through the Valley of Death, I will fear no *evil* . . . " He reached in and extracted the shank from Carlos' twisted fingers.

"Pray faster, Mr. Davenport," I grunted. "He's stronger than he looks." Someone snickered. I thought I heard a suspicious smack from behind me, the kind made when an open palm nails the side of a face.

Meanwhile, Carlos turned on me again, *"Puta madre. No me jodes, mamón."* I laughed. *"Me estás refrescando con tu español animado; sigue, sigue no más . . . mientras tenga la bondad acompañarme al cuarto de seguridad. Ándale pués."* I tightened up on the arm bent up behind him and steered toward the cool-down room near the stairwell.

I locked him in and returned to the dining room, where Dav had things under control; that is, until Palco arrived. "Well, well, it's a pleasure being here among you *punks* again. Anyone for a number twelve boot up the ass?" he said grinning and slapping his key ring possessively. Dav took Palco's shoulder and edged him back out into the front hall. Sinbad saw his chance.

"So you speak spic, *Meeester* Stuart?" This sarcasm drew snickers, but at the moment I wasn't in a carefree, "let's chat" sort of mood.

"Yeah. He told me you and Sugarbear were sexually inappropriate."

"Like it's non'a your mutha-fuckin' business, you honkey piece of shit!" snarled Sinbad.

"'Fraid it is," said Dav from somewhere behind me. "We here at YDC are charged with the safety and dignity of our students . . . you and Sugarbear are getting in our faces! And, lots of folks whisper that you are abusing your fellow students. It stops tonight. No more butter at meals . . . I'll see to it myself . . . and no more racial badmouthing. That's *over*, too. Those unhappy with that order can thank these two," he said, pointing at Sinbad and Sugarbear. It got quiet.

Pats of butter were the necessary ingredient for either anal sex or painless masturbation for those fully circumcised. As such, its value was roughly equivalent to gold. Twice a week when sheets were changed, they were checked for semen patches. Guys jacking off onto the Commonwealth's sheets were officially written up. And since the two-students-per-room overcrowding had been put in place, sheet check had become an obsession. Why they checked expost facto was beyond me. Our real job was to prevent sexual abuse . . . not simple "emissions." Whether those emissions were nocturnal or assisted didn't compute as a sensible governmental concern.

Personally, I thought the Commonwealth was unhinged over the prelaundry condition of its sheets, particularly in reference to a group of caged, hormone-crazed teenagers, but what did I know? I was free but couldn't figure out how to get laid, either.

To let everyone know we were serious, Davenport insisted we lock everyone in for the night before nine. We checked each guy for butter, shanks, and the filched shop rags they ejaculated into to avoid soiled-sheet punishments. That left the crowd in a sullen mood. Rabbit stood at his door and held his breath in protest. I stopped on the other side of his door to give him a thumbs-up of encouragement. "You look good slightly purple, Rabbit," I commented.

Downstairs Dav paced back and forth. "We've got to change the dynamics here. Now that 'good time' and field trips are forbidden him, we have much less control over Sinbad. Instead of doing Sinbad's bidding, we've got to make the others understand that he is the primary source of their discomfort!"

"What about the sexual abuse?"

"No one will snitch as long as Sinbad is top dog. We can accuse but probably can't make it stick. The best case we've got is Country."

"Why don't I go up and talk to him?" I suggested.

"No. Wait for him to make a bathroom call, then talk to him. Meanwhile, I'll ask Williams to help us get him moved to another cottage."

"OK, Mr. Davenport; then I'll finish the cat petition tonight."

][(

These days the dorm filled twice a week with newcomers fresh off the streets. I chalked it up to the seasonal heat in Pittsburgh. Dav chalked it up to America's increasing social disintegration. Whatever the case, we began to get the weekend overflow from Pittsburgh on Monday afternoons, in addition to the traditional Friday crowd. Many moved on to other cottages the next day.

That worried me because it often meant that the real bad asses were now spreading like self-replicating viruses from our cottage into other cottages traditionally populated with students in for less serious crimes: smoking a joint, ranking on a teacher, truancy, and the always-dangerous "underage drinkers."

In Pennsylvania, where nineteenth-century blue laws kept even most grocery stores closed on Sundays, a sixteen-year-old drinking a Sunday beer on a buddy's porch was juvenile detention bound if even one old lady up the block had an outrage attack and reported it. True—most such kids didn't make it straight to the Morganza, but even one moderate "acting out" episode while in some city's temporary juvenile detention center meant a second hearing, another experience with a capricious justice system, and eventually a case of the uncontrollable sweats in the Morganza's Tower dormitory.

Years later it also raised the likelihood that one more very angry and institutionally trained criminal was out on the street, harboring a bitter rage. As Dav put it, "They shouldn't send 'em here if they don't want to get 'em back even more dangerous."

My take was, "We need *two separate* justice and detention systems. One to try those who have done violence and another to try those who haven't."

"How would that work?" asked Richard.

"Preliminary hearing to determine whether violence and aggression were a factor. If 'no,' you get tried in Justice System Nonviolent, where rehab is the goal. If 'yes,' it's Justice System Violent, where protecting society is the goal."

Dav thought about it for a minute. "So, here in this cottage we'd have all the Curtises and Billys and someone else would have Kamensky, Sinbad, and Sugarbear?"

"Yep. Sinbad and his soul mates wouldn't be watching TV and drinking hot chocolate. More importantly, they'd have no innocents to prey on."

Dav frowned. "The hard part would be courts determining what 'violence' meant—just putting your hands up to defend yourself shouldn't count." Stumped by that reality, I shrugged and went back to working on Country's "cat rocking" petition.

]|[

By 11:00 p.m. I had nearly completed the first draft of Country's petition. That done, I began an incident report on "jelly babies" for his file in support of the same.

I'd taken up the usual end-of-upper-hallway easy chair position and plugged in my portable record player to give them some Wes Montgomery. This time it didn't calm them down. Neither did Coltrane. Without butter, rags, and cool air, the whole second floor was in a serious funk.

Someone yelled at Country, who was in his room crying. "Chill . . . punk, weren't for you we'd be gettin' butter!" Country went quiet.

I responded, "No, Sinbad pissed off Dav—not Country." Disgusted, I turned the lights off and went downstairs to pee, grab one of Mrs. Moxon's sandwiches, and leave my petition in the outbox for the typing pool. The cottage was eerily silent, so I ducked into the dorm's foyer to see if anyone was there. Palco and Davenport were locked together in a whispered conversation. I ducked out so as not to interrupt and stepped into the night.

The moon, now almost half full, cast a bright orange glow from behind the nearby hill. I climbed. Cicadas called to one another, and a cool breeze from the bottoms along the banks of Chartiers Creek carried the sounds of bullfrogs. Somewhere a farm dog howled at the moon, and a light flickered below me in one window of the cottage's second floor. *Odd. Their lights are turned out at the main switch.* The fine hairs on the back of my neck stiffened then saluted.

I dropped the last bite of sandwich and hurried back. Inside, I stuck my head into the foyer, where Palco sat alone, legs sprawled wide, supine in his chair. "I saw a light flicker upstairs." Palco shrugged. I headed toward the stairwell as Dav materialized, slightly out of breath and holding a flashlight. "I went up to check on Country, Mr. Stuart," he whispered.

Relieved, I sat down on the stairs. "How's he doing?"

"Couldn't spot him. Must be sleeping on the floor. It's dark and those little windows don't help much." He was still whispering.

"Well, I don't think anyone is really asleep, Mr. Davenport. It was tense up there so I turned out the lights to calm them down—they didn't even want to hear music."

Dav spoke in his regular voice. "We've got to get a handle on Sinbad's little army. They should have moved him to White Hill—or a federal detention center—after the post office robbery. That enhanced his bad-boy rep here. Got him even more converts. Now I . . ."

A keening howl from the hallway a half flight above us interrupted Dav. The howl was answered quickly by an angry bellow. "Shut th' fuck up, you nappy splip-lipped punk."

"I seen sumpin' outside. A face was lookin' me. Duppy seen me. Ah's gonna turn."

"Oh Lord!" grumbled Davenport. "I'll go up again." He disappeared with the flashlight. I saw another quick flash of light before Dav came back down, panting, "Country and Sugarbear are at it," he commented.

Upstairs Country howled again. "Duppy back! His eyes all lits up. He *cookin'* me. I'm turnin'. Lawd help me! I'm *turnin'*."

"I seen his light, too!" someone else shouted. "Check outside," said Dav. "Some dog's howling out there." I took a flashlight and stepped out into the hollow of the hill. No dog, nothing outside. But another light flickered inside on the second story—Davenport's flashlight in the hallway.

Suddenly I heard shouting from inside. I hurried back to relock the security doors behind me and dashed upstairs where all hell had broken loose. Palco shouted at me on the way past. "What's with you, Weasel?"

"Duppy's got me!" screamed Kamensky from above. I rocketed past Palco. "Sounds like we got duppies up on 2."

Palco, apparently unfamiliar with duppies, simply stood there, slack-jawed. Frankly, it was a good look for him. Someone screamed again and I heard Dav's voice. I couldn't make out what he said, but he didn't sound much like his normal, calm self. I took the steps two at a time.

Country shrieked, weird and high-pitched. Rabbit giggled. Even Golightly and Sugarbear were losing it.

"Mr. Dav, Mr. Dav," someone yelled. "He's gonna get us! Help us, Mr. Dav."

I found Davenport sitting at the top of the stairs, holding his flashlight in one hand, the other clamped over his mouth, jiggling like Jell-O, trying not to laugh himself to death. I helped him up. He motioned us back down.

"Mr. Stuart," he said between giggles when we reached the

half-landing. "I didn't realize that it was my flashlight making the duppy trouble until I shined it in and saw Kamensky glued to the Plexiglas, his eyes as big as saucers. 'Fuck me, I ain't done nothin',' he said . . . and I couldn't help myself. I told him, 'Yes, you have! You been doin' *boys.*' That's when he started shrieking. What got 'em all going was Country 'turnin'.'"

Dav tried to say more but was doubled over laughing by this point. "Mr. Stuart, you . . . better go up and . . . turn the light on." I left Dav there howling to himself and flipped on the main switch at the top of the stairs. I tried to imitate Dav's business voice: calm, commanding, and familiar.

"What's all the hollering up here? I'm trying to write reports."

"We got duppies!" wailed Kamensky. "Gonna eat us!"

"Duppies leave when the lights is on," offered Country.

"OK, I'll leave 'em on. If any of you stick chewing gum wrappers in the sockets, they go off again and I go home for the night. I'm not going to listen to some duppy crunching on your bones."

"Ain't you scared of duppies?" hollered Sugarbear.

"*Aren't* you scared of duppies, *what*?" I answered.

"*Aren't* you scared of duppies, *Mr. Stuart*?"

"No. I'm white. They favor dark meat."

Rabbit snickered. "Can you play *white* music?" shouted Sinbad, sounding serious for once. I stopped in front of his door.

"You don't deserve it," I commented dryly.

"Ah know . . . when you gonna send me to White Hill?"

"Last week, Sinbad. They'll tear your head off over there. Place is full of huge Aryan brotherhood types. It will present a challenge . . . you'll love it." Sinbad grimaced through the Plexiglas window.

From several doors down Rabbit crooned, "Really? How big are they?" *How does the little shit hear everything?* I wondered. I flicked the lights on and left before I was tempted into another episode of substandard professionalism with Rabbit.

Like most staff members in our cottage, I'd begun to fantasize about slipping a noose over Rabbit's neck whenever he started his snickering or that bullshit "ooh, ooh" routine . . .

. . . *My thumb twitched involuntarily as I jerked the noose tight and threw the loose end of the rope over the upper bunk's rail, whipped a good Boy Scout's half hitch into it, and pulled till Rabbit's eyeballs popped. . . .*

Finally I managed to turn off the sick fantasy. But more temptation was only steps away. On the way down the hall, Sinbad motioned me back to his window and pointed down toward his lock. Had it not been for Rabbit's infectious, fast-acting, "do something sick" virus that had invaded me, I'd have kept on going.

"Step all the way back—both you and Sugarbear. Face away. Hands on head." To my surprise, they moved to the window quickly and obediently, so I opened the door. "Twitch and I'm replaced by Palco." They nodded. "OK, what did you want?" I asked.

Sinbad, facing away, nodded, *"Please* don't send me to White Hill."

I answered softly, *"Please* don't bother Country, Carlos, Curtis, Rabbit, or any of them again. Understand?" They both nodded. "You screw up again, Sinbad, and Dav and I will ask for the detail that escorts you to White Hill. I'll even give you enough lipstick to survive the first week . . . by the way, they don't give methadone there. They lock you in a room and film you sweating and puking on yourself."

"Don't jive me, Mr. Stuart," answered Sinbad, twitching subtly.

"No jive. You're doing easy time here. This is paradise . . . no Aryan brotherhood. No exercise yard lynchings to keep wiseass black guys in their place. Mr. Davenport is the best thing that ever happened to you. You're just too smug to know it."

Downstairs, Dav was still recovering from his giggles. "Should I go up and explain?" he asked, trying to be professional again.

"No way! Your duppy impersonation got Sinbad and Sugarbear afraid of being sent to White Hill. I told them you and I would personally ask for the escort detail if they messed with any of the kids again."

"In the hallway, you said that?"

"No. In their room. Against the window, facing away, hands on head."

"Well, well, we may be seeing the start of an epiphany. Nice work, Mr. Stuart."

Someone upstairs started shouting about "turning" again. I went up to the landing and flicked off the main light switch. The effect was instant—rather like a massive dose of Thorazine.

chapter 16

The Price of Identity

Exhausted, I pulled only one shift on Tuesday, managed to finish the final draft of Country's ludicrously copious "cat time" paperwork, and hand-delivered it to the Hill before five.

On Wednesday I was in tie and sport jacket for my lunch with Her Majesty. There was a small, elegant executive dining area in an alcove off the formal reception hall. An assistant seated me. I stood when the director walked in a few minutes later, accompanied by two well-dressed colleagues. The first, a young female, was Her Majesty's new administrative assistant, who looked vaguely familiar.

The other colleague, a tweedy, dyspeptic-looking middle-aged white guy, nodded but said nothing. I studied him casually. He wore a Timex, needed a haircut, and, unlike Lawdawg, wore only one piece of jewelry—an old-fashioned stickpin that held his tie in place. Had it not been for the stickpin, I'd have figured him for some sort of displaced academic. But your average professor doesn't own a baguette-cut, three-karat Russian emerald tie pin worth more than a nice ranch-style house. He caught me checking out the pin, so I turned back to Her Majesty's new assistant.

She, unlike Champlin, was breezy and pleasant. "I'm Patricia, a friend of Angela's. Just graduated from Pitt. So you are the one who Angie takes to the Crawford Grill." She grinned. "Boy, her dad is fried."

Her Majesty frowned. "Patricia . . . this is a *business* lunch." Patricia shut up but winked at me.

"Now, to business. Mr. Stuart here has some ideas we should hear about a particular case . . . William Terrell. Proceed." She nodded, and I explained.

"William doesn't belong here. Neither do several of the others in our cottage. They simply aren't security threats. I've written a petition for a new hearing on William's original sentence." I outlined Billy's situation for the three of them, then the director commented.

"It's a good petition. Nearly a final draft, according to Judge Simpson here." Her Majesty gestured toward Stickpin. "Judge Simpson is president of our advisory board and the senior appeals court judge from Delaware County. He is advising us in the event we file this case under YD's aegis." Finally, the judge unpressed his lips and spoke.

"This review appears to have merit . . . but you must realize that several of the issues you raise are, uh, judicially delicate."

I nodded and leaned forward. "How can I improve the draft?" I asked.

"I'd approach the relationship between the original complainant and the presiding judge more obliquely."

"Really?" commented Her Majesty, sounding surprised. Without breaking his eye-lock on me, Simpson nodded. Patricia noticed and did a visual ping-pong back and forth between us.

"OK," I commented. "How oblique is oblique?"

He raised one graying eyebrow. "Delete all reference to it." He abruptly changed the subject to an upcoming state budget recommendation, ". . . which *might* enhance funding for the Morganza and White Hill." The director looked nervous. I kept a straight face and struggled not to laugh.

Compared to my old man, Judge Simpson was a rank amateur at intimidation and power politics. He might have been skilled enough to make it in Pennsylvania, but down in West Virginia where the tax base was lean and the daily needs far more desperate, Senator Byrd-style hardball was an elegant artform. Didn't he know that he was supposed to have that imaginary legislative money in hand before he blackmailed anyone with it?

At home, behind the Cotton Curtain, Simpson would have lasted, at most, six to eight minutes on a slow news day. And against my old man, who'd once had the governor of West Virginia in our living room begging him not to send West Virginia University Medical Center's entire patient population to Pittsburgh hospitals in a National Guard ambulance caravan while CBS, NBC, and ABC filmed it, Judge Simpson would have had a career as fleeting as the half-life of a very rare laboratory-created isotope. That's how my old man had played it, aces in hand, when the Legislature stiffed the medical center he ran for its penny-a-bottle "pop tax" allocation. National Guard ambulances were already lined up and waiting—as was a CBS news producer—when the governor threw in his cards.

Because of my old man, I was far more amused than troubled by Simpson but didn't bother to react. "Delete" translated to me as "press this button harder, it's already scaring the snot out of the judiciary." The soup was good. The stream-caught trout even better.

"The sweet corn is from the farm next door," the director offered brightly when Judge Simpson declined it. About twenty minutes later the judge rose. "I have to get back to a meeting with the governor in Harrisburg. Three p.m. sharp." Pure bullshit—it was already 12:50 p.m. and Harrisburg was three full hours away on the traffic-choked turnpike. The director rose and escorted him out, leaving me with Patricia, who leaned forward.

"I don't believe he just said what he did. Do you suppose he meant it as blackmail?" I smiled.

"Friend of Ange . . . all I heard was a judge making a suggestion. They babble all the time. What did *you* hear?" She paused and stared as if trying to read my mind. I gave her nothing.

"You're good! Angie said you were a wild man, but you seem very collected to me." She leaned back. "So what are your intentions with Angie?"

"She's been a friend since my freshman year at WVU—I tried to date her then without success. She offered friendship. I took it."

"So do you know she's nuts for you?"

"Nope. I don't even believe you. But thanks for thinking the best of it."

"So what is the girl in Mexico like?"

"Not that it's public business, but she's just like Ange: smart, attractive, interesting, and frank."

"Oh my God! You are *sooo* bad! No wonder her dad's pissed."

"I've never met her dad. But I keep hearing the 'pissed' bit."

"Never met him?" I shook my head. "Angie assumes the two of you have spoken before." I shook my head again. "Wouldn't know him if I fell over him."

"Wow! Too strange."

"I agree," said Her Majesty, who had returned. "He's even complained to me about you and your 'affair' with his daughter."

"I'd love to be having an 'affair' with her, but she's a friend. A friend who likes to dance and talk at dinner. I've never even been inside her apartment."

For whatever reason, Her Majesty smiled. "Don't change your petition for Billy. And don't claim any company time for writing it . . . if that is acceptable, I'll support it—at arm's length."

"Fair enough." I stood and shook on it, then turned to Patricia. "Does Ange know her dad is outright fantasizing?"

"I'm not sure."

"Make sure." She nodded. On the way out I stopped to ponder the Morganza's black and gilt colonial-style crest painted on the portico peak above the tall, glass-paned front door. I'd never noticed before, but underneath the crest of two rampant horses it read: "Virtue, Liberty, Independence."

)|(

Later that afternoon I took Her Majesty's advice and backed one day out of my time report. Just to be safe, I wrote it up as "Per director, project unrelated to primary job description." Since, as a trainee, I wasn't allowed to sign anything, I hoped that whoever initialed it would leave it as is. Dav was off, having worked with me overnight, so I had to put up with Palco and Street—a worthless older guy from custodial who substituted for us sometimes. Street neither shaved regularly nor changed his shirts frequently. His gray stubble and dirty fingernails spoke volumes about why custodial sent him to us whenever we were desperate enough to take him.

Mrs. Moxon caught me during a lull about two thirty. "Grab Country. We are going to look at kittens." She winked. Short, dowdy, and comfortingly old-fashioned, she reminded me of the quintessential aunt who quietly held families together when everyone else flipped out.

"Will they approve it?" I asked.

"Already approved."

"How?"

"One of the psych techs is a niece of a friend. She'll sign it when she comes in tomorrow." Mrs. Moxon was one amazingly well-connected housemother. Officially she was involved in none of the "treatment and evaluation" stuff. Unofficially she knew everything and everyone who actually counted.

I caught Country stacking freshly washed plates in the kitchen and waved him away from his task. "Hey! Mizz Moxon and I are going to visit the back farm and see some animals . . . want to come with us?" Country nodded enthusiastically.

On the far side of the property, not far from the Hill, one of the original barns had been converted to house trucks and old farm machinery. The remains of an extensive hayfield surrounded the garage, one end opening to the overgrown, oak-lined lane where the farm's horse-drawn wagons had once passed at the end of each work day.

Tucked into one end of the barn-like garage were stalls and cages for chickens, rabbits, and guinea pigs . . . all remnants of a once-robust 4-H program that had flourished from the '30s to the early '60s. Some of the more rural students still participated . . . though few of them were from our cottage, where city-bred bad boys had become a specialty.

Country went straight to the rabbits, stroking one of the big one's ears and whispering to it. "Can I hold it, Mizz Moxon?"

"Sure. Do you know how?"

"Yazz'm, the mens at home keeps 'em." Country carefully extracted the biggest male and cradled it under his chin, following us as we strolled to one corner where a mother cat nursed her litter, their eyes barely opened. "Ah loves babies," smiled Country. "Can I hold one?"

"Certainly," Mrs. Moxon said, smiling, "put 'Mr. Big' back first." Country took the rabbit back and gently tucked him into his cage.

"He seems OK with animals," whispered Mrs. Moxon.

"Can I sit with kitties?" Country asked us. Mrs. Moxon nodded. We left Country sprawled on the hay in the cat's stall, watching the kittens intently from a yard's distance. Outside, we circled the barns.

"I started here in the forties. It was nicer then . . . more farmwork and poor, addled kids—most were unfortunates, rather than evildoers. The work was good for them. By the sixties the kids were meaner.

We had to watch out for them hurting the animals. Things began to change. More kids; nastier crimes; much more citified . . . and much less emphasis on old-fashioned discipline. Then we went completely liberal . . . 'Don't offend anyone. Talk to the lawyers first.' Every decision reviewed from the Hill." She sighed. "Let's check on Country."

Inside, Country had borrowed a spotted kitten and tucked it under his chin. Rocking back and forth, he sang to it . . . a lullaby of some sort. When he saw us he hurried to put it back with its mother, explaining, "It meow to me."

"That's a good sign, son," said Mrs. Moxon. "Do you want to come here every day and see that kitten?"

"Yazz'm, kitty's name 'Mizz Small.'"

"Good. Let's walk back. We've got to get ready for dinner."

Halfway back to the cottage, Country asked a favor. "Ah don' want Sinbad and dems knowin' 'bout Mizz Small."

"We won't say a word," Mrs. Moxon promised.

][[

That night was quiet. We had only one brief duppy sighting, and this time it was solved by flipping on the lights and playing white music, The Doors. The downside was the students insisted that Richard and I change places. They wanted me upstairs with them, explaining, "Duppies don't take to white folks, Mr. Richard." Richard was upset.

"That's just racism backward."

"I know," I responded, "So, which do you prefer . . . a perfect world, or a quiet one?" Reluctantly, he went with quiet.

Later that night when we were on a break, Richard asked me, "What's it feel like to be white?"

"It's neither interesting nor notable. I feel nothing. Nothing at all. There isn't even any sense of identity or community in it . . . if you get run over by a car in the street, other white people will walk right over you, then later describe you as, 'some guy in the street,' and not even stop to help because they simply do not identify with you."

"Wow! Are you saying that is what equality is like?"

"Yep. Equal in America means *no one* gives a damn . . . that's the 'white' secret as I see it."

"Oh, man. That's *cold*," goggled Richard.

"No . . . that's real, Richard . . . when Martin Luther King talks about becoming equal, I wonder if he knows that, the U.S. Senate and Klan aside, there is no white club. There is a 'rich' club, a 'Jewish' club, a 'Catholic' club, a 'Protestant' club, a 'Confederate' club, and lots of country clubs. But no white club. No secret membership.

"A working-class or middle-class white is absolutely nobody. Invisible. Being ordinary, mainstream white, at least in the North, means no breaks, no favors, no slack, no money, no special identity. In short, no damn nothing."

"Man. That's cynical. It can't be that way."

"Well, perhaps I am cynical. Certainly I don't know what it's like being black in America. But I do know that 'white' is, for most of us, absolutely *nothing*."

"So, what are my people striving for . . . a mirage?" he asked, a pained look on his face.

"If they are smart, they are striving for the 'rich' club, the 'connected' club, the 'country' club, because plain old 'white' isn't a ticket . . . you are totally on your own."

Richard looked a bit dazed.

]|[

A few days later, I bumped into Richard at a late-night diner in Little Washington. I could tell he'd been mulling over our conversation. Over grilled ham and cheese sandwiches he said, "Look, David, I don't think you realize what it's like to be a minority . . . or treated like one. I think that shapes your views."

"I'm sure it does. But I lived in Mexico City where 'gringos' are outnumbered at least one-thousand-to-one, and some people call you names, make derisive comments about your skin color, attitude, and culture . . . you also have far fewer legal rights than the locals and, in spite of all that, I loved it because I had more identity as a 'minority' there than I do here as supposed mainstream. It's odd. And it's only my personal experience. But there it is!"

Richard shook his head. "Mind boggling . . . but being black in America is a special case. Slaves."

"I agree. Given our history, blacks got a raw deal and continue to get a raw deal. But there were many more black slaves imported to

Mexico than to the United States. Could one difference be that blacks here tend to buy into the Klan stereotypes, that is, allow themselves to be defined by those very whites who are the lowest common denominator—despised and totally out of the mainstream—and not even realize that true mainstream America doesn't know much about them . . . or the Klan . . . and, just as with its own 'nobodies,' doesn't really care?" Richard stared.

"What you are saying is that Plain Jane White carries virtually no identity investment, while Plain Jane Black carries a huge one."

"Change one word and replace 'carries' with 'imposes' and finally we agree! You really do need to go into government, Richard."

"It doesn't even bother you to discuss your race, does it, David?"

"Nope. No investment required. No loyalty oath taken. I'm free to hate everyone . . . including my own race."

"I'm not free to do that . . ."

"I know. But you *know* it and aren't in denial . . . that's why I'd vote for you as president."

chapter 17

Daddy

Thursday consisted of a rare, single shift, then dinner with Ange. At ten, Mrs. Moxon sent Country to feed the menagerie of animals in the tractor barn, accompanied by the young female psych tech who was to sign off on his animal contact therapy.

Mr. Reddy was back from vacation and noisier than ever, bragging about some damn thing in his yard called a Pandora . . . at least that's what I think he called it. At one point he turned to me, feet up on the front office desk, and asked, "Does your family have a Pandora?"

"No, Mr. Reddy . . . I've never even heard of one."

He smiled expansively. "Ah. Perhaps they don't have them down there."

I nodded, trying not to grin over the arbitrary barrier historians, geographers, and Mr. Reddy placed so much social importance on, the Mason-Dixon Line. It was as if daily life was fundamentally different in Point Marion, Pennsylvania, from the West Virginia hamlets three hundred yards across the state line. Hell, even the family names were the same. In fact, the biggest differences were in liquor laws and age of consent. In West Virginia you could marry your sixteen-year-old second cousin with no hassles, but you couldn't buy hard liquor in a bar. In Pennsylvania, you couldn't marry a female younger than eighteen— and she couldn't be a cousin—but you could drink yourself to death most anywhere . . . except on Sundays, of course, when you couldn't even buy a jug of milk. Life is replete with irony.

In any case, I was obviously from that "behind the Cotton Curtain" class of whites who had no Pandora, and Reddy seemed content with this.

)|(

An hour later the young psych tech, Mrs. Moxon's "niece of a friend," returned with Country. He was whistling through the prominent lips that had got him labeled a "splip" (big lip) by the other blacks.

Mrs. Moxon's young tech came over to ask Mr. Reddy and me which of us was responsible for up-keeping Country's file. Reddy answered, "I am, but the workup has been delegated to *trainee* Stuart here." With that Reddy excused himself, waving her toward his own seat. "Back in twenty," he said, flashing his gold tooth and adjusting his tie.

Reddy gone, the psych tech, her prim Mennonite hair bun seeming incongruous in our little zoo, sat across from me, smiling. "I am approving your request. He, so far, is very gentle with the animals. Gradually decrease supervision over the next two to three weeks. If all is still well, Mrs. Moxon says the kitten can come over here."

"So what did you think of Country overall, Miss, uh . . ."

"Bowers . . . I think Dexter is very sweet, naïve, and, uh, a bit impaired intellectually. Why do you ask?" *A bit . . . holy smokes!* I goggled and expanded on my theme.

"I don't think he belongs here. I was thinking of petitioning for a halfway house where he could get more remediation . . . fewer bullies, too."

"I heard you were an activist of sorts. Shall I do a complete workup . . . one that can be passed on to one of our consulting psychologists for review?"

"Yes, Miss Bowers, that would be much appreciated." She looked a little like a girl I knew by the name of Bowers back in Morgantown— lovely, in an old-fashioned farm girl sort of way. "Is everything all right?" she asked. That's when I realized I was staring at her. Jet-black hair, creamy cheeks, bright gray eyes, and a lovely mouth, she reminded me of a brilliant, determined girl in a Jane Austen novel.

"Oh, sorry! You remind me of a girl in Morgantown. Her dad, Morgan Bowers, lived out on the Point Marion road."

She smiled. "That's my uncle Morgan! He has several daughters."

"What a coincidence! I would like you to say hello to your cousin Sarah."

"Surely. And I will do a workup on Dexter." *Surely? Now I know we're talking Jane Austen.* I smiled at her.

Reddy drifted back when she left. "You hitting on Mennonite girls out of boredom?" He grinned, his narrow, meticulously crafted mustache twitching, "Or has the heat tricked your brain into believing it's worthwhile?" I smiled and went back to my charts while Reddy relaxed, hands laced behind his head, imitating a Cheshire cat.

About forty minutes later I finished the morning "dailies," irritated that Reddy had watched me write, relaxing while I worked. I pushed them over to him for signatures and stood to take a break. Reddy clucked. "Just one more rewrite on this one should do it, Stuart." I turned toward the kitchen but paused to glare at him from over my shoulder.

"By the way, Mr. Reddy . . . Mennonite girls don't drink, dance, swear, or play cards, but they do it like minks and love it from behind," I lied. "Just thought you'd like to know." I savored a glimpse of Reddy's "You got me!" face as I walked into the kitchen.

Mrs. Moxon was chatty as she prepared dinner. "I can make a place for the kitten. . . . By the way, they tell me you speak Spanish. Is that so?"

"Yes, ma'am. Some at least."

"Did you learn it in West Virginia?"

"No, ma'am. I lived in Mexico for a while."

"Really? Well, we have a talent show each October on Halloween, and there is a role for a bullfighter that is never used because no one here understands the music or the instructions. Would you and a student participate?" *Aha*, I thought, *I'm starting to see how things get done around here.* Unlike Judge Simpson, she was far more like Senator Byrd . . . if I wanted perks for Country, which she could deliver, rather than merely dangle, she wanted a bullfighter in return . . . an unstated quid pro quo. Impressed with her, I accepted.

"Good. Good. What a stroke of luck." she smiled. *Yeah, right,* I laughed to myself. *The kind of luck that gets a compliant psych tech into the building immediately, instead of the usual six-week's written notice, followed by another month of bowing, scraping, begging, and suffering seriously chapped lips.*

〗〖

I punched out at five, retrieved my evening clothing from a hanging bag in the Rambler, which, as usual, was parked behind the cottage, and showered on site—a big mistake. The substantial student commentary wore thin quickly. "Get *down*! Mr. Stuart's got a *hot* date," someone razzed me from the hallway. Moments later I heard Rabbit's sick giggle.

"Rabbit . . . if you are hiding out there in the hall gooning my ass, I'm going to write you up!"

"Righteous!" cackled Curtis. "Curtis," I called, "just for that you get to be the *toreador* in the talent show!"

"I get *what*?"

"You're the bullfighter," snickered Carlos, fingers to his head, mimicking horns.

"Why are you here, Carlos?" I asked as I walked past, buttoning my shirt. Dav answered from around the corner. "Early shower. Fresh clothes . . . our little warlord here is going directly to White Hill after dinner." At the mention of White Hill the other students sneaking around scattered and shut up. As I turned my tie to tighten up its four-in-hand knot, Dav winked at me.

My date with Ange was early dinner at a small restaurant across the Monongahela from Downtown, where we could review Billy's petition then take in a late concert at the Syria Mosque. I wasn't sure who was playing, but Angela had never subjected me to anything like medieval chamber music, so I didn't really care.

Snarled in traffic on one of Pittsburgh's hilly one-ways, I arrived late to find Angela already seated and absorbed in Billy's petition. She didn't notice me, so I coughed. She jumped. "Oh! For a moment I thought it was my father . . . he's followed me several times to check on where I go. I didn't think much of it till Patricia called me last night to tell me Dad knew we'd been in the Crawford Grill. Now I'm nervous. Dad's become a bit unhinged since all the riots—and Mom dying. It's like he has to choose sides or something."

I eased into the booth. "Let's just enjoy dinner. Who are we going to hear?"

"A jazz ensemble. . . . Here, I've made notes in the margins," she said, handing me the petition.

"Will this get the job done?" I asked.

"I showed it to one of the younger partners. She says yes . . . unless there is unseen pressure to avoid a judicial embarrassment. That will depend on where it's heard. If it is reviewed in Beaver Falls, it's dead . . . the fox guarding the henhouse. If it's heard in Allegheny, Washington County, or over in Harrisburg, citified values will prevail and Billy will get another hearing. So it's a venue issue."

"Thanks, Ange . . . can your people help?"

She shook her head. "No! Too political. Bad for the firm. The law is one thing, and practice of the law is another," she said, pouting.

I laughed. "And are you still determined to go to law school?"

She never got a chance to answer me. A horrified expression crossed her face, and suddenly I couldn't move, couldn't talk, couldn't do anything except watch Ange being pulled out of the booth by a huge black guy built like an NFL linebacker. A thickly muscled black arm under my chin, a palm on top of my head, I wasn't going anywhere. Ange stared wide-eyed at someone behind me and shrieked, "Dad! What are you doing?!" From over my shoulder, an angry but impeccably educated voice stated matter-of-factly, "You have just had the very last date of your life with a piece of white trash, young lady."

I struggled to break free as someone at the cash register frantically dialed the police. There was some sort of commotion to the side but, though I tried, I couldn't turn my head to decipher what was going on. My head buzzed and I got sleepy. The next thing I remember, I was on the floor, looking up at a cop and an ambulance tech, who was pressing a big rubber oxygen mask over my face. A few minutes later when the oxygen came off, a jacket-and-tie, middle-aged white guy was giving a statement to the police.

"I own this place, and I want to press charges . . . the black girl screamed, 'Dad, what are you doing?' He was very well-dressed. Tall, thin. Educated, I think. But he had two black street goons with him. He and one of them were out the door with her kicking and screaming within thirty seconds. The other one choked this guy here," he continued, pointing at me.

The cop turned to peer down at me. "Can you confirm?"

I shook my head. "I didn't see anything except her disappear and a black arm under my chin—but her dad's a surgeon. She's Angela Whitson-Montgomery. Paralegal. Pitt graduate. Twenty-two. Don't let them hurt her. She thought her dad was losing it over her dating a white guy . . . except we're not 'dating' and her mother was white." I felt delirious. I was probably saying too much but couldn't really control the words.

The cop rolled his eyes. "A surgeon? Here in town?"

I nodded. "Big shot in the black community, I'm told."

"Just great!" He shook his head and turned to someone over my shoulder. "Get this on the radio *and* call the chief to warn him that we've got *another* high-profile racial incident."

"This isn't really high profile," I amended, but no one seemed the least bit interested in what I had to say.

Ange, who was only one fifth of the alleged high-profile racial incident, counting Dad, two goons, and me, was, according to the cops, found later at Dr. Whitson's place, sedated and locked in her bedroom. Dad had bailed out and barely beat the cops to the airport. A day later it was revealed that he took an unexpected trip to Africa—a continent I suspect he'd never before seen. No one ever identified the two goons.

Angela, according to her friend Patricia, had been assured by Daddy's black lawyer that I'd filed kidnap, false imprisonment, and assault charges against Dr. Whitson. This was pure bull . . . I wouldn't even sign the restaurant owner's complaint. Even so, Angela hung up on me the first time I called. Two days later she did pick up, if only to shout, "You betrayed me by criminalizing my father. Don't ever contact me again!" I'd tried to do the right thing by not piling on. But, just as with my own father, no one seemed to get it. After the phone call I retreated to my eagle's nest on Beau Street, ate dinner, which consisted of a room-temperature can of Chef Boyardee spaghetti with meatballs, and a $1 quart of high-octane, handmade whiskey that had been illicitly "estate bottled" over in rural Preston County, West Virginia.

About 5:00 a.m. I woke up, feeling somewhat out of sorts . . . not that surprising since I'd apparently stepped up on my old man's footlocker to piss into the sink only to pass out and fall into it. The front of my shirt reeked. A deep faucet indentation added temporary character to my freshly bruised forehead. On the upside, I could still see myself in the mirror, so I had obviously not been blinded by a batch of radiator-distilled corn whiskey. Bargain-hunting for $1 whiskey instead of paying the standard $2 below the Cotton Curtain carried risks not unlike slipping one cartridge into a revolver then spinning the cylinder before pulling the trigger.

When other humans don't respond to good deeds, one—that would be me—sometimes requires validation from a higher authority. And Mason jar whiskey definitely carried an air of higher authority. Reasonably satisfied by the combination of cottonmouth and nauseating hangover leavened by the validating gift of continued sight, I stripped off the piss-soaked shirt and went to bed.

Late the following week I called Angela again, hoping she'd cooled down enough to talk. She hung up on me, and Daddy's attorney obtained a restraining order, preventing me from further contact with her. *You're welcome*, I reassured myself as I sought childish revenge by tossing the pieces of her shredded picture into the sink and pissing on them. One unshredded eye stared back at me in stern reproach.

At the Morganza things remained tough, and I was testy. We had a minor melee one Sunday in mid September when the *Ed Sullivan Show* featured The Doors. The white kids went nuts over "Light My Fire," especially the part about, "The girl we couldn't get much higher." I think Sullivan had insisted on a minor word change, but everyone knew the real lyrics. Problem was, like Angela's dad, the black kids went reactive, snarling about why Sullivan didn't invite people like Wes Montgomery on the show. As usual, Sinbad smiled dreamily and skillfully incited the others. Me, I locked 'em all up early—no butter. No rags. No bitching tolerated.

]|[

I had already given up on Ange and no longer felt conflicted about pissing on her likeness when Her Majesty's assistant, Patricia, unexpectedly phoned the cottage one morning. It was already early October. "David, we need to talk. Can you come up?"

"No. We're short-staffed and overflowing down here . . . but I'm off at eleven p.m. tonight. You up that late?"

"Umm. Maybe."

"Coffee at the Little Washington Diner?" I suggested, curious at the cautious tone in her voice.

"OK. 11:20?"

She was waiting in a booth when I walked in. "I have news. Two things. First: Young William's petition has been referred to Delaware County. The director is nervous about that. It smells of our lunch conversation with that judge. Our attorney filed an appeal to move it to a district with no judicial interest in the outcome, but we got Delaware."

"Simpson?" I commented. She nodded.

"I also did something else . . . Angela called me. I know there was a restraining order on you . . . I didn't try to talk her out of it . . ."

I interrupted and scowled, "Not your business!"

"It's relevant to your job here . . . anyway, what I didn't know until the farm's attorney obtained it was that you refused to sign any complaints in the, uh, restaurant incident."

"Didn't need to . . . Daddy screwed himself by locking her up and sedating her. It's just a matter of time till he loses his license to practice here in Pennsylvania. That restaurant owner isn't going away. Where the hell is 'Daddy,' anyway?"

"Still in Ghana. Look, David, I gave a copy of the complaints to Angela. Now she doesn't know what to say. She really believed you had filed them."

"Daddy needs a *much* better lawyer. The one he has now is a liar . . . he also needs a shrink. If he's not careful he'll sentence himself to permanent exile someplace in the third world . . . and he'll lose his daughter when her brain unscrambles."

"He's already losing her . . . you should talk to her."

"Can't. Court orders aren't one-on-one negotiable, if she informally changes her mind. She has to petition the court to vacate the restraining order. Besides, *she* isn't prevented from contacting me."

"She's too humiliated . . . and too proud."

"That's her problem! I did *more* than my half on account of our friendship." I rose to go. I started toward the door, but Patricia called out.

"Do you love her? Is that why you refused to join the complaint?"

I turned. "No . . . at least, I don't think so. I thought the whole thing was blown out of proportion. The cops tried to convince me otherwise, so I thought about it for a day or two, then thought about one of the screwed but no-excuses black guys I work with and decided that I'm not handing 'Daddy' a 'white man holdin' me down' excuse. A rich, spoiled, second-generation, Dartmouth-educated surgeon twice my age doesn't deserve that psychological out. Besides, he called me 'white trash' in front of Ange." She cringed. I stood and left the diner.

Back at the rear steps to the eagle's nest, I was intercepted by Landlady Sister number one, who handed me another message. "We heard there was another disturbance at the Morganza late last week. Was anyone *killed* this time?" she asked, her seventy-year-old eyes bright with hope.

"No, ma'am. Several Band-Aids and bruises, nothing dramatic. Now that it's fall and cooling down, things are calm there." I opened the note in my hand . . . Billy's preacher had called to schedule an "urgent" meeting.

Shaking her head as if disappointed, she retreated into the dimly lit rear kitchen where her sister kneaded her hands in anticipation of a report. I climbed the wooden stairs, flung open both windows to cool the place down, and stepped up to piss in the sink.

]|[

Lonely, I wrote a long letter to my fiancée in Mexico City. It was liberating to write again in Spanish. It took me into a bright, colorful world, full of food and flowers, where fate, rather than a person, was the accepted culprit in most of life's travails. *Odd*, I thought as I wrote. *Here in the States we have the economy, technology, and a decent government, and yet we crap out by blaming the guy down the street—black or white, but nearly always poor . . . or very rich—for everything that goes bad for us. In contrast, Mexico, which is flat-out screwed economically, technologically, and governmentally, blames it on fate.* In human terms, I considered Mexico the more advanced.

The next morning I got up at about ten, showered downstairs after the other roomers had gone to work, then went to the bank and ordered a cashier's check for $300 U.S. in my fiancée's name. On the way to the urgent lunch meeting with Billy's preacher, I stopped by the post office and sent it to Mexico, registered. It contained money for our wedding.

Chapter 18

Billy, I Have Something to Tell You . . .

I met Billy's preacher at the same diner in Little Washington where I'd seen Reddy. The first words out of his mouth were, "Billy's mom has been found dead at their cabin."

"When? How?" I asked.

"Yesterday . . . cause is listed as 'natural.'"

"Who found her?"

"A member of my congregation," he answered, averting his eyes.

I responded sarcastically. "Oh, let me guess, Reverend . . . let's see, uh, would he be a farmer with a rope and a *pony*?" Oddly, my hands shook, and my voice sounded exactly like my old man's.

The preacher nodded and went pale. I took a deep breath.

"Convenient." I sighed.

"Too convenient! I don't know what to do."

"Is there anyone to handle a funeral?"

"I'll do it . . . perhaps take up a special offering . . . it will have to be soon."

"OK, Reverend, do you want to go out to the farm with me . . . or shall I tell Billy alone?"

He took a deep breath. "Are you proposing to tell him today?"

"Actually, I'm not sure what's best for him. I'd prefer to talk to one of the psych techs. Should I call now?" He nodded.

I went to the payphone on the wall and called Mrs. Moxon, who located Miss Bowers.

I filled her in. "Oh, no! I should phone the psychologist on call. Can I get back to you?" "Sure," I answered and went back to sit with the preacher. "I'm waiting for a senior psychologist's advice. Did you order anything to eat?"

He nodded. "A bowl of chili for each of us. What will happen now to Billy, legally?" he asked.

"Well, I'm not the expert . . . but having no family will become a factor. Who will they release him to if his new hearing is granted or reviewed by social services?" The preacher shrugged.

"It is bleak," he said, watching the phone. I spooned pooled grease from the top of my chili and watched it slowly congeal on the chipped off-white bread dish.

"Look," I said at last. "Why don't you head back home and work on arrangements? It is going to take a while to get advice here . . . and Father Ralph at the chapel will help me tell Billy." When he stood to go I suddenly had a thought. "Is there any place you can think of to send Billy? Someplace church-related?"

He smiled. "Either my niece or my older brother in Dayton might take him in. He has a large farm. His kids are grown and out of the house."

I was to clock in at 3:00 p.m. but pulled in to the Hill's semicircular, dried-mustard-colored brick driveway about 1:45. I found Patricia at her desk in the director's front office.

"Tell me what happens, legally, if Billy has no family to take custody of him."

Her eyes widened. "Why? Did something happen?"

"Yep. Mom was found dead this morning. But I need to talk to a psychologist first. I talked to Miss Bowers two hours ago but haven't heard back from her."

"Let's go find her. I'm going to go in and tell the director right now." She disappeared into Her Majesty's office. Both came out thirty seconds later. The director took charge, leading us down to the social psych unit office at the end of the hall. "Betty," called Her Majesty. The Bower girl's head popped out from behind a booth, the phone wedged between her jaw and shoulder.

"This is so frustrating . . . I've been on hold at Pitt for nearly an hour. Before that it was Allegheny General. There is only one clinical psychologist listed today and I can't find him."

Her Majesty leaned into the nearest booth, snatched a phone, announced, "Then we'll get a private one," and dialed, waving us all out.

]|[

Thirty minutes later I'd briefed everyone, including Mr. Davenport and Mrs. Moxon, whom I'd insisted be there, as well as a female psychologist, a friend of Her Majesty's, who'd rushed over from Washington & Jefferson College and was already deep into Billy's chart.

"Don't tell him anything" she said. "He can't process this. Wait till the funeral. It may not be fair, but he'll be victimized here if he goes into a grief cycle in front of the others in his cottage. You all have to be on the same page," the psychologist continued.

"Well, what *do* we tell him?" pressed Mr. Davenport, anxious to get back to the cottage before students began to return from school.

"Keep it simple, straightforward, and not much in advance of the funeral," she responded.

"How far in advance is 'not much?'" I asked.

"The night before."

"What? So he throws a fit all night?" protested Mrs. Moxon.

"Well, what do you propose?" asked the psychologist.

I butted in. "Take him up to Beaver Falls the night before. Make sure his preacher is available. Let him see his mom's body . . . then be there for him while he's in his own bed."

"Is that practical?" she asked.

"I can take a day off and do it, if anyone can get the paperwork to permit it," I said, looking around at the others. The psychologist nodded. "That's good. Yes."

Her Majesty interrupted. "I think that is very humane. I'll see to it. I don't know whether we are permitted to send a trainee as the sole escort. Patricia, ask the counsel to give us an opinion . . . quickly." The counsel appeared. Predictably, he shook his head. "I'll have to research legal precedent." Her Majesty glared at him and abruptly approved my trip "under my own aegis" without even looking over her shoulder at me. Lawdawg smirked.

The preacher called about 4:00 p.m. The funeral preparations were already in place, so Billy and I, armed with Her Majesty's emergency Bereavement Pass, were on the road in my old Rambler by 5:15. The preacher met us just after seven at his simple, white-painted country church about a mile from Beaver Falls. The preacher took Billy's shoulder and broke the news in a soft voice.

"I don' unnerstand, Reverend Jacob. Where'd Momma go?" Jacob, a pleading look on his face, turned to me for help.

I turned Billy to face me. "Billy. Your momma's *dead* and gone. Just got tired and died. I'm taking you home to sleep in your own bed, so you can say good-bye to her in the morning . . . then we will bury her next to your dad out here behind the church."

Billy stared at me, looked accusingly at the preacher, then back at me again. "I'm sorry, Billy," I said. His face tightened and he started to cry.

Later, after nightfall, I followed the preacher's old Chevy pickup along a back road that turned to dirt. Deep in a patch of tangled woods, a small house, supported on a foundation of crooked cinderblock pillars, emerged from the twilight that filtered into a small clearing.

The house had once been white, and its porch probably had once been nearly level, but that had to have been years ago. No electricity, the preacher handed me a flashlight and a roll of toilet paper. "I'll be here for you at seven a.m. My wife will fix breakfast . . . nothing to eat here. Will you be OK? It's, uh, rustic."

"I'll be fine . . . Mrs. Moxon packed us a bag of fruit and sandwiches at the farm." That drew a response from Billy. "Chocolate?" I nodded and nudged him forward. Once inside he struck a box match and lit an old-fashioned wick oil lamp. The scents of kerosene and hot glass momentarily took me back to childhood summers in the mountains. Inhaling the memories, I surveyed Billy's place.

The front room's dining area consisted of a plank table, two regular chairs, a third turned upside down, and a dirty, food-encrusted high chair, which now sat empty against a wavy, bubbled plasterboard wall. The scene was desolate.

The kitchen—formed by the other end of the front room—consisted of a big galvanized steel washbasin supported by four cinderblocks and an old, handmade farm cupboard, once apparently painted a soft mint green. Now it looked like the dingy, pea-soup green walls of our cottage at the Morganza. Next to the cupboard stood a gritty, enameled two-burner propane stove, also propped up on cinderblocks.

"Why's the chair turned up on the end of the table, Billy?"

"Daddy's. He killed diggin' coal for Reverend Jacob's church when I was little." *Hmmm. That means we also have a mystery father for "little sister."*

"Do you remember when he died, Billy?" I instantly regretted asking him this. His face tightened up again and he started bawling.

To help get his mind off of this, I asked Billy about "facilities." "Out back. No light." I went out with the flashlight and peed. While in the smelly one-holer, I heard a rhythmic squeaking. *A hand pump?* I wondered. Sure enough, when I went back inside Billy had started a pot of coffee on the propane stove. He handed me a big tin mug of the bitter, turgid brew and pleaded, "Read me the Bible, Mr. Stuart? I like the Christmas story."

"Did your momma read to you, Billy?" Staring down at the Bible in his hand, he shook his head no.

I exchanged a Mrs. Moxon sandwich for the Bible he held out to me and read. He settled into an old wicker chair nearby, ate, and rocked. "Is that Momma's chair?" I asked. He nodded.

By the time I finished the Christmas story, Billy had withdrawn into himself, staring off into nowhere. It was nearly ten, and I was beat.

I asked, "Where shall I sleep?"

"In bed. Got one in Momma's room." I took a look. The house contained one broken-down iron double, no sheets visible. "Billy . . . you sleep in the bed. I'll go out and sleep in the Rambler. Its seats make up into a bed."

"OK," he said, sounding hollow and even more unfocused than usual. Highlighted by the one kerosene lamp, I could see him through the shack's gritty front window. He was still rocking in Momma's chair when I lowered the Rambler's passenger seat to make a bed and threw a sleeping bag on it as a cushion. I rolled a window down on a crack, ate half of one of Mrs. Moxon's cheese sandwiches, and watched the stars overhead till I drifted off. It seemed like only a few minutes until the preacher's horn wakened me.

Not even sure Billy would still be there, I got up and threw back the sleeping bag, shivering from the morning chill. I jerked on my shoes and caught up with the preacher before he reached the front door. That startled him badly.

"Where'd you come from?"

"I slept in the car," I explained.

"Ah, so you didn't want to sleep in Ellen's bed . . . well, I don't blame you. The sheets were missing when I came with the coroner yesterday. I thought that was odd. She took in wash, so always had clean but old sheets . . . payment in kind."

"'Ellen' is Momma, then?"

"Yes. She was barely seventeen when she bore her common-law husband William Jack Terrell a son . . . Billy. Jack got killed in a mining accident, digging overlooked coal in an old, closed-up mine about ten miles from here. The spoil pile shifted on him. He had offered to pay his tithe in coal. With winter coming on, I accepted . . . and I didn't even think to ask where he'd get the coal." *Ah, we got guilt here.*

"So who is the father of little sister?" I asked. "That," he answered, "Lord forgive me if I'm wrong, is tied up with both her fate and Billy's."

"Mr. Rope and Pony is a possibility, then?"

He nodded. "I don't know, but he always liked 'em young and stupid, and . . ." Just then Billy unexpectedly opened the door and ended our conversation mid-sentence. "I was 'fraid you done left me, Mr. Stuart. It ain't right here without Momma."

"I'm sorry," I said.

Billy in tow, I followed the preacher's truck back to the church, where his wife, a big, plain but very pleasant-faced woman of about forty, met us. "Breakfast will be ready at the house in half an hour. I've been helping to arrange things here. Come in, Billy," she urged. "Let us say a prayer before breakfast."

I waited out front, smoked a Pall Mall Red, and drank a Coke while they did whatever one does in the sanctuary of a country Lutheran church before burying a cognitively deficient thirteen-year-old kid's mom.

)|(

Breakfast next door in the parsonage was the first nice thing about the whole trip. It consisted of a turkey-egg omelet, fluffy from the fresh cream whipped into it, hand-cured bacon, homemade wheat bread with blackberry jam, and a huge pile of home-fried potatoes and onion. Billy, to my surprise, ate an ample breakfast, asking for seconds of the potatoes. While he finished his meal, I used the bathroom to shave, put on a fresh shirt, and polished my shoes with a handkerchief.

At about nine the preacher's older brother, his wife, and their thirtysomething daughter arrived from their farm near Dayton to meet Billy. From their country accents, they sounded more open than the Jacobs. Full of hugs and smiles, they were much more outgoing. Billy, of course, had no idea he was being auditioned.

A half hour later, we discovered that Billy didn't even understand why he couldn't wake his momma up from her repose in the coffin, which had arrived in an old, sun-faded black hearse from a local funeral home.

"Momma. Momma! They gon' *bury* you if'n you don't wake up!"

The preacher's family gathered around Billy, trying gently but without success to extract him from the coffin. He looked over his shoulder at me and wailed. "She *is* daid." I stepped forward to help.

Instantly I wish I hadn't. Between the emergency room and attending autopsies at West Virginia University, I'd seen a number of coroner's cases . . . and old Ellen sure as hell was one of them. The country funeral parlor makeup job and her threadbare, high-necked, off-white dress could hide neither the narrow ligature bruises partially encircling her throat nor the startling dark-purple lividity on her cheeks and forehead.

Ellen looked like she'd been strangled from behind then left facedown after she'd died. Billy wailed, "Wake up, Momma!" over and over as she was lowered into a six-footer at the rear of the graveyard next to the small wooden marker of one W. Jack Terrell.

As they lowered Ellen, my mind replayed my own father's recent funeral all the way through to the "dust to dust" part. As at my father's funeral, I refused to process any emotion. *I don't do funerals,* I reassured myself.

The service over, I left Billy with the preacher's wife and asked Jacob to take me to the farmer who'd found Ellen. At first he refused, but when I commented on the ligature bruises and lividity, he stopped arguing and listened.

"I wondered. There was an incident nearly twenty years ago involving the same person and similar accusations . . . subsequently dropped. I was still in seminary, so I don't know all the details firsthand."

"Did someone else die?"

He nodded. "A young woman." He nodded again.

"Take me to his place," I repeated. "I'm not going to touch him. Just talk." Seeming uncertain, he nonetheless steered me to the truck.

The preacher was antsy from the moment he pulled his truck off the road to park in front of the large house. I understood why. Billy's nemesis, the farmer, had an impressive spread. A big brick house with white trim and long, wraparound front porch, probably dated between 1840 and 1860. Forty yards to the left sat several expansive white barns perched on nineteenth-century hand-cut stone foundations. Each had its traditional steep ramp that led up to the wide barn doors. The whole scene was typical of a bygone era in Pennsylvania and eastern Ohio. He even had two silos.

I could count nearly forty milk cows just from where I stood . . . all well-fed and well-groomed, their udders bulging. Hogs grunted from somewhere nearby, but I couldn't spot them. The peek-through slats of the nearest barn oozed champagne-colored straw from bales of hay stacked high inside.

"Should we go knock?" I asked. It proved unnecessary. A big man wearing bibbed blue overalls and a billed John Deere feedstore give-away hat came out and walked toward us. "Jacob. Who you got there?"

We stepped out of the car. "A young fella who works at the Youth Development Center with Billy. He wants a word with you."

"Get him off my property, Jacob! I'm callin' the sheriff." The preacher blanched and started to turn back toward the driver's door. I stayed put and smiled.

"Unless you own the county right-of-way, I'm not on your property, Mr. Grasty." He stopped.

"How you know my name?"

I took an unauthorized step onto his pristine front lawn. "I read court files . . . I work for the Commonwealth's Division of Justice . . . and I don't really want to talk to you . . . I just want to *tell* you that it's un-Christian to fuck a brain-damaged woman, strangle her till her bowels evacuate as she dies, leave her laying there till morning, then pretend to find her." He shook, his eyes widening to the size of saucers.

"Shut up, you! Shut up! People can hear."

"Did you bury the sheets she soiled, or did you bring them here and wash them?" I asked as he moved toward me. I stepped back until my heels touched the edge of the asphalt lane. "Hadn't you better go back in, Grasty, and call that sheriff? I'm all for a conversation with him. I'd love to see you do thirty years down there in Western Penitentiary."

He bellowed again. "Shut up, you!" A woman's head popped out of the door behind him and said something I couldn't hear.

"Tax collector with Jacob, Mother . . . I'm not paying more taxes. That's all there is to it." I reached out to touch Jacob on the shoulder. "I'm finished. Let's go."

Grasty was still standing there yelling as we pulled away. "Do you believe what you accused him of?" the preacher asked.

"Most of it. But it doesn't matter if it frightens him enough to keep away from Billy."

"What could I have done?" he asked, shruging.

"Probably much less than you did do. He won't mess with Billy's life again . . . least, I don't think so. But what you can do now is help me . . . no one at the farm thinks Billy will get a new hearing, but I have an idea."

"Is it legal?"

"No, but it is just . . . I have an idea of how to get Billy to you, if you can take care of the rest."

He sighed. "All right, tell me!"

Back at the parsonage I retrieved a silent, brooding Billy. Dreading the drive back to the Morganza, I plied him with Snickers till he went pale and refused another. I also reminded him that having a fit up on floor 2 at Cottage 6 would encourage Sinbad and Sugarbear to make nasty talk. He nodded. He might not have been focused enough to fully process his mom's death even though he watched them bury her, but he sure as heck understood the capacity of Sinbad's crewe to torment the sad or weak.

][[

That evening when I took my break out back, there was a fresh snap in the air. Big Jill caught me as I smoked.

"Hi, sweetie. How'd it go up there in the sticks? Mr. Davenport told me about Billy's mom. I came over to check on him."

"It went OK. She was so young . . . only twenty-nine."

"Pretty and dumb . . . that's serious trouble in farm country. They marry big women to work and breed their kids but lust for the cute young ones."

"Come on, Jill. We don't know what happened," I lied.

"Trust me, sweetie. That was once my world. I *know* how it is." With that she let herself in and went to check on Billy in his protective custody cell.

Dav asked no questions at all except, "How can we help Billy, Mr. Stuart?"

"I don't know, Mr. Davenport—I'm fresh out of smart college boy ideas."

"It was decent of you to go up there on your own time," he commented, patting me on the shoulder.

"Well, my dad died just ten days before I started work here . . . I think I was the victim of an empathy attack."

"I didn't know that," said Dav in his gentle voice. I looked down, shrugged, and headed upstairs, pulling the old armchair out into the hall again so I could plug in my record player. Someone yelled from down the hall, "Can we have Coltrane?"

I eased old 'Trane out of the stack and spun him up to speed before babying the needle into the outermost groove.

About forty minutes later, Curtis hollered, "Can you read Bible to us, Mr. Stuart?"

"I'm not in a Bible mood tonight. How about *Moby Dick?*"

"Whose dick?" jeered Sugarbear.

"It's a whale story . . . and after that crack you have no choice . . . disrespecting a great book. You are a problem person, Sugarbear."

"Aw, you *hard*, Mr. Stuart."

"Shut up or I'll read your last court file out loud to everyone. Then they can decide who is hard." It got very quiet. "They call me Ishmael . . ." I began.

A while later Golightly bitched, "Why's the whale got to be *white*. I don't want no *white* whale."

"Because the white whale is so unusual . . . nearly all whales are black or gray."

"Yeah, Golightly. You got to get over your color obsession," ragged Sinbad. "I want to hear it." Golightly muttered something I couldn't quite hear then shut up. I read uninterrupted for another thirty minutes then slipped quietly downstairs for a sandwich and updated Dav.

"I'm worn out, Mr. Davenport. Something is very wrong with Mrs. Terrell's death. Ligature marks at her throat. Postmortem lividity on her cheeks and forehead." Dav grinned. "OK . . . as college boys go you are usually pretty easy to understand, but now, Mr. Stuart, I finally have to ask for a translation."

"Oh, sorry, Mr. Davenport. I think I spent too much time listening to my father dictate postmortems for type-up. From what I saw, she appeared to have been strangled then placed facedown after her heart quit beating. The blood pooled in her cheeks and forehead—then congealed there as her body cooled."

"Oh, dear! This *is* trouble," said Dav. "Did you say anything to the sheriff?"

"No. I'm not sure of anything. At my age, and with only a B.A., any county coroner's testimony would absolutely drown mine in court."

"What if they dug her up?"

"You should have heard Billy screaming at her to wake up before they buried her."

"Oh, heavens! Well, the least you should do is write every detail before you forget. Hold onto it just in case."

"Good idea!" I went upstairs again. Feeling lonely, impotent, and nostalgic, I played Ange's favorite tune, "Clair de Lune," tried to picture her photograph, whole, and unpissed on, then switched gears to María in Mexico City. Her favorite was "Cuando calienta el sol." As the record player turned, I wrote about Billy's mom like a man possessed . . . capturing every detail I thought relevant, including Grasty's exact quotes.

By 3:00 a.m. I felt better. But it seemed even more surreal to see those events on paper. *Stuff like this only happens in cheap detective novels,* I assured myself, still influenced by my dead old man's most frequent complaint, "You imagine things, my son . . . you need psychiatric care. Sooner or later your delusional fantasies will get you into big trouble." It's odd how powerful a parent's voice, even a dead one, can be as it rattles around in your head demanding an audience. The reality was that my dad sometimes seemed to be unable to separate fact from fiction. "Projection," the shrinks called it.

At four I tired of the snoring from Kamensky's single, so I went downstairs and started to update charts with Davenport. "Did you write down the Beaver Falls stuff?" he asked.

"Yes. But seeing it on paper makes me wonder if I simply went hyper from the funeral and Billy's agony . . . none of it seems real now. How is Billy, Mr. Davenport?"

"He's finally asleep. He's in that 'sleep for twenty minutes then reawake with a start to the nightmare' stage. There isn't a lot we can do. If he's overmedicated, he won't process and begin to move on. Right now, being here is pretty safe for him, but in a month or two when he wants to grieve in peace, this is going to become the worst possible place on the planet. He needs a real home." With that Dav shook his head and tossed me Country's file. "Here's another disaster waiting to happen."

"Why do you say that, Mr. Davenport?"

"They brought that kitten into the back pantry today. Rabbit was here—playing 'sick' again to avoid school—and saw Country rocking the cat. He got jealous and ran out of the room. That little freak is trouble. Keep a close eye on Rabbit, Mr. Stuart. This morning he had that evil look he gets."

"Why did you work two shifts today, Mr. Davenport? I thought double shifts were my specialty."

"I need the money. Family obligations."

"You got a big family?"

"Yes . . . but one doesn't ever talk about it here. Like I told you on the first day, no addresses, names, genders, ages, towns . . . the walls have ears, and information like that, once it's out, can come back to haunt those you love if the wrong one of these characters breaks out and decides on revenge. Anyway, I'm going on vacation in a week. I need a change of scenery. North!" He chuckled. "I suppose you head a different direction," he teased.

"I do, but 'vacation' for me is *two* 'curtains' away . . . crossing the Cotton Curtain is home—not a vacation. But that second curtain . . . now that's a whopper."

"What other curtain?"

"The Tortilla Curtain—Mexico." I laughed. "Bright and colorful, beautiful, dark-skinned women with big eyes . . . flowers, music, dancing, ancient ruins. Snowcapped mountains as high as eighteen thousand feet. Cactus whiskey."

"Eighteen thousand feet! You're kidding!"

"Not . . . and the women . . . whooh."

"Stop! You are killing me. So how dark are the Mexican girls?"

"Some are blondes—not as interesting to me. But most are dark, and they go all the way to black."

"Black. Black like *black*?"

"Yep. More black slaves were imported into Mexico, by far, than here."

"Really?"

"Yep. Your brotherhood doesn't stop in south Texas . . . goes all the way to Argentina—it just changes to Spanish."

"So what is your favorite: black-black, or touch-of-coffee black?"

"Here. I have a photo of my fiancée. Look." I flipped open my wallet and shoved her picture at Dav, who gaped.

"Mercy! She's gorgeous! And dark. Most folks here would think she's black."

"Yes. My favorite . . . to answer your question. I had a roommate last year at college—the draft forced me back to the States—who saw her picture and moved out before he even met me."

"Really?" asked Dav. I nodded. Dav went on, "You don't sound all that angry about the disrespect."

"Huh? Not genuine disrespect . . . just garden-variety ignorance. Plenty of that to go around. Somebody has to know you to disrespect you. Like Palco calling me 'Weasel.' That's disrespect. Now, Kamensky or Sinbad calling me a honkey-this-or-that when they get upset is mere ignorance. Rude, but ignorant. Angela's dad hates me but doesn't know me . . . or know enough to believe that his daughter, who is half white, is far too nicely raised to sleep around. So now he's stuck himself in Africa and I've lost a friend. Classic ignorance."

"Why is that not disrespect?"

"Because, in my view, respect is *earned*, while ignorance is *learned*. Angela's dad never even gave me a chance to earn his respect simply because I am white. *That's* racism!"

Mr. Davenport stared at me for a moment, his brow furrowed. His mustache wrinkled at the corners. I couldn't tell how he'd respond, but I was nervous. I knew he didn't like to talk about race issues all that much, and I hadn't really meant to go on like that.

"Sorry, Mr. Davenport. I didn't mean to run off at the mouth."

"No apology needed, Mr. Stuart. I, uh, was wondering something is all."

Without even thinking about it, I said, "It's respect. I respect you . . . earned."

chapter 19

Dammit! It's Rabbit Again . . .

"**D**ammit. It's Rabbit again!" Dav's voice echoed into the Tower's old-dial phone. "And I can't find Palco."

"I'm on my way." It was Davenport's first night back from vacation and should have been a fairly quiet Monday in late October. But there had been racial demonstrations again in Little Washington and Pittsburgh's tattered Upper Hill District the previous Friday night, after Dan Rather announced on the CBS evening news that seven white men had been found guilty of murdering civil rights workers down in Mississippi during the summer of '64.

With those convictions, white America probably thought it was throwing a bone to black America, without realizing that the entire civil rights movement was the phenomenon of an era of rising expectations . . . as public unrest nearly always has been throughout the history of large societies. Thus, that bone—seven useless white guys from our nation's Heart of Darkness—merely raised expectations further, stoking additional demonstrations. A number among piously liberal whites were wounded . . . and dumbfounded . . . that this judicial gesture didn't generate widespread, kneecap-scuffed gratitude in Black America.

While the current demonstrations were exuberant, but much better behaved than those during '67's choking-hot summer just three months earlier, they gave temporary street-level cover to precisely the types of antisocial monsters who filled both our Tower and Pittsburgh's

Western Penitentiary. The local courts in Allegheny County went into action quickly. In short, the actors who came to us that Monday were the usual—a combination of black, white, and plain old mean. Looters, killers, maimers, and the stupid "doofuses" who always seemed to be in the wrong place at precisely the wrong time when some nearby sadist beat a bystander upside the head with a brick.

That night during an intake session we admitted the one who became known as The Bricker. He had left an innocent brickee comatose and bleeding from the ears within sight of Pittsburgh's Civic Center. The innocent victim—whose only crime, the court record stated, had been his white skin—was tossed on a gurney and taken to the neurosurgeons at Pitt, whose theme song, I assumed, was the old rock and roll tune, "Talk to Me." The bricker's last name was Nantahela. That caught my attention because I'd always thought of Nantahela as a place in North Carolina's Cherokee country, rather than a surname.

Racially, there was no telling what Nantahela was or wasn't. He was medium-complected, wore his hair in a '50s bad boy ducktail, and looked one hell of a lot like Elvis when he'd made his first real splash. Whatever he was, or wasn't, he proved to be one mean, highly energetic, and genuinely sadistic son of a bitch.

Within minutes he was on top of Rabbit . . . I saw it happen from the Tower and headed for the stairs. Dav locked the dormitory door behind me when I came running in. It took both of us to peel The Bricker off of Rabbit, who was shrieking in what, for a change, sounded like genuine pain.

It took Dav and me another few seconds to realize that our new bad boy was fully clothed and energetically attempting to sodomize Rabbit with the wooden handle of a potato masher.

The Bricker was the only kid, other than Kamensky, who Dav and I ever had to gang up on in order to cuff. Yet even as our newest bad actor flailed around on the floor, Dav was calm. "OK, fellas, show's over. This character isn't going to be eating people food or peeing in a commode for at least a month. Think about that as you *relax*. That's it; relax *now*." The din quieted.

"Good. Good," Dav droned on. "We'll settle this, then have some hot chocolate . . . you new ones need to know that this place can be downright pleasant when everyone is calm and cool . . . agitated is counterproductive."

With that he lifted Nantahela as if he weighed just twenty pounds and led him to the door, arms behind him, dancing gingerly on tip toes. By then Palco was letting himself in with his security key.

"Hey! I leave you guys . . ."

Dav interrupted him. "Assist Mr. Stuart, please . . . we need a quick removal of Rabbit . . . and we need the nurse." I was already wrapping Rabbit in a sheet when Palco reached me.

Rabbit had been roughed up but, even though I didn't check too carefully, he didn't appear to be bleeding rectally . . . a good sign. I carried him up to Kamensky's room—now our only single—shrink-wrapped, crying, and angry while Palco took charge of the crowd behind me. The downstairs isolation room already contained our newest bad boy, who began to maul the mattress in the padded lockup.

I could hear Big Jill puffing up the stairs as I arranged Rabbit on Kamensky's cot and told Kamensky to gather his personal stuff and wait out in the hall.

"I ain't giving up my room for this honkey punk," he whined, chewing frantically on his raw lip meat. Jill grabbed him from behind and steered him out. "You just calm down now . . . time you grew up." Kamensky shut up. Big Jill had once lifted him off the ground in a bear hug when he was pounding another kid's face at Sinbad's bidding . . . and Kamensky had not forgotten just how strong Jill was when riled.

I left Rabbit with Jill and headed downstairs again. Three cottage staff and a nurse simply weren't enough for intake nights. We needed a fourth for precisely this kind of situation. I was irritated enough to dump on Palco, "Dammit! Don't get lost on us during intake shifts!" Dav nodded in agreement but spent his time calming the students, who were watching the shadow of someone in the Tower window to see if he would move. I looked up. A few days earlier I'd made a cardboard cutout of what looked like a tall male guard. For intake night, I propped him up in the Tower as an experiment.

"Oh, that's Slim. He's a cop in Canonsburg. On 'administrative leave' right now for jackin' up a kid in handcuffs. He's a psycho . . . like a snake, he doesn't move around much . . . till he strikes. Do you characters want to meet him?"

"No."

"No, suh."

"Nah."

"Uh, uh."

"Maybe you're right . . . he's a snap-out artist. But he's going to make the hot chocolate, so don't piss him off." *Murmur, murmur* was the response.

As I headed to the kitchen to make the chocolate, Dav whispered, "You are outrageous." "Thank you!" I grinned. Dav had just given me another idea.

"Mr. Davenport, I wish you'd put Slim's name on the duty roster every intake night. We deserve a fourth staff member." Dav chuckled.

Jill caught me in the kitchen as I was preparing the hot chocolate. "You got to heat that fast and check on Rabbit. He's not really hurt bad, but I have a doctor coming from the county clinic in Little Washington. Now, I gotta go . . . I got a girl going into labor in the women's unit." She disappeared, followed moments later by the sound of the outer doors locking.

Ten minutes later I rolled the big coffee urn filled with hot chocolate into the dormitory, along with a stack of paper cups. Palco bitched, "You two just don't understand discipline." I ignored him and said to Dav, "Mr. Davenport, Jill had to attend to another emergency. I need to check on our student."

Dav interjected, "I'll go up, Mr. Stuart. You stay and handle the chocolate." Palco retook his seat at the foyer door and folded his arms over his belly, watching me pour and pass out the cups. When I turned to stare at him, he shrugged and mouthed, "I'm security." For that I made him get up off his fat rump and beg for a cup of chocolate.

Palco took a swig and smacked his lips. Moments later the house security phone rang. I nodded for him to pick up as I counted heads and checked off bed numbers on the mimeographed cottage census form. On the phone's third ring, I stopped and turned to see why Palco wasn't answering.

Curtis, who'd become one of our regular students to be sent down for the night to "fill the cots," briefed me. "He done disappeared, Mr. Stuart. Took his chocolate and done left." I leaned over and reached for the phone. Dav's voice was taut. "Need you up here. Now!"

I turned to Curtis. "Thanks for the information, Curtis. Do me a favor?"

"Yeah?"

"Finish the census for me. Stand here by the phone and dial one for Slim up there if anyone even twitches."

"Yessir."

I waved at Slim and gave him a quick thumbs-up as I let myself out and dashed for the stairs, where Dav was motioning me.

"Rabbit's jammed his door from the inside and the light won't go on," he said, panting. "I'll go get the screwdriver and hammer," I answered, dashing to the stairwell's custodial closet to find the tools. Kamensky's room door opened to the outside, so the hinge pins were exposed just enough to pop them out with a big screwdriver.

We got the bottom two pins out quickly, paused to start on the top hinge, and heard a thump and gurgle inside, followed by an odd cracking noise.

"Mercy!" shouted Dav. "I can't get the top pin out."

I stepped onto a chair and took a look. "Somebody jammed a penny into it. Now it's bent around the pin." Inside Rabbit's temporary quarters he banged the wall frantically.

Kamensky, who sprawled in the armchair at the end of the hallway, was enjoying our frustration. "You guys having a mutha-fuckin' problem getting that punk out ma' room?"

Dav, to put it sedately, went nuts. "Break it down *now!*" he snarled at Kamensky. "Or you do a goddamn year in isolation. You think you're crazy now? Hell, you'll have convinced yourself you are a *Chinaman* by the time I let you out!" About eight milliseconds later Kamensky was pulling on the bottom of the door with all his might.

Moments later the door tore away from the top hinge. Dav used Kamensky as a springboard on the way in. There hung Rabbit, his legs kicking frantically to find something solid. Hands clutched to the twist of sheet from which he was suspended, he gurgled, trying to save himself.

Apparently that didn't make Dav all that happy, either. "You sneaky little worm. You waited till you thought we had the door off to jump." Rabbit, now lit by the hallway light, gurgled, his eyes bulging. Dav put his hands on his hips, stood under Rabbit for a moment, then flung an arm around Rabbit's legs and jerked his pant legs down. Rabbit gasped.

"Told you I'd help you do it next time! Told you! Repeat the Lord's Prayer after me, Rabbit!"

Gurgle, came Rabbit's response.

"Well, then, *think* it," Dav said calmly. "Mr. Stuart, come over here and help me strangle this little pain in the ass; he's still kicking." Rabbit's mouth formed a tight, panicked, "O."

OK, I told myself, *Don't panic. Even a guy like Davenport has his breakpoint.* I pulled out the dressing scissors I wore in my belt, calmly reached up, and cut the sheets from around Rabbit's neck. To my relief, Dav nodded and winked. Kamensky, watching from the door, went running down the hall, arms flailing. "They've snapped! They's cuttin' on Rabbit! Gonna kill us all. Save me!"

"Kamensky, shut the fuck up and go sit down, or *I'll* kill you myself," crooned Sinbad from behind his Plexiglas window across the hall.

]|[

"Rabbit—excuse me, Lester—asked us not to write it up . . . he said he wants more counseling," I explained the next day at a meeting up on the Hill with Her Majesty and a few of her assistants, one of whom was the ubiquitous Lawdawg.

"You must write it up. And one of the students . . . Kamensky . . . claimed you two threatened to kill Lester," Lawdawg said crisply.

"Kamensky—you mean the U.S. Post Office headline grabber? No. Mr. Davenport had told Rabbit that the next time he, Lester, play-acted a hanging, he was going to pull on his legs . . . no more rescue role. Lester waited till he thought we had the door off, then jumped about six inches off the top bunk, hanging from a light fixture he'd first disconnected. Since Kamensky had pennied the door to jam it, it took us another twenty or thirty seconds to get inside. Once inside, Mr. Davenport tugged on his pant legs to make a point while I cut him down. He was not even blue-lipped. It's a pantomime we've been struggling with. Mr. Davenport surmised that some negative reinforcement might help."

"So where is Davenport, and why isn't he here?" Her Majesty asked.

"He and Mrs. Moxon took Lester up to the troubled children's ward at Pitt. He'll be an in-patient there for two weeks of intensive therapy."

"Oh? Did we know that? Did we authorize it?" whined Lawdawg, fingering the gold band of his monogrammed Rolex. I shrugged. "I wouldn't know. I'm a trainee. I just cut him down and carried him downstairs to the doctor."

"How long till the doctor arrived?" he asked. I felt like I was being cross-examined, so I retorted, "You mean, from the time we cut him down?" Lawdawg sneered. "Of course, or did you think I meant since breakfast? Champlin was right . . . you are 'slow.'" I smiled as though he'd said nothing, then answered.

"About two minutes and twenty seconds, I reckon."

"'About two minutes and twenty seconds, I *reckon*,' what?" he mimicked.

"You know, till he had an oxygen mask and the doctor was examining him. Nurse Dicks anticipated the outcome and called for a doctor STAT from Little Washington Clinic."

"Oh! Did we know that?" he turned to Her Majesty, who'd been sitting quietly, listening.

"*I* knew it," she announced in a soft voice, then turned to me. "Why did this happen, given the probability that it might happen?"

"Two reasons, Doctor. First, Lester was assigned to 'dorm-filling' again despite *six* written recommendations in fourteen weeks not to mix him with any newcomers. Second, we are too short-staffed on intake days. We need a fourth staffer when they arrive."

That got Lawdawg going again. "'We *need* a fourth staffer, *Ah reckon*,'" he taunted.

"Yes . . . except it's *I* reckon. And, for your official record, I created a big paper officer cutout that I keep in the Tower. His name is 'Slim.' I asked Mr. Davenport to add him to the duty roster so that the snoopers would think he's real. We need a fourth. Till that happens we need a make-believe fourth. Can you play along and add 'Slim' to your duty roster?"

"Possibly," answered Her Majesty with a smile. "Does 'Slim' have a full name?" Lawdawg rolled his eyes and stomped out.

"No, Doctor, he's a furloughed cop from Canonsburg. I've billed him as a classic Strother Martin type: distant and brutal. Fortunately, the students haven't asked to meet him." Her Majesty laughed.

"Put Slim on the temporary duty roster. And ask Mr. Davenport to come see me." With that she rushed out to take a phone call. I headed toward the door. Patricia caught up to me outside, where I'd stopped to look up at the "Virtue, Liberty, and Independence" insignia.

"You always stare up at that on the way out." She pointed.

"Yeah. The irony of the state seal drives me nuts. Here we engage in bureaucratic bullshit, lock 'em up, make them totally dependent, then have the gall to tell them how to *conform*. There has to be a better way, and, ironically, it's right up there over the door! . . . So, what's up, Patricia?"

"I wanted to talk about Angie. She needs a favor. Her father wants to come back from Ghana."

"So soon? Didn't take him long to soak up the Dark Continent's mysteries, did it?"

"Don't be cold! He needs a statement that you weren't really assaulted."

"It was assault *and* battery. I got choked. But the legal stuff has nothing to do with me. I already told you, I neither filed nor signed anything."

"Angie's lawyer wants to know what your price is. Name your price."

"Wow. You are serious, aren't you? I'm not listening to this." I continued down the hall.

][[

At the cottage I stopped in the pantry to check on Mizz Small. Country's new kitten was calm, just like the mother cat. Its fur had been meticulously brushed. Country rocked her obsessively and brushed her two or three times a day. Mrs. Moxon had sewn a pink bonnet for Mizz Small. When Country visited her, he'd carefully tie on her tiny bonnet, rock, and sing to her.

The kitten meowed often and had learned to roll partway onto her back, her head erect, awaiting the bonnet, in anticipation of being rocked. Mizz Small's bonnet hung on a hook near the row of dirty work boots worn by the students who worked in vo-tech.

Country also had a bonnet he put on when he rocked Mizz Small. It had come in a package one day, Mrs. Moxon told me. "From someplace in Georgia, I think. Country said it was his grandmother's. She's the one who raised him."

"How'd he wind up here?" I asked.

"Grandmother died—the matriarch who held the family together— then his mother headed north for work. He doesn't remember exactly."

"That package means someone is still on the family place . . . and knows where he is. And cares enough to send him a keepsake."

"Why, yes. I suppose it does."

"Can you find out who it is, Mrs. Moxon?"

chapter 20

Cat Missing

Late October was a relief in many ways. My mom seemed better and fortune had unexpectedly smiled on me. At home in Morgantown one Monday afternoon, the wall phone in mom's kitchen rang while I was preparing to freeze green beans from her garden.

"Hello. Stuart residence."

"John Martin Campbell here. Chair, anthropology, University of New Mexico. Look, Stuart. You were on the alternate list for a spot in our graduate program. One of these characters here this past fall busted out, so I have an opening for spring. It will be tough starting late . . . you up to it?"

"Uh . . . when does school start?"

"Third week of January. It's simple. I'll call you back in ten minutes. You'll say 'yes' or 'no.' Not 'uh.' Got it?" Click.

Mom overheard part of the conversation.

"Is everything all right, David?"

"Yeah, Mom. I just got a call offering me a spot in the master's program in anthropology at New Mexico."

"When?"

"January."

"Did you have to give up your place at Cornell when you went to work in Canonsburg?"

"Yes, Mom, Cornell wouldn't hold my place, but it's OK. I can reapply to schools around here this winter or next."

"Did you tell them why?"

"Yes, Mom."

"I see . . . what's New Mexico's program like?"

"Top ten in the English-speaking world."

"When do you have to decide?"

"About six minutes from now . . . it's not a big deal."

Mom stared out the kitchen window, an odd, faraway quality in her voice. "I was going to be a poet, you know. I received a scholarship to begin at Barnard in the fall of 1940. But we were destitute after the Depression and the scholarship only covered tuition. My mother was afraid to borrow the money for room and board . . . and in those days they didn't have student loans."

"Was that your dream?"

She nodded, tearing up. "Grab the dreams, honey! They are so fragile. So fleeting. Grab!"

"If I go to grad school, where does that leave you?"

"With a dream still alive, even if it's not my own." The phone rang again.

"Campbell here. You ready, Stuart?"

"One question first, Dr. Campbell. Why me?"

"You've got the solid GRE scores and we've never had anyone from Appalachia. The dean wants diversity. Yes or no?"

For the moment I forgot about the Morganza, forgot about my troubles with Angela, and even forgot about my fiancée in Mexico. There was only one thing to say. "Yes, sir."

"Good! Be here a week before classes start—and don't screw up out here. Got it?"

"Yes, sir." Click.

Mom smiled at me. "My little boy. I love my little boy!" Then she disappeared into the newly decorated downstairs bedroom that had been mine and cried.

)|(

Back at Canonsburg the next day, the world seemed different. Lighter. Softer. It occurred to me that New Mexico was much closer to old

Mexico, so María would be happy, and I'd dug out the anthro texts I'd used in Mexico and tossed them into the Rambler's trunk so I could reread them at night in Little Washington. Dav noticed the difference almost immediately. "Your momma doing better?"

I decided not to tell him about grad school. "Yes, Mr. Davenport. Some better. I'm hopeful."

"It's a process. Can't rush it all that much . . . takes time . . . and it's tough." I nodded, again wondering about his family, but didn't ask.

Rabbit was still checked into the kid's psych ward up in Pittsburgh. It was a blessed relief. He and three or four other students occupied half the cottage's staff time. Between the extremes of our practiced abusers and their determined victims, there existed a large community of students who were more ordinary. *Odd how politics, the news, and bureaucracy are all driven by the extremes*, I reflected, wondering what the world would be like without the Sinbads and Rabbits, or, for that matter, the H. Rap Browns and Bull Connors.

In fact, everyone on the farm seemed calmer. Dormitory admissions slowed. There were fewer fights and name-calling. Halloween was coming in a few days, and with it, our talent show. I was prepping Curtis daily for his bullfighting role in our skit.

Many of the students, of course, wanted either to be rock, R&B, or soul stars. The hallways were full of students prancing and chanting Aretha Franklin's "Respect," James Brown's "It's a Man's Man's Man's World," and there were the inevitable Elvises. Billy tried out with a Merle Haggard tune. Country wanted to wear his granny's bonnet and sing lullabies, which Dav and I discouraged. Other guys wanted to show off their "street" dancing, nowadays called funk.

Even Sugarbear and Sinbad entered, practicing some closely guarded "comedy" routine. At first I was amazed, so I asked Dav, "Why is participation in this show so competitive?"

"Two reasons, Mr. Stuart. First, it's their 'acting out' that gets most of these characters sent here in the first place. Second, it's about respect and hierarchy. Gives them another chance to project, impress."

"I'm particularly surprised that Billy is trying out," I commented.

"Yes," he chuckled. "Merle Haggard isn't a big draw with this crowd, but Mrs. Moxon is working on it." He winked. "The show is the kind of thing that gets these kids' minds off of their outside problems for a while."

And, boy, did some of our students have "outside problems." Reading files and helping with the dailies gave me a portrait of an often-ignored world in America—one that badly needed fixing.

Fully half of our students had one or more members of their immediate families doing time. In about three-quarters of our families, there was no working male or no male at all. More than half of our students had been born out of wedlock or to "common law" parents.

One night when I was bored, I listed the parents known to have finished high school. We had just nine known of a potential 130 or so. "Mr. Davenport—is this possible?" I asked, showing him the table I'd made.

"The high school grads are probably understated—these intake records often have mistakes or were filled in by a case worker making a guess—but I'm not surprised. My church community became very emotional a few years ago when they sent the National Guard to open up Central High in Little Rock. Education is like magic. Our community needs a *lot* more of that magic."

"So does West Virginia, Mr. Davenport. It's still a big deal to graduate from high school. Senator Byrd hand signs a letter congratulating every high school graduate."

"Really?"

"Yes. My high school class was lucky. We lived in a university town, so more of us expected to go . . . and could go. You have to walk through campus to get from one end of town to the other. Lots of West Virginia University students live right at home. But in most of the state it isn't like that. If you are born in some out-of-the-way coal town, getting to go away to college is a major deal. It's not like here in Pennsylvania where there are colleges all over the place and jobs to work while you attend."

"The Cotton Curtain," he said, grinning.

"Well, Appalachia. Part of Pennsylvania is Appalachia, too."

"I'm not buying that, Mr. Stuart."

"Tell that to the feds. They think Appalachia goes from North Alabama to North Central Pennsylvania."

"What makes it 'Appalachia?'" retorted Dav.

"Wish you hadn't asked."

Dav cackled in response.

" . . . But I think it's a combination of culture, economics, and geography." The conversation would have gone on, except Country came to the desk where we were working on predinner reports. He was upset.

"Ah cain't fine Mizz Small. Ah axed Mizz Moxon and Mr. Reddy. They hain't seen her." I got up to go help him look. "We'll finish Education and Appalachia later, Mr. Davenport."

Country and I looked everywhere for Mizz Small but could find neither her nor her little bonnet. Unnerved, I handed Country back to Dav, who assigned him chores, then stepped outside to check around the cottage. Nothing. So I walked over to the barn where mother cat and several of her offspring still lived . . . the core of another generation of the barn's mouse-catchers. There was no indication that Mizz Small had returned.

Stumped, I detoured on my way back to the cottage, taking time to climb the hill and hop over the old wooden fence encircling the graveyard. The first chilly fall rains had already begun to dull the oaks' bright red and gold leaves. I wanted to walk in the leaves again and smell their heady, pungent scent before more bad weather brought them down and transformed them into a mass of lifeless, rotting brown. I hated late fall and winter—wet, snowy, and depressing for months on end. Unlike Mexico, Pennsylvania and West Virginia went into a numbing gray mode every November and usually stayed that way till April.

Inside the graveyard, I found Jill sitting under an oak, crying.

"You OK, Jill?"

"No! Someone's been here and disturbed Emma and Ella. Their rosaries are gone." She was right; there were boot prints and heel scuffs all over both of their graves. Fresh marks from a set of heavily treaded vehicle tires ended at the fence.

"Any other graves messed with?" I asked. She sobbed and shook her head.

"Help me cover them up so no one disturbs them again?" she asked. I hesitated.

"Please, sweetie."

"OK, but quick. I've already been gone nearly half an hour, hunting Country's kitten. It's missing, too." I helped her scoop leaves and dead grass over the two crumbling concrete markers and left.

"What took so long?" asked Mr. Reddy when I returned. His frown lines were as crisp as his shirt.

"Looking for Country's kitten. Not outside. Not back at the barn . . ." He interrupted.

" . . . And not up in the graveyard, either. Mrs. Moxon saw you up there on her way back from the chapel. You are supposed to stay out of there, Stuart."

"Sorry. I saw Nurse Dicks up there and stopped to ask if she'd seen the cat."

"I don't care, but someone on the Hill has an obsession about that graveyard. Don't get seen up there—I am not writing reports on account of you. Got it?"

"The director didn't seem too upset about it . . ." I deflected.

Reddy grinned suddenly. "Her Majesty will soon be upset about everything *but* that graveyard."

"What does that mean?"

Reddy gave me his best gold-toothed smile and said "Poof!" spreading the fingers of both hands in mimic of a magic act.

Later, I asked Mr. Davenport to tell me what he knew. "Rumors, Mr. Stuart. Rumors of an administrative shake-up on the Hill. Some, including Williams, say that there are powerful political forces pushing for a change."

"What kind of change?"

"A new director. Conservative. Law and order. Old-fashioned discipline. The heck with 'students' and 'rehabilitation.' You know, 'Let's show these miscreants who's boss and throw away the key.'"

"Hmm . . . if everyone here was like Kamensky, Sinbad, and Sugarbear, I might agree. But we've got all these kids here who either don't belong at all or *could* go the other way."

"Exactly!" said Dav, matter-of-factly. "But this is one case of politics where, for the oddest of reasons, folks who are not natural allies will wind up in agreement."

"Like?" Dav scanned the immediate vicinity to make certain Palco wasn't lurking nearby.

"Like, the one you call Lawdawg up there. He *hates* the director . . . she's black and more educated than he is. He's choking on it and boot-kissing the State Bar Association to become president. They say he's a 'Let's throw the key away on the blacks' type. Then there's the traditional staff . . . black *and* white . . . very conservative. Many once worked in the adult penal system. It doesn't translate well to these kids.

And some of the black staff are panicking over the segments of our black community that are disintegrating into chaos. They want to get tough, too . . . but for very different reasons than our chief counsel and his buddies. Now, we never had this conversation, OK? I don't want to be in the middle of this."

"I understand," I said.

"Do you?"

"Some. I grew up in a conflicted world, too. A different version. Mom's family was upper class. My dad's people were straight working class. Blue collar. South Philly. My dad wasn't usually allowed inside my maternal grandmother's house . . . had to wait outside on the porch. Their different attitudes and politics were too weird for me to grasp. So I don't want to be in the middle of this, either."

Dav's eyebrows went up. "*South* Philly? As in, south of South Street?"

I nodded.

Dav emitted a long, low whistle as a prelude to his reply. "It's not fun, is it?"

"No . . . I'd rather be in Mexico."

"What keeps you from going back?"

"I'm *gringo*. Not allowed to work, vote, or own property outright."

Dav shook his head, looking confused.

"I'm not crazy, Mr. Davenport. Honest. Ordinary people treat you better in Mexico. It's only the government that craps on you for being *gringo*."

]|[

At 11:00 p.m., everyone locked in and the dailies written, Dav punched out. That left only me and Richard on the late-night shift in the main cottage. It should have been quiet, but "The Bricker" had seen Davenport leave from the window of his room and started raising hell the instant he heard the downstairs' outer door close behind Dav.

"Stay away from me, you baboon!" he shouted at Sugarbear, who predictably swallowed the bait.

"Baboon? I ain't no baboon, mutha' fucka'." Pow. Something, a fist or a foot, flew. That's all it took. Hollering at them had no effect whatsoever. Several minutes later Richard ran downstairs to alert Palco, who was in the kitchen stealing food.

The three of us went in together, peeling the two apart. Stuck together like magnets, they were spitting, clawing, and biting one another. But, in tackling Sugarbear, our Bricker had taken on a bit too much. Sugarbear had already left several noticeable tooth marks on his tormenter's cheek and ear.

Palco drug Nantahela downstairs, kicking and hollering, "I hate 'coons and faggots!" That sent another dozen students into orbit, fists pounding rhythmically on the Plexiglas doors. The din was head-splitting.

"Whoa! Aspirin time," groaned Richard. "I can't handle this, David."

"Help me strip Sugarbear's room, then you can head downstairs." We worked fast, Sugarbear protesting, "I didn't start it!" I locked him in with only a bottom sheet. We stacked everything else out in the hall. The rhythmic pounding intensified.

"Quiet. Absolute quiet! That is what I need from all of you." I went to the stairwell and flipped the switch, but the hallway didn't go very dark. Bright moonlight lit up the room's outer windows. *Huh. I need to watch moon phases more carefully. No wonder everyone's gone ape*, I noted while staring out at the nearly full orange-tinted moon, which backlit the skeletal thicket of leaf-thinned oaks on the hill behind.

I couldn't tell whether it was flipping off the lights or the fact that they had to choose between banging on their doors or listening for the satisfying sounds of Palco bouncing Nantahela off the downstairs wall that finally quieted the students.

Whichever it was, everyone could hear Palco. "You will never, ever spit at me again," he growled. ". . . In fact, you will never even *look* at me again, you miserable piece of shit!" Palco's voice conveyed a distinctly eerie strain of hysteria, ending in a high-pitched emphasis on "shit." Something bounced hard against the wall. The building seemed to shiver in response.

Richard, now downstairs, yelled at Palco. That resulted in another ominous thump. I rushed downstairs to find a bewildered Richard pulling frantically on the lockup's door.

"He locked himself in with Nantahela, David." Richard panted, still tugging futilely on the handle. The locked room emitted thunderous pandemonium. I dashed to the security booth phone and called the state police.

"Stuart here at Cottage 6 on the Morganza. A student and our security chief are both in a locked room. Sounds like a struggle . . . no . . . I'm a counselor . . . can you help?" The nearest detachment was on old Route 19 on the outskirts of Little Washington. I lit a smoke right there in the cottage and yelled in to Palco.

"We're getting help, Mr. Palco. State police on the way." More growling and thumping emanated from the padded room. Then I called Big Jill. The state police cruiser's flashing lights reflected through the dining room windows even before I stubbed out my Pall Mall. Richard paced. "This is unbelievable!" In a philosophical mood, I retorted, "In this place *all* things are possible, therefore believable," and hurried to unlock the rear door for the police.

"Thanks for coming so quick."

"An early Halloween, huh?" commented a big, burly trooper. "Is Palco in there?"

I nodded as he grinned. His partner walked up, fitted a big slide hammer to the isolation unit's door lock, and rocketed six pounds of metal down its shaft. It took two tries to pop it.

Inside they found Palco out colder than a mackerel, sprawled on top of The Bricker, who didn't look too good, either, mashed and bloodied up.

"You two having a hot date?" asked the trooper, who pulled Palco off the kid. Palco groaned and Nantahela bitched, "Couldn't breathe with that fat motherfucker all over me." Jill, already at the door, clucked her tongue at Nantahela's trash talk and started to clean up Palco. I took The Bricker, triaging him, and plugged the biggest leaks first, just as I'd done many times in the emergency room at WVU. An ambulance arrived about five minutes later and the techs took over. Trooper number one grunted at Richard and me to help them get fat-assed Palco up onto the gurney; he had a nasty, pulsing scalp bleeder that pumped thin, rhythmic spouts of blood like a miniature Moby Dick. "Thar she blows!" I chuckled, musing.

"Looks like Palco's key ring went the wrong way for once," commented Jill, her tone of disapproval plain as she thumb-pressed a bandage to his scalp bleeder.

They wheeled him out as Nantahela crowed, "Damn right. I made him eat his own key ring! Won't fuck with me again."

"You're the one with the bigger problem," I commented. "These fellows will be taking you to the hospital, then another lockup, I reckon."

"Got that right," said the trooper who'd inquired about Palco. "Stretch those arms out behind you, hot shot."

"What for? He attacked *me!*"

"We'll let a judge sort that out." He cuffed Nantahela while the other highway patrolman patted him down. Our petulant Bricker, struggling against both of them, pulled back and groin-kicked the trooper hard. That got him bug-squashed for the second time. They dragged him out, still kicking, heaved him into the cruiser's rear seat, and locked him in, then backed their unit out.

Poor Richard looked tired and disheveled. "Really, I can't handle this."

"I don't like it, either. We wind up spending all our time and energy on the head cases and don't get to do much for the ones we really could help."

Richard nodded. "It's like the Greek, Sisyphus."

I nodded in return. "Yep. This system is like pushing one big rock up a steep hill."

"Have you found Country's kitten yet?" asked Jill as she closed her medical bag.

"No. I forgot. We were dealing with Palco and Nantahela."

"*Both* of 'em's a waste of time," she grunted as she snapped her bag closed and headed for the back door. "You'd best find that kitten, sweetie!"

chapter 21

Happy Halloween, 1967

The festivities began outdoors on the administration building's front veranda. A bright, clear day, I guessed it was the only day of the year when the folks on the Hill actually interacted with groups of our students. Except for the psych techs and social workers, who occasionally came down to the cottages for state-mandated one-on-one's, the contact between students and Hill staff suffered from, uh, "underdeveloped potential."

The miniature bullring Mrs. Moxon had set up was well-done. The bull entered when I cued the "Virgin of the Macarena" on my record player, enhanced by a portable amplifier.

Sugarbear had, after constant wheedling from Mrs. Moxon, finally agreed to be the bull but firmly declined to wear a costume with a guy playing the hind legs behind him under the same cloth—a scenario too ripe with the possibility of butt-focused retribution to suit Sugarbear. Mrs. Moxon had finally relented and shortened the costume's hind end to convert it into a one-man bull.

Sugarbear looked odd as a two-legged bull while he trotted around the miniature arena, snorting and hooking his horns from side to side, but the students cheering him on seemed not to notice.

When the music reached its crescendo, a dandified Curtis stepped out of the Hill's Old Main in carefully sewn bullfighter's tights, red sash, black cap, and an old four-button vest tarted up with a number of small, gold Christmas bows. He looked splendid, slimmer than usual, and proud as he arched his back in a damned good imitation of a bull-fighter's stylized "I piss on all of you, laugh at death, and intend to rav-ish that blonde in Row One once this is over" entrance.

Sinbad goggled. "That fat Curtis? . . . Mr. Stuart, you should've axed *me* to be the bullfighter."

"Couldn't, Sinbad, you just don't look the part . . . too tall."

"Mutha'f . . ."

"*Roland!*" snapped Mrs. Moxon. "Don't you dare!" Sinbad shut up and did a predator's sidelong eye dance to determine how many had heard her use his detested first name. Satisfied that it hadn't been many, he glowered at Kamensky, who leered and leaned forward as if he might make a wiseass comment.

Kamensky caught Sinbad's gaze, settled back into his metal chair, and muttered, "We're cool" several times. Some of our predators were nuts, in the ordinary clinical meaning of it, but rarely too far out of it to catch the scent of another predator's ire, especially that of a preda-tor like Sinbad, who owned a coveted top niche in the gangster world's food chain.

When Curtis whirled his cape and stepped forward to confront Sugarbear's horns, someone yelled, "*Get off*, Curtis, my man . . . you *bad!*" Curtis responded with a second twirl, head back, wooden sword behind him.

Predictably, Sugarbear, cackling in his goofy way from underneath the brown cloth, tried to hook Curtis with his fake horns. Curtis, to my surprise, grinned, neatly sidestepped Sugarbear, and smacked his butt with the flat of his sword. Goosed by the wooden blade, Sugarbear jumped. The students laughed.

Our bull, however, didn't see the humor in it, and just before he charged Curtis for the second time, he was quickly redirected to the side of the ring, Mr. Davenport and a dignified-looking older man pressed tightly against each of his brown clothed shoulders. The bull-fight was quickly declared over, and the students gave the two boys a standing ovation.

It could have turned into a major incident had Mr. Davenport and the other guy not moved with lightning speed. Apparently, both of them were accomplished mind readers, often anticipating a student's next move even before the student seemed fully aware of his own intent. "Now, how'd you know I was gonna do that, Mr. Dav?" was a common student comment.

Several juggling acts followed the bullfight. Then, like herding cats, the cottage staff moved several hundred guys in small, unfocused groups toward the farm's auditorium. Finally, we packed them into assigned seats and settled them down with candy bars while those participating in the stage acts got ready. Mrs. Moxon had been careful to schedule the order of acts so as not to reinforce the prevailing pecking order. Thus, Sinbad and Sugarbear's comedy act, to their substantial irritation, was cleverly buried in the middle of the program.

Their shtick was for the audience to guess which staff member they were mimicking. Their opening send-up was a full-bellied guy rattling his keys and threatening to "put a number twelve boot up your . . ." then pushed their butts out, pointing to them. The students shouted, "Palco, Palco!" without prompting. That drew a laugh from everyone except Palco, who seemed suddenly to focus on his pocket calendar while feigning utter boredom.

"Now, *Clarence*, I am *disappointed* by your language," Sinbad crooned, clicking two pencils as if he were knitting. "Who? Who?" shouted Sugarbear.

"Mizz Moxon!" shouted the audience.

Then came Sugarbear with, "*You* are *there*. Good. Good."

"Who? Who?" crooned Sinbad.

"Mr. Dav, Mr. Dav!"

Next, Sugarbear adjusted imaginary glasses. "That is reasonable— now you *gentlemen* need to calm down." The emphasis on "gentlemen" referred to my second day on the job. Not yet knowing Golightly's name, I'd called him "son." He'd responded, "*You* ain't my father!" I'd come back with, "That's a reasonable statement of fact; does 'gentleman' work for you?"

"Yeah. That's cool. Now, how 'bout you treat me like one?"

"Glad to. But you have to *act* like one."

"Who? Who?" they chanted.

"Mr. Stuart," responded the crowd.

What fascinated me was how accomplished most of those acts were . . . and how very much most of the farm's residents wanted attention that moved beyond fear to approval. As bad as some of these kids were, there appeared still to be a part of many that wanted to please. In fact, that seemed a common theme through most of the acts.

The finale was a big dance number to Aretha's "Respect," twenty students doing their Wylie Avenue dip in perfect unison, their identical gray head silks worn over chemically busted hair. Dav groaned at their stereotyped role as the curtain went down.

My only downer was that Country, deeply depressed over Mizz Small's disappearance, refused to attend. He was in his room, alternately crying and brooding. And Billy didn't get to perform—a Mrs. Moxon decision, to protect him. She was probably right, but he sat next to me, staring blankly at the stage throughout, totally unable to comprehend the Morganza's world, which had swallowed him. Poor Billy was a Jonah—swallowed whole by the whale, totally lost in its belly and in need of deliverance.

][[

Back at Cottage 6, I read ghost stories while we ate a late dinner of orange- and black-tinted spaghetti and meatballs in the TV room. Dessert consisted of a huge tray of spice cake topped with black and orange icing. A large, carved jack-o-lantern lit the stairwell landing, courtesy of Mrs. Moxon. I ended by reading selections from Edgar Allan Poe's, "The Pit and the Pendulum." Then we escorted the students upstairs and locked them in their rooms. Dav and I spent the next hour getting small groups through the shower routine, while Richard and Big Jill administered meds, Palco standing by.

After lights out at ten, Dav and I took breaks in turn, since we were both scheduled to work through the night. I had a full twenty minutes so lit a Pall Mall at the back door and strolled over toward Willow Cottage, enjoying a clear night, the smell of damp leaves, and the sight of a waning deep yellow moon.

I intended to check the barn again for Mizz Small, but when I saw a light up in the graveyard, I turned to climb the hill. Sitting in front of the markers with a bright battery lantern to keep her company, Jill greeted me. "Hi, sweetie! I'm not on duty—I'm just keeping watch over them tonight."

I leaned over and hugged her. "They all doing OK?" I asked.

She whispered, "Yes. I've been reading to them. They like that a lot."

"What are you reading? Bible?"

"No. They wanted a story after I sprinkled holy water on each to protect them. I'm reading *To Kill a Mockingbird*."

"Ooh! My favorite," I commented. "Has anyone else been back to disturb them?"

"It doesn't feel like it."

"Are you going to be here all night, Jill?"

"No. Just until midnight has passed."

"You need anything?"

"No, sweetie . . . got my rosary . . . my kids and I are fine." I squeezed her shoulder and headed back, my break time nearly gone. Though I couldn't quite make out the words, I heard her reading to them as I moved through the scattered oaks, guided by both familiarity and the pale moonlight.

)|(

In Cottage 6, our students, lights out notwithstanding, were still hyper from the combination of holiday festivities, their liberal Halloween intake of sugar, and, as it turned out, my earlier ghost stories. Stationed in the upstairs hallway, I played an old scratchy vinyl 78 of Billie Holiday that I'd borrowed from my grandmother. Elsie never ceased to amaze me. Her record collection ranged from Puccini to Rudy Vallée to Robert Johnson, W.C. Handy, and early Billie Holiday.

Until I'd gotten into her old, hand-wound, floor model Victrola and its cabinet of stored treasures up on her third floor, I really had no image of her other than as a tired, aging, white-haired lady wearing black square-toed shoes and an off-white apron. Born at home in 1887 on Forbes Avenue in Pittsburgh, she had lived in Ridley Park on Philadelphia's Main Line since about 1919.

Some huge family secret to do with her marriage had generated the move from Pittsburgh nearly a half century before, so I had no idea until I reached my teen years that she'd once had a life, as I defined it. She still missed Pittsburgh terribly—almost fifty years after leaving it—so I sent her short letters describing nearly everything I saw or did when I went to town. In return, she "loaned" me a few vinyl treasures on condition that I not identify her "unorthodox" tastes in front of the rest of the family. "It's a secret," she'd said, pursing her lips. Nearly everything else about the family was also a "secret," so I never had much to say about her or our relationship . . . anything, for that matter, when others were around.

"Who's singing?" a disembodied voice asked from an under-door crack down the hall.

"Billie Holiday. Thirties or forties, I think. Not sure."

"It good." Then quiet. For most of our students there was no history. No Billie Holiday. No George Washington . . . or George Washington Carver. There was no collective past. No great books. No great ideas. No great events. No great memories. History and tradition are stunning social gifts generally withheld from those born to America's poor, fragmented, and underschooled families.

Does no past mean they simply can't conceive of a future, either? I wondered as Billie's voice drowned out the sounds of breathing and jostling for floor position near the hall's residence doors. But even Billie couldn't mask the unfamiliar sounds of steam thumping through the cottage's radiators that, until then, had been turned off for months.

I dozed, slipping into a dreamy state. My fiancée smiled at me. We chatted. *"Ay, corazón, como te quiero. ¿Cuándo regresas al D.F.?"*

"En la semana santa, preciosa. ¿Dónde quieres casarte?" I responded.

"Get *out!*" shouted someone. "Mr. Stuart's talkin' Spanish."

Carlos's bitchy, nasal voice answered to whomever it was who'd spoke, "You 'choco-pops' got a problem with that?"

Sinbad snarled, "You're sick, man. They shoulda' kept your racist ass at White Hill." Sinbad's irony jolted me—it hadn't been a black girl whose nipples he'd razored. But sociopaths don't process their own behaviors, so I shouldn't have been surprised. Carlos snarled back, so I shook myself fully awake, pulled myself out of the chair, and started down the hall before we wound up in the middle of another door-shattering, window-smashing racial disagreement.

In one way, though, I had to agree with Sinbad. Carlos, it turned out, had been too much for the shrinks over at White Hill. In a classic Pennsylvania bureaucratic move, they had redumped him on us three days before Halloween, accompanied by a White Hill staffer and two state troopers who left quickly before the cottage's front door had even closed behind Carlos. "And just who do they think will be watching him now that he's back?" asked Dav, who shook his head in disgusted resignation.

"Carlos," I now hissed on the way past his cell. *"No me piques . . . no mas del racismo. ¿Comprendes?"*

He answered in English. "Nah. I don't understand you—your Spanish sounds *Mexican* . . . kind of like a dog talking." Someone cackled from under a door.

"Being a dog would be a massive step up for you," I retorted, unable to muster any pretense of professionalism. I didn't take kindly to anyone who peed on my sustaining images of Mexico. Thinking of Mexico—especially my fiancée—was the only thing that filled my brain with warm and happy images.

Contemplating twitchy little Carlos had precisely the opposite result. I had begun to actively resent several of the badasses at Cottage 6. We might have been able to do some good for the tragic screwups had violent pricks like Carlos, Kamensky, Sinbad, Sugarbear, and Tattoos been sent away to someplace very dark, very lonely, and very permanent.

In that sense, our halfdozen badasses had extraordinary power. They not only hurt people who were in their way but also consumed vast amounts of time, energy, and scarce resources. That altered the fates of the weaker ones who received much less attention. Whatever their IQs, the bad boys controlled Pennsylvania's juvenile system. They, not folks on the Hill, prioritized our use of resources, defined our security procedures, and limited both the hopes and freedoms of the other students by assuring that our entire system was designed to deal with *them*. In short, they were grandiose, merciless, cunning, narcissistic, and high maintenance . . . rather, I imagined, like most politicians.

The only real difference between them and your average politician, I assumed, is that the politician maintains power through the inferred promise of reward (graft, votes, or policy favoritism) while our problem people maintained it through the inferred fear of pain and violence. "If we actually had the means to rehab characters like Sinbad and Sugarbear," I'd once wisecracked to Dav, "we'd have to see to it that they became surgeons so they could still cut on someone and get paid for it."

"Ah knows, but it hain't me. Smell really nasty, it do."

"Probably a dead mouse or something under the radiator," commented Dav from behind the chair. "I came up to let you know I'm taking a break, Mr. Stuart."

"OK. Is Palco downstairs?"

Dav nodded, adding, "As always" rather loudly, for the benefit of the students. A few minutes later Country's roommate, Curtis, piped in. "It does stink in here, Mr. Stuart . . . I can't sleep."

"OK. I'll check on it when Mr. Davenport comes back." It went quiet again.

When Dav returned, he tapped me on the shoulder. "Need a break, Mr. Stuart?"

"Yes, but Country and Curtis got that smell in their room. I'll check before I go downstairs if you have the time." He nodded. I walked down the hall, unlocked Curtis and Country's door, flinched from the odor as I opened the door, and asked them to step up to the window. "That where it stink," pointed Country, who, for the third day now, wore his grandma's bonnet, inviting merciless teasing from the usual bullies. "Then stand by the door," I suggested. They moved. I swept under the radiator with my flashlight. Nothing except an old soiled cum cloth. I extracted it gingerly with the tip of my ballpoint pen and moved closer to sniff. Nope. Not the source.

Next I ducked under the bunk bed. In retrospect, I wished I hadn't. There in the flashlight beam I spotted what I thought at first might be a toy soccer ball, but when I reached for it, it leaked and deflated. I gagged from the smell. . . . I'd finally found Mizz Small, a hangman's cord tight around her little neck and still wearing her neatly tied minia-ture bonnet. The kitten had probably been dead for two or three days. I grabbed one stiff paw and slid her out gently. Behind me Country wailed and made a dive for her.

"She's rotted, Country! Don't grab . . ." Too late . . . he squeezed the fetid ball that had once been Mizz Small. The ball deflated further, and the kitten's innards oozed down his shirt. Dav came into the room and recoiled. As I walked Country downstairs, I could hear Dav giving instructions, moving Curtis in with Kamensky for the night. Dav was firm. "Now, let me explain this, *Master* Kamensky . . . one twitch . . . one comment . . . one *anything* where you make contact with Curtis here and you will have problems that you simply do not want."

I know Kamensky responded to the Davenport magic because I heard no comment or protest. *If Pennsylvania could clone Davenport we'd be down to forty students on this farm within five years*, I decided, also realizing that I would never be able to do it like Dav. I lacked Dav's presence, his psychological wholeness and depth of character.

Country didn't cry. Instead, he wailed, softly and eerily. Once outside, he stood by the back door, still moaning. I went to the trunk of my Rambler to grab the trenching tool I used each winter when shoveling sand under tires in order to make it up the hill to our home in Morgantown.

Armed with flashlight and shovel, I walked Country up the hill behind Willow Cottage, where Big Jill lay asleep in the waning glow of her battery lantern. *To Kill a Mockingbird* lay open across her belly. I wondered if Jill ever went home. I'd never once seen her leave the farm. Then an absurd thought went through my head. *Maybe she lives here.*

I leaned down and switched off her lantern. She jerked and coughed, "Who . . . ?" Country still wailed softly.

"It's me and Country, Jill. We found Mizz Small. Dead. Can we bury her here?"

"Oh. The smell! . . . I didn't expect anyone . . ."

Country made soft moaning noises to the rhythmic scrape, scrape of my shovel. The ground already half-frozen, it was tough shoveling. When the hole was about twenty inches deep, Country placed Mizz Small gently into the hole and blubbered while I shoveled the dirt back in. Jill said a prayer, "For the soul of an innocent animal," and tamped her carefully arranged black glass rosary onto the tiny mound of dirt.

I whispered to her, "You are a saint," then added, "Any way to get Country to stop wailing?"

She shrugged then turned to him. "Baby Jesus thanks you for bringing Mizz Small to be here with his children. They will play with her forever, you know." Country sniffled. I walked him down the hill and straight into the showers, where we tried to rid ourselves of the scent of death in hot, billowing clouds of steam.

chapter 22

Who? Who?

For the next week I must have sounded like I was imitating Sugarbear and Sinbad at the talent show. "Who? Who?" began nearly every conversation with students. It flustered me that I had succumbed to anger and transformed into an irritating version of Investigative Reporter, but I simply had to know "Who? Who?" had hung Country's kitten.

Even the ordinarily taciturn Father Ralph was smoked enough to say a prayer for Mizz Small at the next chapel service. His sermon focused pointedly on the expiating relief of confession for sins visited upon the small and innocent. No good. As before, like *Hogan's* Sergeant Schultz, no one knew anything.

On the upside, no one dared say or do anything to Country or his roommate, Curtis. They seemed to sense that hanging Mizz Small and stuffing her under Country's cot had, like the fork-in-my-ass incident, pressed a deeply primitive button deep in the darkest recesses of my own unrefined soul. I didn't like that part of me, but I faced the brooding reality that I wanted to pull a short noose tight around the guilty bastard's neck, slowly kick a chair out from under his legs, give him the finger, and walk away as he swelled up into a fetid ball. My primitive revenge fantasies created enormous inner anxiety. *Help! I'm losing it.*

To hide my inner discomfort, I settled for "Who? Who?" delivered calmly in a flat, cold monotone. No preludes. No follow-ups. Every time I received no response, I stared icily then walked away.

Finally, Mr. Davenport confronted me. "Nearly every one of them has come to me on the QT and told me they didn't do it, Mr. Stuart. I think it might have been that Nantahela, before he was kicked out."

"Really?"

"Yes. They know you are angry. I think it would be good if you commented at dinner. You have the cottage's full attention now."

"I do?"

"Yes . . . and some respect with it. It's time for a values message. This is the only time it works . . . the only time they will really hear." Dav patted me on the shoulder and went back to his dailies. He'd just offered me a small piece of his magic.

At dinner, as the prayer ended, I stood and coughed. "Gentlemen, I have been deeply offended by both the cruelty to that little cat and to Country. As life unfolds, most of us are destined to lose things, people, or pets that we love . . . and need. We all want and need both love and respect, even if it comes so rarely that we deny wanting it to protect ourselves from the fear of its loss. Country needs love and respect now. If you aren't strong enough to give it to him, then I expect you to be strong enough not to take it from him, either. Thank you for considering my views." I sat down and ate. It was quiet.

After dinner I worked on the monthly files while Dav monitored the second-floor hallway. When Dav came down to clock out at eleven, he commented, "They are whispering about your dinner comments upstairs."

"It won't get me answers, Mr. Davenport."

"Perhaps not. But it may get Country some slack. He's still wearing that bonnet and no one has said a word to him about it since dinner."

Dav proved to have assessed the situation correctly. I drew shower duty the next night. Country started into the shower with his quarter bar of soap, still wearing Granny's bonnet. Done, Sinbad stepped out from under the showerhead next to Country.

"Man," he crooned, "you gonna mess up your gram's bonnet. Here, let me hold it for you." Country's lips went even more slack than usual as he stared at Sinbad and tried to assess the situation. Unsuccessful, Country turned to me with a "Help me, I'm confused" glance.

Sinbad jerked his head. "Then give it to Mr. Stuart, man; you gonna rune it." Country glanced at me again then untied it and, to my surprise, handed it to Sinbad, who stood there patiently, towel wrapped around him, till Country was finished and had dried his head. As Sinbad slipped past me, I did a Davenport "Good! *Very* good" and nodded at him.

]|[

I think the boys now understand how wrong it was to kill the cat, I told myself to reinforce the idea that my need for small hopes had been sensed from on high—and a few crumbs tossed. *Perhaps I am making a difference*, I reassured myself late that night. But reality hit at the end of the week when Patricia called from up on the Hill. "David. The director wants to see you this afternoon. I need to talk, too. Can you come up now?"

"I'll ask." I turned to Mr. Reddy. "The director wants me to come up to the Hill." Reddy shrugged. "Now," I added. Reddy put his hand out. "Give me the phone, Stuart."

"This is Reddy. Did you wish something from my employee? Uh, huh . . . I see . . . hmm . . . I can release him in twenty minutes. He'll need another ten to walk over there." With that Reddy hung up.

"What did they say?" I asked.

"Don't know. Didn't ask . . ." Reddy stared. "If you are going to kiss Her Majesty's ass on *my* shift, you are going to do it on *my* schedule." I sat there doing nothing, save staring at ordinary morning entries for exactly twenty minutes to the second, then rose without a word and walked out past Reddy who, head down, had been intently consulting the second hand of his watch. As the trainee, I might have had to follow Reddy's directive, but nothing required me to beg for his forgiveness, especially since he'd just made it clear that ass-kissing was abhorrent to him.

Up on the Hill, I stopped for a moment under the yellow, rose, and black rampant horse-adorned motto over the front door and looked up at it again. "It *is* ironic, isn't it?" said the director from somewhere over my shoulder.

"Yes, Doctor. You wanted to see me?"

"Here on the terrace is good. It's a beautiful afternoon; besides, everyone listens inside. Billy's petition for a new hearing has been denied. The Bar Association has actually lobbied against it." I flinched. In fact, my head began to throb as if an ice pick had just been jammed into my right eyeball.

"Judge Simpson?" I asked. She nodded. "We filed an appeal. You will need to appear in person next week. See Patricia for details. And I'll be leaving soon. No precise date yet fixed . . . but I should like to ask you a personal favor."

"*Me?*"

She nodded.

"What is it?"

"Dr., uh, Angela's father, wants to come home from Ghana. His lawyer wants a deposition from you that you were not assaulted."

"Look. I already indicated that I formally refused to press charges. If he wants more, he can acknowledge that I am a human and ask me himself. But I won't deal with that lawyer of his."

"Do you want him to find a white lawyer?" she asked, sounding irritated.

"Race isn't the issue. His lawyer is a liar. As Dr. King puts it, it's about character, not color."

She said nothing.

"Did Daddy phone you from Africa?" I asked.

She nodded.

"Then tell him to find a new lawyer and set up another phone call. I'll talk to a new lawyer . . . unless he starts screaming like the other one did. I miss Angela."

But she didn't seem to hear me.

"You OK?" I asked. Looking as if she might cry, she shook her head and put her palm up to silence me. She looked deflated. She had gone an entire conversation without using her favorite "aegis" word. I stepped through the foyer into the immense, high-ceilinged reception hall, looking back over my shoulder. Her Majesty didn't look very majestic sitting alone out on the veranda. She hadn't even moved. Hunched forward, her chin drooping, she gave the impression of someone whose sense of purpose had been vacuumed clean.

][

Patricia also seemed distracted. "Oh! I didn't expect you, David."

"Why not? You asked me to talk to you."

"Yes, I guess I did."

"I can come back tomorrow if that's better."

"Oh, could you? . . . I'm discombobulated right now . . . we are in the midst of some kind of palace coup." I backed out of her office, patted the Gibraltar safe on the way past, and paused to flip off the painted horses out front before descending the Hill's imposing front steps.

I dawdled on the walk back to Cottage 6. Clear, crisp late fall days were rare enough to engage me in a temporary thrall. The sprawling orange brick vo-tech complex contrasted with the darker red brick of the farm's high school. Parked nearby, a Commonwealth green truck created a picture-perfect counterpoint to the yellow-and-red-streaked leaves clinging to the oaks in the hills behind it.

For a few minutes the scene's bright splashes of color erased the Morganza's dark, gothic persona, until Mr. Reddy's shouts from the porch of our cottage broke the spell. "You coming back, or what, Stuart?" I walked faster.

"So what did Her Majesty have to say that was so damned important?" he demanded as I drew near.

"Billy's petition . . . some sort of hearing coming up—I'm supposed to attend. She didn't stick around to give me details."

"That all?" he asked.

"Yep."

"I don't like her style," he said. I shrugged and inched past him.

Just after 5:00 p.m. Patricia called again. "Hello, David. Are you working all night?"

"No. Till around midnight. Then I get some sleep for a change."

"Can you meet me?"

"Sure. Little Washington?"

"No. Here. I'll be working late. Can you meet me out front in the drive?"

"OK."

I spent much of the evening distracted and fantasizing about her possible motives. Upstairs in the hallway it got me into trouble. "You listening, Mr. Stuart?" asked Englan, a tall, flamboyant white kid who'd become a new admittee after being busted for selling weed at some sort of anti-Vietnam political rally on the Pitt campus. Eighteen, he was into theater and had arrived in the tie-dyed shirt, mannerisms, and spiky hair to prove it.

Now, of course, he was having one seriously miserable time dealing with the kind of streetwise predators he'd never even imagined,

Industrial Arts. Paint shop, right.

much less known, in his clubby, middle-class, college-going world. Since I was the staff member who he apparently perceived as most like him, he followed me around like a puppy dog. Lucky me.

When Englan first arrived for a 120-day stay, he proved to be the only student everyone from the director on down agreed upon. "What the hell are they doing, sending us kids like this?" Dav had exclaimed after our cottage's intake interview.

"The outside world has gone nuts on law and order in reaction to the riots," scowled Mrs. Moxon. Even Reddy, apparently oblivious to his own tendencies toward fascist-leaning ideas of discipline, was stunned. "Lord! If this is what they are doing to middle-class *white* kids for a half-lid of herb, how many new black kids are we gonna get for failing to say, 'Yes, Sir, Boss,' to some f-ing Irish harness bull?" While Dav flinched at the string of racist innuendos, I retorted, "Lots. This is the way the government has always dealt with protesting miners in West Virginia—try 'em for treason if they even look cross-eyed. Shoot their wives and children if they actually do something un-American, like demonstrate."

"Ah, come on!" said Reddy. "They don't shoot white women and children or try union members for treason."

"Nineteen twenty-one, Mr. Reddy," I said. "The feds tried over three hundred striking miners for demonstrating down near Logan, West Virginia, after an episode they referred to as 'The Battle of Blair Mountain.' Twenty-four of those guys were busted for outright treason. They machine-gunned a tent camp full of women and children, *then* sent in the U.S. Air Force."

"I'm writing that down," Reddy said, leering, already scribbling on a legal pad. "Gonna make you eat this note if it's B.S." His gold tooth flashed as he rattled the note at me. Inwardly, I was thrilled that Reddy might actually check it out and choke on the reality. I disengaged to get ready for the regular afternoon influx from the farm's proprietary classrooms.

I clocked out at 11:45 p.m. after working a straight thirteen hours and forty-five minutes. I was so tired that I forgot to meet Patricia; I was already on the old stone bridge that crossed Chartiers Creek when I remembered and did a "U-ey" on the arched span's far side and drove back to the administration building.

Patricia was still waiting when I pulled up. She leaned into my open window. "Park next to my car. I'm driving." *This is getting interesting.* It also proved to be unexpected. Fifteen minutes later we were on Route 19 north, headed toward the outskirts of Pittsburgh's declining South Side.

"Where are we going? Your apartment?" I asked. From her huffy reaction I must have sounded a touch too anticipatory. "I don't know why Angela cares about you. You go after every woman except her."

"Uh, how did Ange wind up in the middle of this conversation—she's written me off. I'm under a restraining order, remember?"

"No. I forgot. That isn't still in force, is it?"

"Yes." She slowed down and I figured it out. "So you were taking me to see Angela?" She sounded contrite. "That *was* the plan."

"I'm not doing jail time just so she can have the last word . . . or blackmail me into perjuring myself with some kind of deposition."

"I'll stop and call her," she said, sounding apologetic. We pulled up to a pay phone on the old Brownsville Road, next to the small, brick Carrick Post Office. She stepped out and phoned Angela. From the vantage point of my opened passenger window it sounded loud and argumentative, but I wasn't one to judge, especially since Patricia got back in, slammed the door, peeled out, and headed back to the Morganza without uttering a single word.

I showed the maturity and good manners not to interrupt her fuming. Those manners paid off twenty-five slow minutes later when I stepped out of her car and unlocked my gray Rambler. She pulled away but braked abruptly before she reached the end of the brick drive. She stuck her head out of her window when I pulled alongside to pass her. "Follow me. If Angela doesn't want you, I'll take you."

"Uh, I'm taken."

"OK. Then I'll *borrow* you." She pulled away. Like any ordinary male lemming, I followed her over the cliff.

Patricia had a cute back-of-house studio in a large, old Victorian only eight blocks from Beau Street. "I'm angry at Angela," she eventually explained.

"Let it out," I coaxed, adrift in a sea of musk-scented testosterone.

"OK." She smiled, then talked nonstop about Angela. She was still venting when I fell asleep propped up on her foldout bed.

]|[

The following Monday morning found me back in Morgantown by seven. Mom was still sleeping when I arrived. Too early to go to the bank or go grocery shopping, I took a nap in my absent twin brother John's bedroom while Mom slept in my redecorated one.

She woke me about eight. "Honey, I have to go to work. Can you meet me at the Mountainlair for lunch?"

"Sure, Mom." I dozed for another hour, got up, gave the grass its final mowing of the season, showered, and met her for lunch.

She ate the usual: a small side dish of cottage cheese, a glass of iced tea, and a free dinner roll. Raised during the Depression, Mom was simply incapable of either spending money on herself or throwing anything away. She even rewashed her used Saran wrap, hanging it to dry on a small towel bar over the kitchen sink.

Guiltily, I ordered a burger, which she insisted on buying for me. She'd do damn near anything for her "little boys" yet balk at a buck's worth of pleasures for herself. Dad's life insurance had finally paid off, and she had begun to receive bits and pieces of his TIAA retirement annuity, but, true to her roots, it didn't really matter how much money she had—she still felt poor.

Several of her colleagues at West Virginia University's Student Counseling Center came over to sit with us, among them the Drs. Carruth and Comer. Mom had the huge luxury of working with decent, highly trained, highly effective but unpretentious, people. True, there was one she'd taken to describing simply as "The Little Nazi Bastard," and another whose attendance record was iffy. But just to hear her comment on something other than "Your father was so tragic" temporarily lifted my spirits.

Working and going to school again was good for her. She'd begun to focus on that. For a few hours each day, she could step away from the old man's death.

By the time I drove back to Little Washington before dawn the next morning, it had already morphed into the season of oppressive skies and cold rains. Mom was still awake and pacing at 4:30 a.m. when I left M-Town. She shivered on the front stoop and watched me go.

On Wednesday, I flew to Philadelphia then took a cab to the Delaware County Courthouse in Media, where I was to "testify" at Billy's rehearing proceeding. Judge Simpson stared and salivated as they swore me in. His eyes followed me like I was a piece of raw meat and he was the boss hyena leading his cackling coterie in from the Veldt to tear chunks of living flesh from my body.

Spread out on the bench next to him was his pack of four fat-assed, pasty-white robed judges who were to preside over the administrative proceeding. To settle my nerves I imagined them making silly hyena sounds. Both judge and jury, they would determine the course of Billy's life—a life which, given their golf clubs, power lunches, and well-diversified portfolios, they could never even remotely grasp.

Simpson asked the first question. "Why did they send *you*? You are a trainee."

"I wrote the petition . . . and I am not on state time here today."

"How touching," he said, sneering. I didn't take the bait. "Just graduated from college, eh?" The puffy-cheeked judge to his left reacted with a condescending grin.

"Yes, sir," I replied.

"Now, tell me, is this *West Virginia* college accredited?" continued Judge Simpson. Another black-robed jester sitting across the bench threw his head back and bleated like a lamb in derisive approval. In control, on his own turf, and buoyed by his flanking peers, Simpson could afford to be mean. Worse yet, he delighted in it. His eyes glittered and his lips quivered, but I kept my cool and slowed my responses, answering in a bored monotone.

"Yes, Wesleyan is accredited, but the presiding judge in Billy's trial is not even a college graduate."

The corner of Simpson's left eye began to twitch satisfyingly. "What is the relevance of that statement?" he growled.

I needed an ally, so I began to invent one. I took even longer to answer, flatly enunciating every word with obsessive care as I kept looking back over my shoulder toward an empty row of chairs. "I a-am . . . quite certain that he didn't . . . follow the law. Mr. Grasty . . . should have been charged with c-contributing." I paused then mumbled something to the empty row behind me.

Finally, Simpson turned his head to look behind me. *Now I have you, you little prick*, I grinned. Judge Simpson snapped.

"Face *me*! Stop fidgeting and answer expeditiously. And just who were you talking to?"

"Ellen," I answered calmly. Rattled, he blew it badly. "She's dead . . . and she's *not* here." *So how does he know I was referring to Billy's mom?* I wondered. Feeling much better I answered, "Oh, but she is, Judge. She's been whispering to me for half an hour about how and why she was murdered."

His face twisted up like the busted spring sticking out of an old-fashioned mantle clock. He turned cherry red as I stared at him and raised my eyebrows. One of the others judges, looking surprised at Simpson, snuck a sidelong glance at him.

"You are *excused*," snarled Simpson, trying to recover from the "she's dead" faux pas. "You are obviously too mentally disturbed to give reliable testimony."

I smiled. "Suits me. Didn't know that you knew Billy's mother." His gavel damn near split its circular, wooden base. I stood and exited without even bothering to look back.

]|[

A full afternoon to kill until my return flight, I took a cab from Media to my grandmother Elsie's house in Ridley Park, only four miles from the airport. She had turned eighty and had reached that age when she was sometimes confused. Still hiding in eastern Pennsylvania from the fallout of her long-ago failed marriage, she had become agoraphobic enough to be perennially lonely.

Elsie lived with her eldest daughter, my aunt Natalie, who had never left home, never married, and never had kids but who, to my total wonderment, worked as a high school counselor. Polar opposites, Natalie's persona was as open and as formidable as Grandmother's was guarded and fearful, at least when she was around Natalie. Perhaps that's why my grandmother didn't want me to rat her out for her wide-ranging tastes in music—she didn't want Natalie to know.

Elsie loved it when my twin brother and I visited because she had someone to talk to . . . instead of the daughter who talked nonstop to her. Their household revolved around the secret of Grandmother's marriage and Natalie's foaming anger at the uncontrollable, changing world around them. It was as if Natalie fixated on some magic juncture in childhood and demanded that nothing—*nothing!*—change afterward. Ever. Not custom; not old-fashioned courtesy; not the patterns on coins, the hemlines on dresses, the faces in the neighborhood. "Nothing shall change" was her mantra.

My aunt and grandmother had evolved an odd symbiosis. Natalie supplied the moral outrage about a changing world and Grandmom supplied a timeless house, still *exactly* as it had been in 1920, and smothered her tendencies toward the off-center flamboyance that had generated "the secrets" of fifty years before. Grandmother's mantra was, "Do not upset Natalie." My reaction to the odd family situation was one of astounded curiosity. Going to my grandmother's house was an eerie, endless treasure hunt to uncover the family secrets.

Alone that afternoon, Grandmother was chatty, matter-of-fact, and wanted to pass on family history, lest even more of it fall into the maelstrom of total secrecy. Grandmom and I looked at family photo albums, which went back to the days of the Densmore, Wheaton, and Vandergrift river men posing in front of their gingerbread-styled riverboats.

I drank tea with Grandmother, explained what had brought me to Media, and asked her advice on what to do about Judge Simpson and Billy. She worked up her focus, emitting singsong "Oh, oh's" until she had thought it through. "I'll phone a friend in Spring Lake, New Jersey . . . he'll know."

"Know what, Grandmom?"

"Whether or not the judge is Republican. If he is a Republican, I can ask Mr. Nixon to look into it. If he is Democrat, well, I don't know anything about *those* people." I smiled and patted her shoulder. How was she to know that her younger daughter and one grandson had already slipped over to the dark side and had voted Democrat? I saw no need to tell her and induce a stroke but did enjoy her fantasy that she could simply call Tricky Dick Nixon—then a candidate for president—and solve my little dilemma.

While I foraged for more food in the old-fashioned refrigerator tucked into the pantry, she went out into the front room to phone someone.

To my amazement, she came back to the kitchen, smiling. "Judge Simpson is Republican."

"Shall we call Mr. Nixon?" I teased. She smiled. "Oh, oh . . . he was *so* nice on the phone."

"You mean, you *already* called Mr. Nixon?"

"Oh, yes. And I am quite certain that someone will properly investigate the death of your little ward's mother. I think that it is quite nice that you are helping orphans. What is the name of this place where you work?"

I shook my head incredulously but answered her question. "It's called the Youth Development Center in Canonsburg. Locally it's called 'The Morganza.'"

Her eyes widened as her lips pursed into a carefully puckered "O." She nodded. "Notorious. Quite notorious. I am surprised that you work there—that is very kind. I am sure they are grateful." I forced back the urge to laugh. "Now, what has this Billy done?"

"He took a pony and a rope to transport a barrel of stale beer to Beaver Falls. He was paid for a day's work with the beer." Grandmother recoiled.

"Beer! . . . *Gentlemen* don't drink beer! And they are *never* seen in public in their shirtsleeves." Her head wagged from side to side in social despair. "The world is no longer so gracious as it once was. I hope your ward finds a home where they emphasize the proper values."

I grinned inside. "I'll see to it, Grandmom." She smiled and relaxed.

I checked my watch. Three. Time to catch a Chester Pike bus down to the airport before my aunt came home and grilled her mother to find out if she had exposed any "family secrets."

That, it turned out, proved to be the last time I ever saw Grandmom Elsie. I, of course, didn't know that when, about ten that night, I locked Billy into his room and told him, "Talked to my grandmother today. She advises no more beer and a suit jacket when you are out in public."

"OK." He smiled. "Do you think I'll be going home soon?"

"I do, Billy. Somehow, I think things will work out." I slipped him and Curtis each a Clark Bar I had signed for and locked their door behind me.

chapter 23

Her Majesty's Dance

Finally, news that Her Majesty would be replaced began to spread like wildfire. Some among the staff, like Mr. Reddy, were openly jubilant. The director may have been black, but many had nothing else in common with her. A black, educated, former colonel of military police, or a retired officer of a distinguished combat unit . . . now *that* would have been a different story. A male kick-ass director—race unimportant—might have been worshipped. But a liberal, doctorate-holding *woman*—no way.

In short, a significant portion of the farm's staff went immediately into a euphoric, "Well, so much for this stupid little experiment in calling them 'students'" mode.

"'Yes, sir!' 'No, sir!' 'May I kiss your ass, sir?'" was Palco's suggestion for a new communication on-campus code.

"How would that work?" I asked.

"Well, in your case, it wouldn't. You see, these little misfits don't respect *weasels*. They respect *tough*, so it would work great for the real staff who understand that respect means 'Don't fuck with me.'"

"Hmm? 'Don't fuck with me' . . . I never thought of that. It has an unusual ring to it." Nearby, one of the perennially eavesdropping students snickered. Palco turned heart-attack red and snarled, "Fuck you!"

"May I kiss your ass, sir?" I responded. Another round of snickering erupted from out in the hallway. "Don't screw with me, Weasel. I mean it. You keep pushing my buttons and I'll find a reason to light up one of your little buddies, like that nappy fairy, Country, or stupid Billy."

In response to his threat I leaned forward and said softly enough that he had to stop rattling his keys and concentrate to hear me, "Palco, mess with any of them and I'll spike your cheese sandwiches with Drano, just like you spit into the kids' food back there in the kitchen."

Palco twitched spasmodically but controlled himself enough to lodge a weak denial. "I don't do that," he asserted, looking into the hall-way for the source of the snickers. I assumed his denial was intended to ward off likely street justice from Sinbad's crewe, who would not take kindly to Palco's behavior. Individually they may have feared Palco, but in a hunting pack, they morphed into a formidable adversary.

⧚

It was a difficult time for both the director's staff and for those in the cottages who had embraced liberal views of student rehabilitation. Some of Her Majesty's detractors began immediately to ignore all orders, decisions, and directives from the Hill.

Her Majesty, in spite of her reputation for being out of touch with reality, was fully aware of this. Proof that she was in touch came the second week in November in the form of an official directive to organize an all-students dance to be held in the Hill's main reception hall during the Thanksgiving season.

This finally drove Dav to comment, "I don't blame her, Mr. Stuart, but this event will be very difficult to control."

"Harder than my trip to see *Cool Hand Luke*?"

In response, he chuckled. "Let us pray . . . and I do mean *pray* . . . not. Do you have any idea what it's like over in the women's unit?"

"No. No one ever talks about it, and I've never even been over there."

"It's tough. When women go bad, they don't usually do it half-way. They are more clever and more volatile. We have no trainees over there. Unsafe." I whistled . . . then indulged my curiosity.

"What are most of them in for?"

"Murder; drugs; prostitution; rolling Johns . . . mutilating abus-ers . . ."

"Who do they murder?"

"Ah. Good question. Usually the men who try to control them. Sometimes family. It's a different psychological world over there."

"So we are going to be chaperones at an 'experimental' event?" I asked.

"Yep. We've had small dances from time to time between honor roll students and the like. Twenty or twenty-five of each . . . but nothing quite like this."

The "I Hate Her Majesty" group immediately tried to put the kibosh on the dance, but they didn't have a prayer, mostly because within minutes of the original directive's mimeographing, the news of a dance had spread from students with choice errand assignments on the Hill to every quarter of the farm.

I was amused by the dilemma Her Majesty had created: Hold the dance and we *might* have a riot in two weeks; stop the dance and a full-scale riot would erupt *immediately*. "Nice touch," I told Patricia over coffee in Little Washington a few nights later while attempting to convince her that she should still be angry enough at Angela to take me back to her apartment and extract meaningful revenge—and not the conversational kind. But she wasn't buying.

"You probably aren't *that* good. Besides, I don't know if I should forgive you for hoping to cheat on your fiancée in Mexico."

"Huh? *You* drug me into that bed several weeks ago with the intent to use me to displace your own anger," I protested. "Then changed your mind!"

"If it was so traumatic, why are you fishing for another try?" she asked, smirking.

Feeling petulant, I answered, "Needy." That generated a truce of sorts, then news.

"Here, read this." She spread a letter on the table.

Dear Governor,

It has come to my attention that there may remain uninvestigated circumstances in the death of one Ellen Terrell in Beaver County, Pennsylvania. Her son is currently a ward of the State at your Youth Development facility in Canonsburg, Pennsylvania. I would be most grateful if you could enquire.

Sincerely,
Richard M. Nixon

I laughed as I read it. Judging from the look on her face, that wasn't the response Patricia expected. "You don't seem amazed, David," she pouted, as if I had intentionally spoiled her fun. "I'm not. I thought my grandmother was nuts when she said she had called Nixon about Billy. I guess the old gal actually did call. If he becomes president tomorrow, it will be a hoot!"

"Your *grandmother* called him?"

"Yeah, she lives near Philly. Frighteningly Republican . . . and it's an election year. She's part of America's genetically connected— DAR, Descendant of the Signers of the Declaration of Independence. Mayflower, or something like it, in the 1600s. Descended from a long line of Yankee capitalists. But, most importantly, great-granddaughter of a minority stockholder/founder of the original Standard Oil, and four greats away from a signer of the Declaration of Independence. Republicans love old bats who just might be flighty enough to leave their estates to the National Committee."

"You are *so* cynical! This is your family you are talking about."

"I like my grandmother, Patricia. But she has no real idea why the pols like her . . . trust me!"

"Well, I don't trust your judgment. Mayflower?"

"I don't know, Patricia. Some damn ship is involved . . . and I don't care. They talked about this crap so often that my brother and I quit listening to it when we were six or seven."

"Well, you should care. A grandmother who can pick up the phone and get through to Nixon? Why are you working at the Morganza?"

"Huh? My mom was broke. First job I could get."

Patricia shook her head like I was hopeless.

"What's with you, Patricia?" I asked.

"You *are* an enigma. Connected, but working at the Morganza. Did you never think about asking Granny to call Mr. Nixon for *you*?"

She had me on that one. "No. Actually . . . it's never even occurred to me."

"So?"

"Uh, so . . . what's 'so' mean?"

"It means we're going to my place."

"Why?"

"I think you guys call it a 'mercy fuck.'"

"Is accepting a mercy fuck pathetic?"

"Definitely."

"OK. 'Pathetic' works for now." I shrugged.

Forty minutes later she abruptly changed her mind again, *after* a ferocious, half-clothed make-out session. "Why?" I croaked.

"I just can't betray Angela . . . and your fiancée. I can't."

"I can handle the guilt," I protested. She threw my clothes at me and locked herself in the bathroom. On the way out I leaned against the bathroom door and rasped, "Screw Nixon." I meant to sound cynical. Perhaps even James Dean-ish. But it came out sounding, well, pathetic. She giggled from behind the door.

My "date" clearly over, I drove back to the eagle's nest, stepped up onto the old man's footlocker and peed into the sink, one hand aiming, the other wrapped tight around the neck of a quart of José Cuervo.

]|[

The dance took place about a week before Thanksgiving. Security was heavy—with both off-duty local police and moonlighting state troopers providing extra presence. The girls came in groups of about twenty-five, cottage by cottage. Each cottage had its own labeled benches set up against the reception hall's walls. Several huge punchbowls filled with spiced cider had been placed near the floor-to-ceiling front windows. Trays of chips and ginger cookies rounded out the snacks.

Her Majesty welcomed the girls and asked a lieutenant to explain the ground rules, then the mysterious Williams gave the sign for the guys to enter.

Our male students gaped. Sinbad's crewe lined up to do their Wylie Avenue dip. Others, like Curtis, reacted like deer in a Peterbilt's headlamps. Some of the girls looked as rough and squinty-eyed as Davenport had implied. But a number—black and white—appeared big-eyed, innocent, and gorgeous. I whistled involuntarily while Richard gulped, "Mercy!"

Dav stuck his head between us and whispered, "Looks like candy. Smells like candy. Might even taste like candy. But it's poison, boys . . . and don't forget it!"

I teased, "My short-term memory is failing me, Mr. Davenport."

"Don't joke!" he answered, deep into his firm mode. "The last male staffer whose short-term memory was shorter than his

'Johnson' wound up dead when a pack of them tore him apart with their bare hands."

"Are you serious?" asked Richard, sounding shocked. I looked at Dav.

"I'm not saving either of you. If you go flirtin', I don't know you." The ominous tone in Dav's voice was new to us.

Rolling his eyes, he motioned us into the positions we were assigned. I drew Sinbad's crewe. Richard got our white and Latino students, and Dav, along with the ominous, black-suited Williams, acted like sideline refs. "Boys return to their benches after every dance. Young ladies, you shall do likewise," boomed Williams.

Meanwhile, Her Majesty and most of the off-campus VIP guests disappeared into the large, adjacent foyer, the scents of their canapés and the refined sounds of their political chitchat provided a surreal backbeat to the coarse noise and raw, grinding hormones on our dance floor.

Motown reigned. Elvis played occasionally, and The Doors, for once, didn't create any racial whining with the women present. About forty minutes into watching the kids dance, I spotted a tall, slender black girl with big eyes, dimples, and a tiny waist. *Wow! Great ass!* She glanced at me and smiled. My groin reacted. I smiled back. In response, Dav whispered in my ear, "Her nickname is Minnie Mouse."

"Unusual," I whispered back.

"She steals 'cheese,' as some call it on the street—goes down on Johns and bites off the tips of their penises. That's what she's in for."

"You're joking."

"Ask Jill," said Dav, sounding smug as he strolled back to the sideline. I did ask Jill a few minutes later.

"Oh, sweetie, don't you go messin' with her. Don't even make eye contact. She's *angry*. Guys who mess with her end up getting a partial penectomy on the spot." Well, that did it. As Minnie Mouse smiled and made eyes at me again, my groin, uh, shrunk. Jittery, I looked away.

The dance ended with one final, old-fashioned slow number, "Goodnight Sweetheart." Someone tapped me on the shoulder. "You wanna dance, lover?" crooned Minnie Mouse.

I twitched. "Ah, thanks, but can't, Miss . . . I'm on duty."

She went all pouty and asked again, a grainy undertone in her voice. "Come on, *lover* . . . I like man meat. Just one dance?"

"Can't, Miss. Sorry." Apparently, rejection didn't suit her—her face morphed instantly into "mad-dog staring you down" mode as she transformed from coy vamp into a teeth-bared, primitive rage.

Several of her girlfriends rushed over and dragged her away from me as she hissed, her hands twisting into claw-like appendages. Pulse racing, I backed up a step or two and caught Dav taking in the scene, looking even smugger than before.

◗◖

Up in the hallway of Cottage 6 that night, it took a lot to get our students settled down. Contraband butter and illicit rags circulated. Grossed out by hearing a bunch of teenagers furtively jacking off, I turned up my portable record player and got lost in Armstrong's "It's a Wonderful World." After Minnie Mouse, I simply wasn't in a mood to play cop, even though I knew there would be hell to pay in the morning as the Commonwealth's agents fretted darkly over "soiled" bed sheets and "masturbation demerits."

I didn't care. Instead, I settled for fretting over how I was going to deal with Billy, Curtis, and Country, who was now wearing Granny's bonnet full time.

◗◖

The next morning when I arrived in West Virginia, Mom seemed better than before but later confided she was afraid of the holiday season. "I'm so sad that Christmas is over for me now that Ed's dead. I've always loved Christmas." Since it was still four days till Thanksgiving, her tone of "it's over" completely undid me. After a cheap, but excellent, early bird spaghetti dinner at the Communtzi family's airport restaurant, she asked me to drive her around. "Turn here, John." I did, without bothering to correct her.

A few minutes later she did it again. "John, can we go right here?"

"Sure, Mom, but this road goes back toward the Medical Center . . . there's nothing to see."

"Oh, I know, but I thought we could drive past Ed's office and see if his light is on."

"Uh, Mom, I'm David . . . and Dad's dead." It was quiet for a moment before the inevitable, "Oh, I knew that, didn't I?" Still, she insisted that we go there.

It began to drizzle again. Within minutes the sound of drops splattering on the Rambler's roof intensified. As night fell, the cold rain changed to sleet. I turned into the short drive at the front of the Medical Center's administrative wing, passing the white marble history of medicine-inspired pylons. My old man's office windows were dark. *Has it not dawned on her that he'll never be there to turn them on again?* I wondered.

"I used to drive over here at two or three a.m. to bring him coffee," she said as the sound of the Rambler's rumbling exhaust notes echoed back from the carved marble pylons. "Do you think he's really dead?" I was too stunned to answer. She sighed in response. "He isn't coming back, is he, uh, *David*? Is he?"

"No, Mom," I whispered.

She began to cry.

"I'm sorry, Mom. I shouldn't have sounded so matter-of-fact."

chapter 24

I'll Take Extra Shifts

As the holiday season approached, many staff members wanted to schedule Christmas sojourns to be with family. I volunteered to work more shifts, requesting only one twenty-four-hour unscheduled period a week so I could visit my mom.

The farm's budget had been trimmed, according to rumors from the Hill, so extra shifts would become vacation hours, rather than extra pay, for junior staff. It didn't matter to me, as deferred salary was easier to hold onto than money in hand.

Meanwhile Preacher Jacob had phoned again, asking me about the farm's visiting schedule.

"Next Sunday, Reverend—it's Visiting Day. Can you make it?"

"No, but my niece Emily will come—she was once Billy's Sunday school teacher. You met her at the funeral. Anything new on Billy's hearings, Mr. Stuart?"

"Dead as a doornail in Delaware County, Reverend. I went to Media and gave testimony, but I don't think it did much good. Anything new with your congregation?"

"Yes. We've been offered a rather unexpected cash donation from a farmer with a pony . . . who no longer attends church."

"Well, that's justice of sorts. I'll meet your niece when she gets here. Make sure she asks for me, OK? Thanks."

On Sunday, I had two important family consultations scheduled.

The first to arrive was Curtis's mother, who brought us cornbread—the kind of cornbread you might actually hurt someone to get more of.

"Hello, Mrs. Rice. How are you today?"

"Fresh from church and feelin' fortified by the Lord. How's my boy child doin'?"

"He's fine. Actually, I want to talk to you about Alabama."

She smiled and fidgeted, perhaps self-conscious in her hand-sewn floral print dress and a much-repaired old-fashioned black hat punctuated by one stubby, tattered peacock feather. Her face as broad and as open as her smile, she struck me as a fundamentally happy, uncomplicated person. But the Morganza always made her fidget. "I'm never knowing a place like this before," she told me the second time we'd spoken.

She smoothed and resmoothed her dress as I seated her. I tried one last time to mentally compose what I was about to say. The pause unnerved her. She studied my face. "Oh, no. My Curtis done sumpin' naughty?"

"No . . . uh, no, ma'am. I was thinking about Curtis and wondering if he might do better . . . someday . . . uh . . . back in Alabama."

"Oh, I do so want to go home again. I miss my people. We been on the same place down there since 'Mancipation. Forty acres . . . and my brother has another twenty acres nearby. I came up here to earn cash. Costs being what they are, though, it's hard to save."

"Well, if Curtis comes home some night on a special furlough . . ."

She shook her head, not understanding.

"If he was given permission to leave here for a little while, uh, that is, and if he was *my* son, I'd go straight to the bus station and take him home to Birmingham and not come back. That's what *I'd* do."

"You would?"

"Yes, ma'am, but it's very hard to get those furloughs."

"Well, then . . . that's *that*! I'll ask the Lord to look kindly on a furlough."

"Thanks for the chat, Mrs. Rice. Let's go see Curtis. Oh, I almost forgot. Here's a photo of him at our talent show. He played the bullfighter." She studied the photo and smiled.

"He's a handsome boy. Yes, indeed, my boy child is a splendid sight all fancied up like that . . ."

I seated her in the visiting room as Mr. Reddy ushered in Curtis.

"Stuart," Reddy said, smiling and snapping his manicured fingers, "You do the honors here. I have administrative matters to attend to—come to my office when Curtis and his momma are finished." I took Reddy's usual position outside the visiting room door when he disappeared.

Physical contact was prohibited between parent and child, so I looked away when Mrs. Rice folded Curtis, her only living "boy child," to her bosom and stroked his hair. According to Curtis's master file, she'd lost two children—both dead before age two—at about the same time Dr. Martin Luther King was writing his "Letter From Birmingham Jail." *Born black on forty acres of scrubby, worn-out red soil a half hour's bumpy bus ride south of Birmingham? No thank you*, I reflected.

After they left I stepped up to Reddy's desk area. "You wanted to see me, Mr. Reddy?"

"Yes. What's this crap about a special furlough that I overheard out in the hall?" My heart sank.

"I read that an occasional Christmas furlough is granted in special cases. I thought I'd ask Mr. Davenport or Mrs. Moxon how it's arranged. Curtis is a good kid and his mom is really solid." Reddy stared at me—no gold tooth, no hint of what might be on his mind. *I'll never figure this guy out*, I thought to myself.

I wanted to say something, anything, to break the silence, but Reddy beat me to it. "I'll never figure you out, Stuart. You spend months fussin' over Billy, so I figure you for stuck on your own kind. Now you go and surprise me by getting soft on one of the blackest kids on the farm."

"Umm . . . ah, well, *is* a furlough possible?"

Reddy waved expansively, showing off his cuff links, and gave me his full-toothed car-dealer's smile. "His momma prays hard enough, so most anything could happen. Now get out of here. I got stuff to do. I don't like my Sundays interrupted."

I couldn't let it go. "I'll work more shifts," I offered.

"Including Christmas?"

"Yes, sir. I can visit my mom after Christmas." Reddy waved me out again, but this time a little softer. Satisfied I'd done what I could, I went out front, poured myself a cup of hot chocolate, and hid in the rear hallway while I ate a square of Mrs. Rice's cornbread. I carefully hid the rest. *No need to share with a rooting pig like Palco*, I rationalized.

An hour later the preacher's niece Emily showed up. I remembered her as the quiet, thirtysomething woman at Ellen's funeral. In fact, she looked rather like the preacher: ruddy-faced, neat, and blocky, but not fat. Like Curtis's mom, she seemed solid, too.

"John couldn't come today," she said, smiling.

"Who is John?"

"My uncle—Reverend John Jacob."

"Ah! I wondered whether 'Jacob' was a first or a last name."

"And you never asked?"

"No, ma'am."

She frowned. "May I see Billy?"

"Sure. I'll take you into the visiting room. No items may change hands, and your purse stays with us. Physical contact is prohibited. We may look in from time to time. Let me know if you need anything."

She smiled. "You sound like me . . . at school. I'm a teacher."

"Do you live in Beaver Falls or in Ohio?"

"Both. School year in Ohio, near my parents. Summers on the family farm here in P.A. with Uncle John . . . now that my husband is gone." Her face clouded. *Vietnam?* I wondered but didn't ask. I left her and went upstairs to get Billy.

"Billy, Mizz Emily, Reverend Jacob's niece, is here to see you."

He smiled. "She nice. She read me Bible when I was little. Sunday school."

"Ah . . . good. She's waiting."

When Mizz Emily's visit ended, I walked her out. "So are you the source for Billy's Christmas story from the Bible?"

She smiled and nodded. "I didn't think he'd remember."

"Oh, he remembers, and I still need to talk to Reverend Jacob. Please let him know," I said.

She reached into her jacket pocket nervously. "Here is my phone number. About midnight is best. I'll handle details of any, umm, special Christmas visit. The note explains the rest."

"There could be *three* packages to pick up, ma'am."

She smiled. "As long as there are instructions, Santa can deal with it."

I took it and held the door for her as she eased behind the wheel of the ancient, factory-gray '53 Chevy sedan and smiled. "Which way to the stone bridge?" she asked. I pointed. "You seem so calm. Almost heroic," I commented.

"Perhaps I am too calm. It does worry me at times, but I've already lost both my husband and my son—my only child. It's odd; I'm only thirty-four and there isn't much left to be afraid of . . . and there is *no* heroism in me at all." She smiled sublimely, slipped the column shift into first gear, and pulled away. I stood out back and watched her turn then drive slowly across the old stone bridge at Chartiers Creek. Reddy was standing behind me. "You practicing to be a hotel parking valet, or are you working my shift, Stuart?"

"I haven't decided, Mr. Reddy. I'm on my three p.m. break right now." He muttered something as he slammed the cottage door behind him.

)|(

The next day Mrs. Moxon caught up with me. "I have a letter back from Statesboro, Georgia. It's about Country."

I unfolded it.

> *Dear Mrs. Moxon,*
>
> > *The current address for the family you enquired about is unknown to us here in Social Services. But the grandmother of your student once lived in the settlement of Egypt on the old McLaw's place in Effingham County about sixteen miles east of town. They are Geechee people. She attended church there, the A.M.E. Church's Reverend Forsyth in our county should know where to find any living relatives.*
> >
> > > *Sincerely yours,*
> > > *William Deaton,*
> > > *Director Bulloch County, Social Services*

"Wow! Doesn't tell us much, does it? Didn't the letter to the bonnet's return address go to Country's family?"

"No. The package was actually mailed from the Social Services office in Statesboro—probably as a public service for someone who couldn't read or write . . . at least, that is what I understood when I phoned them this morning and tried to get Reverend Forsyth's address."

"Did you get it?"

She grinned. "Of course!"

"OK, thanks. Thanks a lot." Later, I caught Mr. Dav when he clocked in for the three shift.

"Mr. Davenport, I have a letter you need to look at." He read it. "Need to find the family, do we?"

"Yes! Got any ideas?"

"Sure. A.M.E. ministers are just one big network. We can find this Reverend Forsyth if he exists."

"Mrs. Moxon already phoned and got the Reverend's address."

"That makes it easy. Let me take this with me. Will you be here tomorrow?"

"No, I'm driving to Morgantown when I get off work in the morning. I'll be back for the Wednesday three p.m. shift."

"A whole day off! You'll get spoiled." He grinned. "By the way, Mr. Stuart, I was hoping for Christmas Eve leave—family."

"Tell Mr. Reddy. I begged him for more shifts yesterday. List me as your stand-in, before someone else puts the pressure on me."

"You got a deal. How soon do you need to connect about Country?"

"Pretty soon—he's married to Granny's bonnet and seriously depressed. I'm worried."

"Is he still hiding all day and talking to nobody?" asked Dav. I nodded.

"Did we hear anything on the clinical psych workup we suggested?"

"No. We're not getting much of anything from the Hill. I'm still waiting on Billy's full-service evals."

"I'll ask Williams about both."

A few minutes later, I opened the sheet closet to take inventory and gasped. There, hidden in the back, was a ghostlike Country, rocking back and forth, eyes closed, to the cadence of an eerie, rhythmic hum. Totally unresponsive to the world around him, he didn't look up at me when I complained, "Country! You scared the crap out of me!"

Instead, he continued to moan and rock even as I stepped over him to count the fresh sheets for an after-dinner, cottage-wide sheet change. The odd, evening sheet count order had come from the Hill, probably in vengeful response for the episode of sheet soiling that took place after Her Majesty's dance, when I'd ignored the postdance masturbation by musically drowning it out with "It's a Wonderful World" in the upstairs hall.

Sheet change was supposed to be done in the morning so that students busted for semen soiling had a whole school day to calm down before displacing their anger at whomever they imagined had snitched on them. Evening write-ups made for the kind of long, hard nights that guaranteed no one, including Palco, got any sleep. I backed out of the closet and left Country rocking in the dark, still safe in the comforting pile of clean sheets.

Back in the dining hall, Dav, Richard, and I waited for the kids to come back from school. "What's for dinner?" Palco asked as he let himself in through the back door. It occurred to me that he'd never once begun his shift by asking, "How are things here?" or "Brief me." Never even a "Hi." So I answered, "Mystery meat with library paste gravy, whipped potatoes garnished with flea powder, and string beans so well-done that you can snort them through a straw."

Richard grimaced. But Palco didn't respond any more appropriately than had Country. "OK . . . so what's the dessert?"

Dav rolled his eyes. "Pig-foot pie."

"No kiddin'?" answered Palco, perking up. "Is that another of those black recipes to please the culturally sensitive crowd up on the Hill?"

"It's a joke, Mr. Palco," said Dav. "Although, the food has been terrible lately."

"Oh, hadn't noticed. Thought the pig-foot pie might be like that jerked chicken we had a couple of weeks ago—pretty good stuff, but they ought to rename it . . . name's enough to slow a normal man down. I don't like the idea of eating anything that's been *jerked*." With that, Palco disappeared into the kitchen. Richard and Dav exchanged deeply pained glances. To break the tension I posed a question. "How do you think he'd go over as the U.S. Ambassador to Jamaica?" They both guffawed.

When foraging, Palco was as easy to track as a bear rampaging through a campground parking lot. The sounds of violated cupboards, doors, shredding plastic bread wraps, and jars of jam and peanut butter being forced open reassured us of momentary privacy.

We took the occasion to discuss politics on the Hill and its effects on our daily operations: We weren't getting clean bed sheets on time; the duty roster was screwed up; the food sucked; the meds were erratic; and the Hill issued weird, spur-of-the-moment directives damn near hourly. Other than Big Jill, we were on our own when it came to getting any medical or psych services for the students. Dav summed it up: "FUBAR—just like in the Army."

"What's FUBAR mean?" asked Richard.

I illuminated him. "'Fucked up beyond all recognition,' according to my twin brother, who is in the Army."

"I hate politics," said Richard, wrinkling his nose. "Our director is a very articulate and thoughtful woman. If they want to make a change in its directors, why do they have to mess up the kids' lives in the process?"

"Collateral damage is accepted in both war and in politics. That's why I don't believe in either," Dav replied.

Huh, I thought he was, "True blue, I'll follow you" on matters of God and country. Guess it's not that simple.

I might have commented had it not been for the fact that Palco, done with his predinner foraging and into his security checklist, had just come across Country hiding in the sheet closet.

"Jesus! What are *you* doing in here, hiding in the freakin' dark? You want a number twelve . . . ?"

Dav hollered, "Leave him alone, Palco. He's having a mental breakdown."

Unfortunately, Rabbit, who'd been discharged from Pitt (another preholiday season cleanout, I assumed) and dumped back on us again, strolled in and heard Dav yelling at Palco about Country. God only knows what he would later receive in return for the precious information that Country had lost it, but pass it on he did. I was on watch in the dining hall when Dav and Richard rounded up most of the students. As the main group filed in, Dav leaned to me on the way past. "Four missing, including Country and Kamensky."

"I'll check, Mr. Davenport. Don't wait for me." First, I checked the linen closet. Its door stood partially open, a stack of sheets scattered onto the floor. The adjacent shower rooms were the only logical place to go from there.

Three white students—Englan, the college boy who should have known better, a new guy known as Little Jerry, and Kamensky—were engaged in the age-old schoolyard stunt of "pass the cap" while taunting an unfortunate Country, who knelt in the middle of their circle, bawling. They were so absorbed in their cruelty that they didn't even notice me standing behind them. I waited till Granny's bonnet came to rest in Kamensky's grasp and intercepted it from over his shoulder.

Kamensky was too surprised to take a swing at me. In fact, he jumped back and gasped, looking frightened. "You big pussy!" I chastised. "Why do you need to saw on Country?"

"Uh, he said I was white. Honest."

"And you think he's dumb . . . hah! You three go to the showerheads and clean yourselves."

"But we're dressed, Mr. Stuart," said Englan.

"That's the point. Cold water and wet clothes will do you good . . . and here we'd almost decided you didn't belong here," I guilted Englan.

His face turned red. "We weren't *hurting* him. Just teasing."

"He's on his knees crying. What do you mean 'not hurting him'? Now move!"

My shout brought Davenport on a trot. "Need help, Mr. Stuart?"

"Yes. Can you take Country upstairs and send in Palco? These three merrymakers will be taking cold showers while the rest of us eat." I handed Country's bonnet to Dav, who nodded.

"Cold water has healing properties—advances the Lord's work. Come on, Country, let's get you home . . . and fed."

"Don' wanna' eat. Don' wanna' do nuthin'.."

Dav reached for Country's shoulder. "Come on and eat for me, son. We're trying to contact Reverend Forsyth in Georgia. Do you remember him?" Country frowned, then nodded.

"Does he know Ah's here?"

"We're working on it. Every day. Now come on, son. Let's go upstairs." Country turned his head to look at Dav's hand on his shoulder and asked in a plaintive tone, "Can Ah's call you 'Daddy,' Mr. Davenport?" Kamensky snickered—a huge mistake.

Dav turned around and said for Kamensky's benefit, "Certainly, Country, you can be the *only* one here to call me that. Suits me fine." Country smiled, even as Dav leaned to me, calm but ominous. "When Kamensky is finished showering, bring him to me. I have a special chore for him." I nodded. Palco arrived, puffing.

As Dav led Country away, Kamensky freaked out. "What's you gonna to do me, Mr. Davenport?" Dav ignored him, focusing on Palco, who had just stepped into the shower area.

"Evening, Mr. Palco." Dav smiled. "We need you to assist in an emergency procedure. Mr. Stuart will explain."

"Glad to." I nodded.

"These three need thirty-minute, fully clothed, cold-water showers to rinse some toxic stuff off them." Palco grinned at the three.

"Well, well. Things are sure looking up here on the farm. Get wet, you punks."

Kamensky, bully that he was, had the temerity to beg, his hands up, "This ain't right . . ."

I snapped at him. "You are either a prick or a victim. You chose to be the prick. Can't have it both ways." As I walked away I heard Palco giggling eerily. *That applies to you, too, Palco*, I told myself.

]|[

Alone in the morning's fog and sleet I drove to Morgantown. Grayness enveloped everything. Leafless roadside trees poked out of the gloom like the brittle hands of a skeleton. There was no sky. No skyline. No color. No warmth. Only the misery of another cold, wet winter in a land that every year grits its teeth, holds its breath, and prays for Easter. Only the bar and roadhouse juke-joint owners took joy in this season. Perhaps, also, the undertakers.

It was so gloomy that our house on Citadel Road wasn't visible until I was in the driveway. Nine a.m. Mom had left me a note: "I love you, David! Pick me up at noon? Keep the faith! Avis/Mom." *Ah, this is good—she is signing things again the way she used to*, I rejoiced. She'd also drawn a heart next to her name. As odd as our family was, there'd never been any doubt in her mind about one thing—it may have been the only thing she didn't doubt: "I love my little boys." That we were men now, she may never have processed.

At noon I picked her up on the curb in front of the counseling center. She stood there in the wet gloom, all bundled in my father's faded tan trench coat, its black imitation-fur collar turned up and her old umbrella flopping in the gusts of freezing rain. I pulled over and swung open the passenger door. She smiled.

"You look happy, Mom."

"I've been thinking. . . . Do you suppose I could visit you in New Mexico once you are settled?"

"Sure, Mom."

"When do you leave, David?"

"About December 28, I think . . . possibly later than that. I'm working extra shifts so my paycheck goes through January. We'll have to have a late Christmas."

"That's OK. I have an invitation at Mother's for Christmas dinner. Since you will be in Canonsburg, I'll drive to Ridley Park alone. Can you spend tonight here? I'd like that. We haven't talked about anything except Ed in a long time. We've never really talked about your year in Mexico." Suddenly, the surroundings seemed less gray and the rain not quite so icy.

chapter 25

The Changing of the Guard

Changes came to the Morganza. Hallway whisperings, secret after-hours meetings, and impromptu victory dances all swirled around Her Majesty's withdrawal from the political field of battle.

"How can this matter so much to staff who barely know her?" I asked Dav one evening in December.

"I don't know, Mr. Stuart, but even my mentor Williams is wrapped up in it. It's about social philosophy, I suppose."

"Can you tell me more about Williams?" I asked.

"Why do you want to know?"

"His name is always whispered, but that's all I know." Dav shook his head. "He's very private. Been here since the thirties. He always steps in between directors—maintains order."

"More 'discipline'?" I asked. He nodded.

And more discipline is what we got as Her Majesty's old administration fled, transferred, or were fired. Judge Simpson seemed suddenly to be everywhere trustees simply weren't supposed to be, and Lawdawg licked his bum like a submissive puppy. Reddy and others winked at each other as they snuck off to see Lawdawg, now often referred to in hallway whispers as simply "The Man."

On Wednesday, December 12, Patricia was at work. She called to update me on Billy's ruling. "The official appeals ruling is in—Billy was appropriately charged, sentenced, and incarcerated. Period. I'm so sorry, David."

"Thanks, Patricia," I said, though I didn't really mean it. In fact I was angry enough to immediately convene a court of common sense, resolve the issue in my head, and make my own ruling on the matter. I picked up the phone again and dialed Reverend Jacob . . .

"OK, then. Someone dressed as Santa Claus will be waiting at the bridge across Chartiers Creek?" I said, toward the end of our conversation.

"Count on it."

"Thank you, Reverend . . . thank you." He hung up, sounding cheerful. I was still shaking off the jitters about what might happen at Christmas if an unauthorized Santa actually did show when Reddy returned, jubilant, from what must have been his latest ass-kissing drill. "Senior counsel wants to see you *now*, Stuart."

I checked out his lips for signs of advanced chapping. He gaped.

"Move it! Don't keep *The Man* waiting, Stuart. You deaf or something?" I eased out of the chair and ambled toward the front door, amazed at Reddy's sudden deference for the bureaucratic tools who worked up on the Hill. *Don't keep them waiting? Speaking of waiting, I can't wait to pack my bags and head to New Mexico*, I reflected as I shivered and adjusted my scarf on the way to the administration building. If I hadn't had unfinished Christmas business to attend to, I'd simply have driven the Rambler to Morgantown and headed West, then and there.

On the Hill I paused to glance up at the prancing stallions over the front door, patted the Gibraltar safe on the way down the side hall to counsel's office, and braced for a main course of "weird" served with a dessert of "gaga."

As I suspected, Simpson sat next to Lawdawg, who looked sleeker, younger, and less dyspeptic than I'd ever seen him. Simpson himself was as smug and arrogant as ever. "Uh, let's see now . . . your trainee status ends on . . . yes, here it is . . . January 17, 1968." Simpson actually paused, as if waiting for me to break into sweating fear at the mere mention of my employment status.

I grinned inwardly. *Amateurs like Simpson are so clumsy with this crap.* As he droned on, I pictured my fiancée in Mexico City. She handed me my dinner plate: two shimmering eggs over easy surrounded by a pile of yellow rice cooked with peas and carrots. Refried beans and fresh jalapeños on the side. After dinner we sat outside by the bubbling fountain in the old courtyard of the military barracks where her family lived.

"Why so many *chiles, querida?*" I asked her.

"To make you *picante*, my love." I reached out to stroke her hair. Someone shouted at me . . . *Which of her jealous older brothers is it now?* I wondered as my hand stopped its forward path.

"I asked you a question." It was Lawdawg speaking. "Do you understand that you will have to repeat your six-month trainee period . . . assigned solely to Mr. Palco? We are moving you to nighttime security. You aren't suited to be a counselor."

"When?" I asked, trying to refocus on Lawdawg without reacting.

"Saturday night, December 23, eleven p.m.," he said, sneering.

"Oh, I thought Palco was going to be off for two or three nights."

"He is." Lawdawg laughed. "You'll be *alone* after eleven p.m. . . . . that's *your* problem." Judge Simpson grinned and commented as if I weren't there. "You told me he was slow, Counselor." Lawdawg smiled eerily at me. "Merry Christmas! Now go away."

Reddy was waiting, expectant, when I returned.

"How'd it go?" he asked, doing his not-too-convincing version of casual.

"Fine. They want me to move to nighttime security and retrain."

"So, you got busted . . . have to redo boot camp," commented Reddy, his gold tooth showing.

"Uh, I didn't think of it like that, Mr. Reddy, but I didn't ask a lot of questions." Reddy's gold tooth went back into hiding.

By age five or six, I'd discovered the cardinal rule of dealing with angry control freaks, which I repeated to myself: *They want to watch you bleed inside. They need you to feel it so they can displace their own failures. Don't give 'em anything. Ever.*

I left a visibly unrequited Reddy at his desk when I departed to oversee the daily return of our back-from-school crowd. That evening after dinner, as Billy, Country, and Curtis helped me prepare a television room snack, I chatted with the three about Christmas. "Santa Claus, you know, comes here to the farm every Christmas Eve. He won't come inside because of the bad kids . . . and Palco . . . but he waits out by the creek with a light to give presents to the good kids."

Curtis seemed skeptical, but Billy's chimpanzee-like brain had never disconnected from a childhood Santa. He asked, "How do we get outside to see Santa?"

"Don't know, Billy, but I heard that the front door opens magically if it's a *good* kid who turns the knob."

)|(

The next afternoon I called Patricia to ask her how Angela was doing, but a female I didn't know answered her office phone. "She no longer works here, sir."

"What? Where did she go?"

"I already explained, sir. . . . *She no longer works here.* I am not at liberty to convey any other information to you."

"Is the director available?"

"She is on vacation, sir. Chief counsel is serving as interim director in her absence. Did you want to request a callback from his assistant?"

"OK, let me have the assistant's name. I'll call later."

"It's Ms. Champlin. She is new to that position, so I suggest you call back next week. The extension is zero-two." Click.

"You look rattled, Mr. Stuart," commented Dav, who leaned over to hand me the evening activity list as I hung up.

"I am. That Champlin person is back on the Hill, Mr. Davenport."

"I'm not surprised," he responded and grinned. "Umm, some say that she did a lot of work 'directly under' chief counsel."

"Jeez, so Lawdawg suffers from bad taste on top of his unresolved control issues," I blurted out. Dav laughed and disappeared to get the day's briefing from Reddy, who was slumped over his desk, frowning.

"You OK, Mr. Reddy?" he asked.

"No," he answered. "Stuart's lack of respect for management is depressing—I'm taking a break."

When Billy came back from the paint shop, we talked again about Santa Claus, who, I reiterated, waited each Christmas at Chartiers Creek to give presents to the good kids who got there first. "Our secret, Billy." He nodded in response. Later that night I repeated the same account to Curtis and Country. I'm not sure Country got it . . . one couldn't really tell. He hadn't been very responsive since Mizz Small disintegrated and oozed all over him. Worse yet, the Hill had suddenly proclaimed his bonnet to be a nonregulation distraction, and Palco had been ordered to confiscate it. "Mr. Davenport and I are trying to get the bonnet back," I consoled him. "It'll probably take a few days." He stared off into an unseen world.

Curtis, still Country's roommate, had conferred with Billy and now grasped Santa Claus so clearly that he pulled me aside to ask where Santa would wait at Chartiers Creek. Within a day or two, whispers of a Santa for the good kids had spread. Sinbad, who'd been in residence the Christmas before, pooh-poohed the Santa bit, but a surprising group of our more credulous students became hopeful that Santa would come.

Dav confronted me with it. "Mr. Stuart, the farm doesn't budget for lots of gifts at Christmas. I hope you aren't raising kids' expectations beyond reality."

"Billy's preacher has the women in his congregation hand-making gifts. Scarves and other knits. The men are making tops, wooden combs, and checker sets. I figured we could move the January reissue of clothing items up a week or two . . . you know, the belts and all. I also gave Mrs. Moxon a personal check for a few extras. She's getting yoyos, harmonicas, and such for the younger kids . . . and flashy 'do-rags' for the guys who bust their hair."

Dav nodded. "Good. Good! It sounds like it might work out."

"It will, I think. Mrs. Moxon and I have been working on a tree, paper ornaments, and popcorn strands. Those who want a Christmas will have projects."

"Good. Good. And what about Sinbad's group?"

"Could you talk to them, Mr. Davenport? It would be nice if they didn't ruin it for the others."

"I'll see what I can do. By the way, I hear the administration wants you to retrain. You OK?"

"Yes. I've been thinking about the future a lot, anyway. But off the record, I'm going to grad school in New Mexico this spring. Right now I am concerned about duty alone here at night. There isn't enough staff, and only one staff member is a bad joke."

"Seems folks on the Hill are intent on making some kind of point, doesn't it?"

"Yes. But I'm not sure what it is, unless they want to guarantee a screwup of some kind. Short-staffing during a holiday doesn't make sense. You warned me that it's an emotionally charged season."

Dav frowned. "I meant, 'I'll be sorry to see you go.'"

"Really? Thanks."

"Yep. Hang in there, Mr. Stuart. Time for you to head up to the Tower. It's intake night. They never stop coming, do they?"

chapter 26

Punish Me! Punish Me!

The next ten days went fast, disproving the adage "Time flies when you are having fun!" In my case that meant unhooking Rabbit from another carefully twisted sheet after some big-muscled new guy ardently rejected his "ooh-oohing" and "ah-aahing" on intake night. In this particular case, "ardent" translated into a quick but nasty beating.

Rabbit didn't complain about the pain but went morose at both the boy's rejection and his own swollen lips. "I look like Kamensky," he wailed. "I'm not pretty anymore!" Jill patched him up before we sent him back to Pitt for another shot at behavioral modification in the kid's psych unit.

Furious at me for having saved him then having lobbied to send him back to Pitt, Rabbit spit at me on the way out the door. I stepped back. "Quit trying to share body fluids with me, Rabbit . . . it's getting old."

Not getting the reaction he hoped for, he screamed hysterically. "*I* killed Country's cat, you old faggot! *I* hung the cat, you stupid faggot. Punish me! *Punish* me!" he shrieked. I blinked a couple of times then stepped forward, wanting desperately to do something like rip his ears off and make him eat them. As if he could read my mind, he quivered in defiant anticipation.

His red-rimmed eyes and drawn-back lips made him look like a pale albino rat. "Dammit, Rabbit, you've split your lip open again," chided

Jill, who rushed over, blocking my path, and applied another butterfly Band-Aid to slow the leak. By way of a thank you, Rabbit, in a very bad imitation of Béla Lugosi, sunk his teeth into Jill's forearm.

"You are a creep," growled Jill. "Even biting me won't make me punish you. You want that too badly. It's sick."

With that, Jill squeezed Rabbit's head in the crook of her free arm and applied pressure. Rabbit's eyes bulged oddly before he relaxed his jaw lock on Jill and begged her to quit squeezing.

The ambulance attendants strapped Rabbit to the gurney and wheeled him out while I cleansed Jill's bite wounds and administered the tetanus and penicillin shots. Palco, true to form, ragged us about the sexual possibilities from out in the hallway. "So you like them apples *big*, eh, Weasel? Well, big you got."

Jill, grim and tightlipped, pulled up her work blues, recovered her hip, walked over, and slapped Palco so hard that her finger impressions took four or five days to subside. I clapped.

"It's going to be a long month," Dav said, sighing.

]|[

Palco went into a somber, brooding mode after several days of the students' snickers over how Big Jill had jacked him up. A brooding Palco, it turned out, was also a singularly primitive Palco. Every time I saw him, it reminded me of the poster admonishing school kids not to be pouty "Lower Lippers" that had once graced the wall of my first-grade classroom at the Demonstration School on the campus of West Chester State Teacher's College. Obviously Palco's first-grade classroom had been disadvantaged—if he'd gone to school at all— for Palco was a classic Lower Lipper. On several occasions while Jill's handprint faded, other staff had to step in between a petulant Palco and an offending student.

Meanwhile, Jill readied for the holidays by spending more time up in the graveyard, wrapped in an old army-gray sleeping bag and reading to her "kids." I snuck up to take her a big thermos of hot soup on my shift break around 11:00 p.m. on Sunday, December 22.

The frost-covered ground and wet breeze made it the kind of night that could have sucked the heat out of an atomic reactor, but that didn't stop Jill.

"Oh, thank you, sweetie, I'm freezing."

"Why do you come up here on nights like this, Jill?"

"I don't know." She sighed. "Maybe it's because these kids have to love me back. They talk to me, you know."

"Your kids don't have to work at loving you back—you're lovable, Jill."

"I *am*?"

"Yep . . . these kids are lucky to have you . . . so are the rest of us. Do you ever go home . . . leave the farm?" She didn't answer, so I babbled, "I mean, it seems like you are always here."

"This *is* home, sweetie . . ." was all I got out of her.

"Well, I've got to get back to the Tower, Jill." I headed downhill, following the soft, jiggly flashlight path she lit for me until I was beyond her light's range.

]|[

It was supposed to be my last shift as a counselor—that is, it would have been if anyone on the Hill had stopped politicking long enough to process my paperwork. Come morning, when I clocked out, then in again, I was supposed to be in security work and docked 10¢ an hour. The thought of working for Palco would have been intolerable had it not been for the anticipation of moving to New Mexico and a spring semester far from the Morganza's institutional madness. That Palco was scheduled to be on leave for most of Christmas helped even more.

Standing in the Tower's window, for the benefit of the dorm below, I nodded to a cardboard Slim and evaluated my underreaction to Lawdawg's administrative punishment. *Am I beginning to mature?* I mused then answered my own question out loud. "Nah, it's not about maturity—it's because my resignation is buried somewhere in his two-foot-tall stack of mail."

Slim, of course, said nothing. In a good mood, I waved down at Davenport, who waved back and motioned me to make a phone call.

I called him right away. "What's up, Mr. Davenport?"

"These guys are restless. Is Slim going to make hot chocolate?" Dav's voice sounded tense.

"Wow! It's late for that, Mr. Davenport. Does this have anything to do with Sinbad and Golightly being down there with the Virgins?"

"Yes, Mr. Stuart. That would be correct." The Hill had insisted on Sinbad and Golightly as fill-ins for Intake Friday. Suicidal . . . so stupid as to reek of active, premeditated malevolence. Some of us suspected that Lawdawg's interim regime actually wanted to spark a riot, in order to justify an even more draconian crackdown.

"Got it. I'll call Palco and send him in."

I refocused on Dav while I dialed Palco. Dav was watching two new partners in crime who had just been remanded to us on the same armed robbery beef. Not good procedure—they should have been sent to separate cottages. If there were any more ways for the new regime on the Hill to screw up, neither Dav nor I could figure out what that might be.

Palco, to my surprise, picked up on the second ring. "That you, Weasel?"

"Yep. 'Slim' is making hot chocolate in five minutes. Get in there and spot Dav so I can sneak down."

"You and that damn piece of cardboard got one seriously fucked-up relationship. Why the hot choc so late?"

"Dav wants it during the Christmas season. Goodwill to our students and all that."

"OK. I'm going. And, Weasel . . ."

"What?"

"Make the chocolate thick. That watery crap you made last night was disgusting."

I watched Palco saunter into the dorm, moved Slim away from the window, and phoned Dav.

"Slim is on the way to the kitchen." Dav looked up and gave me a thumbs-up as his lips moved, making his announcement, which sounded oddly disembodied over the phone: "Mr. Stuart's in the Tower. Old Slim's going to make hot chocolate for you restless characters." I left the Tower and headed for the kitchen, which Curtis, Country, and Billy had set up for the winter season's hot chocolate.

Fifteen minutes later, the hot chocolate cart ready, I wheeled it out of the kitchen, bounded up the Tower stairs, slid low across its polished wooden floor, and put Slim back into the window. I crept downstairs again and pushed the cart to the dorm, knocked, and rolled it in.

"Where's Slim?" asked Dav with a wink.

"Not acting social tonight. Thought *I* should bring the cart in so he doesn't snap out and hurt somebody. He gets edgy at Christmas."

Palco rolled his eyes but didn't make any fatal wiseass comments. An on-duty Slim meant he could nap out in the hallway with impunity once Dav locked himself into the dorm after the hot chocolate break.

Five minutes later most of the kids were sipping hot chocolate and glancing warily at their companions. Dav, who watched the students as I passed out paper cups, had already decided which new one to extricate for the night. He was a genius at extricating the one who was "the pin in the grenade," as he put it. Finally, he pointed to the newest "pin."

"You . . . yes, you," he said, nodding toward a white weightlifter type who had not come forward for hot chocolate. "You are *here*." The student shrugged and glowered at Davenport, so Dav repeated, "*You*, Mr. Muscles . . . are here." He pointed to a spot in front of him. The guy, eighteen or nineteen and even bigger than Kamensky, shrugged again.

Palco stopped sipping and furtively slid one hand toward his key ring.

"I'm waiting," said Dav in the firm, hypnotic voice that nearly always got results. But not this time.

"I don't do nothing for scrawny ni . . . "

"Don't say it, man!" yelled Golightly, who was a fill-in. "You can't say *that* here." An angry murmur went through the group.

Someone on a cot in the back row backed up Golightly. "Yeah, man . . . that ain't cool." That's when Sinbad butted in, his voice smooth and oily. "No, man. Not cool at all. We done spent all summer and fall trying to get past this racial stuff, man. It's uncool . . . don't work for us here. Like Mr. Dav says, 'Everyone loses dignity.'"

Muscles, recognizing the tone of authority in Sinbad's voice, wrinkled his brow, apparently trying to reassess this unfamiliar group's dynamics. He recalibrated, as accomplished predators do. "Well, I just don't want to take crap off of 'nobody,' was all I was going to say." Someone snickered.

Dav ignored the derision. "Good. Don't dish out any and you won't get any. Now, over *here* . . . you and I need to go over some ground rules."

As I collected foam cups and got ready to push the cart out, I overheard Dav talking to Muscles near the doorway, out of the other students' earshot. "You are outnumbered here . . . this cottage is sixty-five percent black. Here, respect is *earned*. Got it?" As I pushed the cart past, pretending not to notice, Muscles nodded.

When Mr. Davenport came up to the Tower to give me my 2:00 a.m. break, he was upbeat. "Well, Mr. Stuart, did you ever think we'd hear Sinbad argue to lower racial strife?"

"Frankly, no, Mr. Davenport, but your persistence on this seems to be paying off."

"Well, it's almost Christmas . . . season of miracles," Dav said, smiling, as I headed downstairs to grab a coffee and eat one of Mrs. Moxon's sandwiches.

I chuckled to myself as I negotiated the stairs. *Dav's too optimistic— old Sinbad is on the cusp of nothing more than a "no methadone at White Hill" epiphany.* In retrospect, even that might have qualified as a miracle.

chapter 27

Sanna's White . . . It Gonna Open for You

The next morning Mr. Reddy and I clocked in as Dav clocked out. I was now security, I think, and Reddy was edgy. "Why are we getting all these new ones just before Christmas . . . and where the hell are we going to put them?"

Dav smiled as he punched his card. "Merry Christmas! See you on the twenty-sixth."

I ignored Reddy's bitching and instead asked, "So, how will my duties change?" Reddy brightened. "Well . . . a lot. You work today till our prisoners [Reddy had abandoned the "student" euphemism with alacrity] are gone to activities, then you clock out at nine a.m. Back at two forty-five, then work all night. Christmas Eve you are back at three p.m. sharp. No call-ins."

"Tough schedule," I commented dryly.

"Not for an eager college beaver like you." He smiled. I stared his gold tooth in the eyeballs and asked it for clarification. "Specific duties?"

"Uh, the usual, *plus* Palco's role. Keep the new ones locked up today till we get some of them placed in other cottages. We won't be able to close the dormitory—request of Allegheny County Juvenile Court—so at night, you will have to alternate watch between the main hall and the dormitory floor."

"OK, got it," I grumbled.

On the evening of December 23, Mrs. Moxon stayed late to help my crew of temporary elves set up the Christmas tree in the big TV room. At her urging, Sinbad and Golightly hung garlands of popcorn over the windows. Golightly's helpfulness was as out of character as Sinbad's, yet he wasn't facing a White Hall threat. *Well, maybe Christmas is the season of miracles*, I speculated, wondering just how Dav remained so hopeful and untainted by the Morganza's chaos, tensions, and turbulence.

After dinner and scheduled activities, my crew of three stayed out of their rooms again and helped to wrap the gifts, which would go under the tree the next day.

Billy and Curtis were as hyper as six-year-olds. "Is Santa going to *do* for me tomorrow?" asked Billy as he wrapped his own gift, a flashlight. Billy was as good at wrapping as he was in the paint shop. "Yep. Santa comes at midnight. Open the front door and walk out."

"How will I know when it's time?" Billy fretted.

Curtis, the brightest of the three, reassured him. "I can read the clock . . . can't I, Mr. Stuart? But if we go to bed at eleven we'll miss Sanna."

"I'll work on that." I smiled. "Seems like you should get a glimpse of him after all the work you've done."

For three nights I'd had them out till nearly midnight, assigning them to clean and decorate downstairs in preparation for Santa Claus. Country would stop and stare vacantly into some invisible place if I didn't keep him busy. Curtis obsessed on the front windows, asking several times, "Where do Sanna park his sleigh?"

"There." I pointed. "Down by the old stone bridge that crosses the creek . . . now back to work, little elves."

]|[

For many of the Morganza's residents, our Christmas, with music, gifts, church, carols, and a big dinner to follow, would be one of the more elaborate Christmases many had ever experienced. Kids whose parents are in prison rarely have lavish Christmas expectations.

Other students who did have happy holiday memories, everyone warned me, often tried desperately to break out, just to go home for a day or two till recaptured. Then there were those prized forty-eight-hour furloughs.

I had petitioned for five furloughs . . . all denied by Lawdawg, of course. Reddy petitioned two . . . both granted. Mrs. Moxon petitioned just one . . . a "Don't you dare turn this down" furlough for Rabbit, just in case he got dumped back on us Christmas Eve. With widespread staff pressure behind it, Rabbit's furlough was granted. Even I was glad . . . at least I wouldn't have to cut him down—or not—right in the middle of handing out presents to the others on Christmas morning.

On Sunday afternoon of Christmas Eve, most of our cottage's students went to the Winter Festival with Richard and Mrs. Moxon. Though not a single student on the farm was Jewish, nor, as best I knew, were any staff, Lawdawg's revisionist, old-fashioned disciplinary administration had insisted for some baroque reason that what had always been called the "Christmas Gala" now be referred to as "Winter Festival."

I didn't much care what they called it, but it certainly had eaten into staff time explaining the mysterious change of holiday from "Christmas" to "Festival"—especially to a bunch of agitated kids suffering from IQs trapped on the lower floors of Homo sapiens' allegedly towering capacity for complex thought.

"We'ze still gonna have Christmas after Festival, right, Mr. Stuart?" asked Country, worried that Santa had been sneakily hijacked. Once again wearing his granny's tattered bonnet adorned with an oversized red-velvet Christmas bow that flopped back and forth at each turn of his head, I didn't know how to take the question till Sinbad butted in.

"Yeah, they fuckin' with Christmas, man—that's jive!"

"I didn't hear *that* word, did I, *Roland*?" Mrs. Moxon protested.

"No, ma'am . . . no ma'am . . . just an ugly slip o' the lip." Mrs. Moxon grunted in response.

I answered the question. "The new administration has renamed the carol sing this afternoon to conform with urban Jewish tradition. Nothing else about Christmas has changed. Tree and treats tonight. Presents in the morning."

Sinbad nodded.

"OK," I said. "Sinbad, go help Richard and Mizz Moxon get the gents together for assembly."

"Aw, Mr. Stuart, why me?"

"Atonement for the slip o' the lip."

"Aw, Mr. Stuart, you *hard*."

Mrs. Moxon smiled. "Appropriate. Consider it a graciously accepted apology, Roland."

"Yes, ma'am," grumbled Sinbad, who looked around again to make certain no one had heard his given name before shouting into the TV room for Sugarbear, "Bear . . . you gather up the misfits."

"Never delegate an apology, Sinbad!" I interrupted. He shrugged unremorsefully and pimp-strutted slowly toward the TV room.

As soon as the "misfits" were out of the cottage, I went to the security desk and got to work. Since my furloughs had all been denied, the pissed-off, in-your-face part of me had decided to issue my own. I commandeered the old L.C. Smith typewriter to execute three furloughs on official letterhead that Englan, our increasingly bewildered but increasingly useful college boy, had "requisitioned" from Lawdawg's office.

While working his pet "I'll bring your coffee, sir" student assignment up in the interim director's office suite, Englan had access to many critical assets. He had proven thorough. As I had requested, he also quietly "borrowed" one of Lawdawg's engraved signature fonts to accompany the letterhead. In return, he'd been the subject of one of my five rejected Christmas furloughs.

I typed out three furloughs, carefully matching the wording of the one in Lester/Rabbit's folder . . . one each for Curtis, Country, and Billy. I dipped Lawdawg's font into a capful of poured ink and hand-stamped each letter. I held Billy's up to inspect it. *Good. That'll teach the grandiose bastard to have a font made because he thinks he's too important to sign his own internal memos.*

Done with the furloughs, I turned to writing up the dailies then checked on the evening meal with the farm's central kitchen. Unbelievably, the Christmas Eve menu consisted of grits with gravy, mystery meatloaf, white bread, canned green beans, and "Winter Festival" Jell-O.

"How festive of Lawdawg," I commented to Country, who stared at me, silent. He had refused to go to assembly after students from the farm's other cottages hooted at him out on the main walk. I tried, unsuccessfully, to explain that it was likely the floppy, foot-wide red bow pinned on his granny's bonnet. He pouted.

Poor Country. Still shattered over Mizz Small, he'd been too distracted to process much of anything except the hideous spectacle of his dead cat, swollen to the size of a soccer ball—not Mizz Small anymore. I don't think he even remembered or understood Davenport when Dav told the two of us a week earlier that he'd finally found and personally spoken with Revered Forsythe in Georgia. "Who dat?" Country had "axed."

In fact, the news was good: Country's two sisters near Egypt, Georgia, which I couldn't find on a map, wanted him to come home. The Reverend himself would act as Country's legal guardian since, according to Reverend Forsythe, neither sister was "sophisticated enough" to handle "custodial procedures" with Social Services in Statesboro, the nearest large town.

"All we need to do is get him there," lamented Dav, who began to despair of a solution for Country the moment Lawdawg took over the Morganza. I wanted to say something to Dav about the possibility of a "Santa alternative plan," but I was outbound to New Mexico—read: "flight to avoid prosecution." Dav, meanwhile, was a case of "You are *here*" and needed the job. Making him into a codefendant, I decided, wasn't the type of Christmas miracle he hoped for.

And Christmas couldn't come too soon: Poor Country was, at most, one more blow to the psyche away from losing it altogether. One more emotional thump and he might wind up catatonic and doing life in some psych ward for the criminally insane. Fortunately, there was a chance, even if a long shot, that "Sanna" would come and deliver Country to his family, when "he" collected Billy for a newfound one.

]|[

The students came back from assembly all jazzed up and, many of them, full of the Christmas spirit. Thus, most seemed not to notice the gratuitously awful, if not condescending, Christmas Eve food—few ate grits and gravy in urban southwestern Pennsylvania. In fact, we were in the very epicenter of the world's best home-fried potatoes, usually slathered with Heinz ketchup, or vinegar for the old-fashioned.

It was Richard who, with awe, first commented at the menu. "What is this white stuff with the brown slime on it?"

I laughed and answered, "Yesiree . . . western Pennsylvania . . . land of cultural mysteries. Grits and canned gravy for Christmas Eve."

Englan, who had come to us as a harmless middle-class idealist but had begun to identify with the kids around him, piped up. "He thinks it's the Wild West out here. He's from some suburb on the Main Line near Philadelphia."

"Who is *he?*" asked Richard.

"The interim director. He thinks it's uncivilized here."

In response, Sinbad laughed. "He right. And where you from, you know so much?" Englan, apparently stressed by Sinbad's direct inquiry, offered, in place of personal information, a neat summary:

"Driven largely by the attitude of its Philadelphia-centric elites, Pennsylvania has never quite processed anything west of the Allegheny Mountains as more than raw, squirrel-eating, log-cabin-living, untamed frontier."

Sinbad gaped. "Log cabins? We got no cribs like that anymore! You crazy like Kamensky?"

I intervened. "Ease up, Sinbad. He's reporting what he hears." Sinbad rolled his eyes but shut up. Englan seized the moment and disappeared.

In fact, it simply didn't register east of Harrisburg that Pittsburgh had generated KDKA, the nation's first public radio station; was the only other real pre-World War stronghold of opera outside of New York; had made the United States a world power in steel, oil, and manufacturing technology; and had played remarkable roles in theatre, jazz, baseball, and public education.

I considered this attitude warped, if for no other reason than, by the summer of '67, Philadelphia was nothing more than a worn-out shell of its eighteenth- and nineteenth-century glory. Arguably it was the first of America's colonial cities to suffer what would later commonly be called "The Rust Belt" but that I came to think of as "The Beirut" syndrome—a partially burned-out, desolate, free-fire zone contested by competing religious and ethnic factions.

But grits for Christmas Eve? *The problem with Philly,* I concluded, *is that, unlike Rome, most of its upper class has survived the decline.*

}|(

After dinner we lit the Christmas tree in the TV room and drank hot chocolate with marshmallows while Richard read the Christmas story from the Bible. When he finished I played a disc of jazzed-up Christmas standards on my portable, then Richard and I took the guys up to bed. "Happy Christmas Eve, fellas!" I hollered as Richard, scheduled to leave at eleven, took my customary hallway watch up on 2.

I escorted Country, Curtis, and Billy downstairs about 10:15. Billy and Curtis wore big green elf hats, Country his outlandish bonnet and floppy red bow.

"Why does they get to help?" bitched Kamensky as we passed his room on our way to the stairwell. "'Cause they can't read," I yelled back. "Santa's helpers can't be squeezed for gift secrets at breakfast in the morning."

"Man! That ain't fair!" whined Kamenksy. "I can't read, neither!"

"Yeah, right . . . just like you're not white," I commented. Widespread snickering shut Kamensky up. He was already pouting and busily repuffing his raw lip meat when we went downstairs and I unlocked the linen closet's holiday treasures. Richard, as cordial as ever, commented, "I'll be at my Ontie's tomorrow . . . I'm dressing up as Santa, so I've got to go soon. I'm sorry."

"It's OK, Richard. I'm grateful for the extra hour tonight. When you leave I'll have to shuttle back and forth between the dorm and upstairs. It's only a hundred feet. It'll work out, I think."

"It's crazy, David." Richard nodded toward my crew of elves. "Will you be all right here alone?"

"I'm not quite alone. Jill and ol' Street from custodial are in the dorm. The courts have reduced sessions for the holidays, so we've only got eight newish ones in there tonight. When Jill goes at eleven thirty, I'll start shuttling." I locked the rear door behind Richard when he punched out just after eleven.

Judging from Curtis's hollering, my elves had quickly lost focus. "Mr. Stuart, I can't 'member whose package this are!"

"*Is*, Curtis . . . the package *is*. I'm coming; I had to lock up after Mr. Richard."

My poor elves were seriously stressed out—unable to read and frustrated at how long it took them to do anything organized, they were in a "We'll miss Santa!" driven panic over work efficiency issues. "Here . . . I'll read the tags . . . you place 'em with the number tag I hand you." They relaxed.

Everyone's brown-bag package was number-keyed . . . orders from the high command on the Hill. "Numbered lists with a precise, and concise, description of each gift will be submitted to the interim director's office by noon, 26 December, 1967," the memo had read. One thing about bureaucratic control freaks seemed consistent—they could never sort the important from the trivial.

In contrast, there were no instructions to open and check wrapped gifts arriving from outside the farm. We opened the few that arrived anyway and repackaged them, just in case they contained sweet little Christmas-season "I love yous" like saws, bolt cutters, knives, a pistol, or drugs. Fortunately, we found no contraband except for one rather flamboyant photo-booth, self-portrait crotch shot sent by one of Golightly's off-campus female admirers.

It took the four of us till 11:30 to arrange all the gifts and set up the hot chocolate cart for midmorning festivities.

At 11:35, nervous about the unauthorized furloughs I was about to award my elves, I clumsily divided one of Mrs. Moxon's cheese sandwiches between the four of us and signed out three Hershey bars. Perhaps it was because I was leaving soon, but my signature on the "Candy Sign Out Sheet" suddenly looked ridiculous. The Commonwealth might not know the name of every kid buried up on the hill behind Willow, but it certainly had a detailed record of where every damned fifteen-cent candy bar went.

Pissed off and reflecting on the Commonwealth's exquisite concern for candy bars and "soiled" sheets, I jumped when the phone rang unexpectedly. I picked up, assuming it was an emergency somewhere on the farm. Instead I heard Angela's soft voice. "Merry Christmas, David!"

I freaked. "Jesus, Angela . . . what's happened?"

She sighed. "I'm sorry, really sorry . . . don't hate me. *Please* . . . it's all so confusing." My elves stared at me for a moment then went back to smearing chocolate on themselves.

I took a deep breath, turned my back on my helpers, and whispered, "Damn, Angela . . . I can't really talk now. I've got a dilemma here."

"OK. I was hoping you'd tell me you don't hate me."

I took another breath. "I don't hate you, but I've been angry. It seems like when I do the right thing, I pay for it."

"Please don't believe that. It's what I like most about you!"

"*Really?*"

"Yes. Don't stop now . . . just because of me."

"OK. Gotta go. I've missed you, Ange. Merry Christmas."

Angela's unexpected validation was the tipping point. I left my crew at the staff's dining table, unlocked the front door, and stepped out. To my amazement, a pair of headlights flashed nearby. An instant rush of adrenaline blasted me into action. I closed the door, rushed to grab the elves' Christmas bags from under the tree, and set them in a neat row by the front door, then stepped back into the dining hall where the boys were staring at me, waiting for instructions.

"OK, guys, I saw a light, or lantern, flash outside near the bridge when I passed the front door; I think it might be Santa. Go get your coats, gloves, and rubber boots." Each grocery bag contained food, cash, candy bars, a change of clothes, and copies of the fake furloughs, just as I'd promised "Santa."

Billy went ape. "Do you really think it's Sanna?"

"I'm not positive. He doesn't reveal himself to adults, you know. Come on! It's almost midnight."

In his excitement, Billy tripped over his boots as he tried to lace them. Country paced and threw his hands in the air. "Billy, don' you be slow, Ah wants to see him."

At three minutes to midnight I waved them toward the front door and said a quick good-bye. Country panicked. "Ain't you come with us?"

"No! Santa will go away if I come out." They gaped at me, looking confused, so I told them, "You'll need those grocery bags," then headed upstairs to check on the other students. Halfway up the stairs I heard the three boys deep in their version of a philosophical conversation.

Curtis was blowing a gasket. "No! *You* touch it first, Billy. You *white* . . . Sanna's white . . . it gonna open for you . . ."

Curtis pleaded, "Just reach out for it, Billy! Quick! I'm comin' out wit' you if it open. I swear it on the Holy Bible!"

I started to panic, not knowing how long "Santa" would wait for them. I didn't dare shout to them from the second floor stairwell, where I imagined every snitch on 2 holding his breath, one ear cupped against his door, to hear what I was saying, so I froze and waited. Just when I was convinced I needed to go back and push the elves out, I heard a click, followed by a cacophony of what I hoped was the sound of rubber boots squeaking across concrete. With no idea of what might happen next, I prayed silently that my elves stayed out of the headlines.

Nervous that they'd either get lost or, worse, that I'd wind up on trial for aiding and abetting, I rushed upstairs to check on Floor 2. My portable turntable had run through its LP and it was still much too quiet up there, so I hastily stacked two Coltranes, restarted it, and turned up the volume before I checked door-to-door.

As best I could tell, no one was either being murdered or abused on 2, and only a couple of newer kids were crying about being locked up for Christmas. So, after reassuring them, I forced myself to sit in the armchair at the end of the hallway. I took deep breaths to calm down, then opened Emil Haury's *The Stratigraphy and Archaeology of Ventana Cave, Arizona*. But trying to act normal didn't ease my curiosity about what might have happened downstairs.

Less than thirty minutes later I could no longer function, much less maintain the "everything's cool here" facade, so I eased out of the chair, slipped downstairs, and went to the front door. I feared that the three of them might still be standing out on the front steps, confused and whimpering like six-week-old puppies, so I swung the door open and stepped out.

The scene was silent and peaceful. All I saw was a light dusting of fresh snow, fading rubber boot tracks headed toward Chartiers Creek, and the pale headlights of a lone vehicle out on Morganza Road.

chapter 28

We Lost Four?

I reclosed the door without locking it, lit a Pall Mall, and took a couple of deep drags to relax. By the time I stepped into the dorm at the far end of the downstairs hallway, Jill had already gone back to the women's unit and Street was alone, crouched nervously near the dorm's outer door.

"You OK?" I asked him. I don't know why I asked—the useless wimp would never be OK.

"It was super quiet a half hour ago when Mizz Dicks left, but now they are noisy." He nodded toward the row of cots. "Like they are *planning* something."

"Actually, it sounds pretty normal in here . . . confined kids make noise. More importantly, bored or apprehensive ones make noise. Normally, you've got a midlevel background buzz at all times. Noise is one of the few dimensions of their lives they can control. Raging noise, of course, is big trouble—usually anger that's about to explode. Absolute silence is also ominous. Don't wish for either."

"Thanks for telling me. You got it here, then?"

"Yeah, I'm good till four a.m. Then I'll need five minutes. That work?"

"Sure."

I nodded at the cardboard figure on duty in the window above us as the nearest students tuned in to our conversation. "Tell Slim 'hello' up there . . . but don't try to make small talk . . . there's something seriously wrong with that guy."

Street frowned and his voice went up in pitch. "Really? Maybe I should stay down here."

"OK, then I'll go up there." I smiled.

His frown twisted into an expression I'd never seen him make before. Tortured.

"Uh, on second thought, if I don't have to talk to him, I'll go."

I took a seat in Palco's usual desk, slumped down, and watched Street retreat. Palco's school desk seemed oddly comfortable and familiar till my memory banks fired up. *This is exactly the way I spent most of high school in Morgantown.* I chuckled, remembering my front-row sprawl in sweet Mrs. Herrera's French class. With Street gone, I went back to wondering how the elves were making out. To soothe my elf anxiety, I began to breathe deep and hum to myself, "Silent night . . . holy night . . . all is calm . . . all is bright . . ."

The security phone rang unexpectedly. I panicked and jumped to grab it, certain it would be perimeter security asking what to do with three loose guys wearing weird hats and claiming I'd let them out to visit Santa.

"Stuart speaking."

"Hey! What's going on?" a jittery Street howled into the phone. "You guys fucking with my head? . . . It's *not* funny! This guy up here isn't real . . . he's a piece of fuckin' cardboard!"

I laughed, relieved. "Yes. Slim is a bit stiff with strangers," I answered as the students near me pretended not to listen. "Did he jump you? . . . No? Then everything is normal. Relax . . ." Street was still flipping out when I hung up on him—he had to be the only staffer on the entire farm who was unaware of Slim's true identity.

An hour later Big Jill knocked on the dorm's corridor door. I let her in and she immediately engulfed me in a bear hug.

"You OK?" I wheezed from under her grip.

"I am so happy! I just wanted to wish you a Merry Christmas, sweetie! Thank you for bringing Santa tonight."

"Uhh . . . is that unexpected on Christmas?"

"I was up in the graveyard singing carols with *my* kids when *yours* left."

"Am I busted?" I asked as a frightening sensation in my legs made me look down, wondering how every drop of blood had managed instantly to escape my upper body and balloon my calves out into painfully gorged sausages. I went lightheaded. My pain-in-the-ass inner self was suffering from serious turmoil. *Well, here's one witness they can depose.* I began to stutter. "D-d-do you, uh . . ."

"Shh!" She giggled. "Don't faint! And don't say anything. It's what I wished for when I was twelve . . . and locked up here."

"Huh? You?"

She nodded yes, released me, blew me a kiss, then let herself out, cheerfully whistling the tune to "Here Comes Santa Claus."

]|[

By Christmas morning when I dutifully clocked out, took a break, then clocked in again, I'd smoked an entire pack of cigarettes and had an unanticipated psychic conversation with my old man. It was his first visitation since he'd died, and the opening line was familiar. "Well, my son, just how do you intend to explain *this* behavior?"

"Um, actually, I don't think it is explainable. I just thought it was the right thing to do."

He stared back. His cold, gray-green eyes slowly burned into my guilty conscience. When I looked down to inspect the damage, a wisp of smoke curled up from one of the charred bull's-eyes in my shirt. The scent of burnt wool was so real I panicked. The old man laughed and disappeared before I realized that the cigarette dangling from my mouth had been dropping ashes onto my sweater as I sat there transfixed by my dad's creepy visit.

According to the morning census and security check, we'd lost *four*, not three, students—one new one from the dorm had escaped along with my elves, probably about the time Street let Jill out. The perimeter boys also discovered that our cottage's front door wasn't security locked. I wasn't all that surprised. On the upside, the old man wasn't there to laugh when they told me two students from other cottages had also vanished between the "Winter Festival" gala and Christmas morning. Thus, I was personally responsible for just half of the night's statistical damage. Just why that pleased me, I'm not sure. No one else seemed thrilled.

Mrs. Moxon, Richard, and Father Ralph nervously speculated on the interim director's likely reaction as they passed out gifts to the students. I answered questions and filled out incident reports for security.

"Who was on duty?" asked the chief of perimeter.

I answered, "After eleven p.m. when Richard left, it was me, the temp, Street, from custodial, and ol' Slim."

"That's it? No one else?"

I shook my head. The perimeter chief gaped. "You're still a *trainee*. No one more *senior*?"

"Nope. It's a wonder we didn't lose more," I responded, sounding as innocent as possible. "And I'm not sure about the status of three of the four we lost . . . I thought Christmas furloughs were in process. I thought they'd be going home today, anyway. Do you guys in perimeter know?"

"No! No one tells us crap anymore."

Predictably, administrative confusion reigned the next day. One of Lawdawg's assistants had found the stack of font-stamped furloughs that I had slipped into a huge pile of master files when I turned in the required gift lists during my quick Christmas morning break.

Lawdawg stormed through the door of Cottage 6. "Look at these!" He shook, waving the furloughs wildly in my face. "I didn't sign these!"

I shrugged. "Don't you think we should look for the boys, anyway . . . to make sure they are OK?"

"You are due in my office Friday at ten a.m.!"

"That's a problem, sir. I won't be here. I resigned last month. Thursday is my last shift."

"*What*? We don't have a resignation on file!" he yelled.

"I gave it to the director weeks ago. Didn't she tell you?" I fudged. He turned bright red and stalked off. Actually, I had given it to Patricia, who promised to slip it into the director's stack of "deferred" mail, but so what.

Dav showed up and clocked in around 2:45 p.m. "How was Christmas here?" he asked.

"Complicated. The farm lost six . . . I lost four of those. The interim director went ballistic a while ago."

"That's no surprise. Who did we lose?" Dav frowned.

"Country, Curtis, Billy—they were on a Christmas decoration detail for me—and one new kid from the dorm. I have a copy of the report for you." I braced for a tongue-lashing when Dav shook his head and scrunched his face in disapproval. Then he studied my face carefully.

"I hoped it would go more smoothly, in spite of the short staffing," was all he said.

"I should have had a handle on it. But at least those three won't go out there and hurt anyone."

"You sure about the new one, too?" Dav asked.

"No, sir." I shrugged and turned away, only to run smack into a gloating Reddy who'd been eavesdropping from about three feet behind me. When I turned he was so close I actually stepped on one of his mirror-polished burgundy wingtips.

Irritated, he and his gold tooth stared down at the damage. "Convenient that you are leaving Thursday, isn't it, Stuart?"

"That depends on one's perspective, Mr. Reddy. I turned in my resignation just a day or two before Her Majesty went on vacation. It was for the end of next week, but I'm already at the limit for comp time. Besides, if I'd known then that I'd be doing something as crazy as working the cottage on Christmas Eve with no one but old Street, I'd have resigned as of last Saturday and had myself a real Christmas." Reddy's gold tooth promptly vanished. Reddy followed.

Mr. Davenport chuckled. "Thursday, huh?"

I nodded.

"He really loathes you, you know."

"That's fair . . . sorry about losing those kids."

Dav sighed. "No, you're not."

"OK, I'm not heartbroken, but I am *worried* about them. I can't sleep." Dav lay his hand gently on my shoulder. "Now *that* I believe. Any idea on where any of them might be?"

"No. And it *is* my fault. I stepped out front to smoke and must have forgotten to lock the door. Once they were gone I half expected that it would be Curtis who was together enough to come back or find his way home . . . his mom seemed so solid."

"Mind if someone calls her?"

A jolt of panic shot through my belly. "No. But what if he's there? Won't she get busted for harboring?"

"Not if she had the good sense to get on a bus and take him straight to Alabama," Dav said enigmatically as he reached for Curtis's file.

I tensed again, not sure what Dav was thinking. "Ah . . . well, I can see that you don't need me here right now, Mr. Davenport. I'm going to take a smoke break before I clock out and in. It's going to be a long night." I retreated as Dav reached for the phone.

chapter 29

It's an Inside Joke

On my last shift, Reddy didn't speak. By way of good-bye, he pointed down to a freshly repolished wingtip and mouthed, "You owe me three bucks." I pulled three ones out of my wallet and slowly placed them on his desk. Richard was off till Friday evening, and Mrs. Moxon had taken two days off. I hadn't slept well, wondering where the boys were.

About 2:30 p.m., Reddy announced that he had business up on the Hill and left. I cleared out my locker and carried a box of my personal effects out to the old Rambler. Sinbad and Kamensky watched me. Back inside, they confronted me. "You leavin', Mr. Stuart?"

"Yep. I go at three today."

"Can Slim make us hot chocolate one last time?" asked Sinbad.

"Slim's not here," I commented.

"Never was, was he?" Sinbad grinned.

I shrugged in response.

"It don't matter about Slim, but you never told us what happened to the whale."

"The captain and the whale destroy each other . . . trapped by their own rage."

"No happy ending, huh?"

"No, but instructive."

Sinbad chuckled. "So you done *instructing* us?"

I nodded.

"Well, the boys want you to come and say good-bye."

"Yeah, right."

"Yeah, come on . . . it ain't no trick."

We stepped into the TV room, where Sugarbear, of all people, stood to speak for the group. "Thanks for reading to us, playing ol' Miles, and doing . . . uh, stuff for us." Sinbad poked Sugarbear. "And, uh, what can we do for you, Mr. Stuart?"

"You all can stay out of White Hill. That's what you can do."

]|[

Just before three I heard Mr. Davenport arrive to clock in. When he peered over my shoulder to see what I was doing, I handed him a small package. "What's this?"

"Something from our house for your house . . . a memento of life behind the Cotton Curtain. My mom picked it for you."

"She knows who I am?"

"Yep. It's been an honor, a genuine honor, Mr. Davenport."

Dav reached out and squeezed my shoulder. "It's mutual . . . *earned* . . . in case you are wondering."

We shook hands before I clocked out; when I opened the back hallway door to leave, Dav hollered, "By the way, it's time for you to get some sleep!"

"*Really*? You heard from . . ."

"Oh, yes. *Good* sleep."

"Thank you, Mr. Davenport. And Happy New Year!"

I heard Reddy ask, "What's that all about?"

"An inside joke." Dav laughed. I pulled the door shut behind me.

On the way past the administration building, I stopped the Rambler to stare up at those rampant horses one last time. I decided that, even if the rest of the motto seemed too cynical for the Morganza, the hope of "Independence" might still mean something, and I intended to find out.

]|[

Back at the eagle's nest in Little Washington, I packed the car, spun Coltrane on my portable, and got my first six hours of decent rack time since Christmas. At 4:45 a.m. I shook myself awake and stepped up onto my old man's footlocker to take one final piss in the sink before carrying his trunk down to my Rambler.

Mom cried when I pulled out of our driveway in Morgantown later that morning. The last thing she sobbed when I hugged her good-bye was, "Oh, David, please don't forget me!" So like her—and so like America: unmoved by the inevitable, the real, and the probable—but terrified of the impossible.

The Hill.

Epilogue

Sunday, July 29, 2007, The Morganza

Forty years and twenty-odd days have passed since I worked my first shift here at the Morganza farm, and it is still hot and humid. Most of its lands have been transformed into a golf course and business park called Southpointe. Fancy buildings sprout up indifferently from nearby hillsides where the farm's child wards once lived . . . and died.

These new buildings, I suspect, will fall down long before the old brick administration building above me yields to the ravages of time. When I arrived a few hours ago, a bit disoriented, I had asked the whereabouts of the old main building at the new Marriot on a steep hill overlooking the Morganza's narrow valley. "We've never heard of such a place" and a shrug brush-off was the response. Odd, since *The Silence of the Lambs* was filmed in front of the building in '91. Odd also since Southpointe's formal transfer agreement with the Commonwealth of Pennsylvania stipulates that the administration building and the farm's cemetery be preserved. In fact, the main building was to be renovated into a community center.

As I stare at it, it doesn't look renovated. Unless, of course, one considers "renovation" to consist of bulldozing piles of raw dirt to close the Hill's curving yellow-brick carriageway, then filling every window with plywood painted an ominous flat black.

The Hill's copper spire.

I step closer to inspect the building's black-iron entryway, which still shouts, "Virtue, Liberty, and Independence" from its incongruously gilded and crested doorway. Perhaps they really meant it when it was painted there in the late nineteenth century. But now, how the hell does "Virtue, Liberty, and Independence" become transformed into a golf course?

I climb the hill and move through the oaks, the Morganza's imposing, copper-clad art deco spire shimmering, mirage-like, in late July's suffocating afternoon heat. Broken glass crackles underfoot as I cross the wide veranda where the farm's administrators once took mint tea served by their wards.

One of the plywood panels, its edge splintered, has been pried back to create an unauthorized entry point. I lean in toward the gap, hoping for a glance at the Belle Age Reception Hall—once furnished with elaborate antiques, some of them made right in the farm's industrial arts complex, now roofless and sitting in the center of an overgrown field about two hundred yards to the northwest.

As I lean past the plywood, a sudden blast of icy air swirls past me.

Not possible, I tell myself. *We are in the middle of one of the hottest summers on record—it should be cooking inside there. Maybe I'm imagining this.* So I ask my wife Cynthia to come over and check it out.

She sticks her head in near the gap. "I'm not going in. It's spooky. Where is the cold air coming from?" I remember Country's duppies as we step away and circle the building to get a view of the rear. Some of the former cottages have been leveled. While she takes photos, I sit in the shade of an oak grove, trying to remember which path—now overgrown—leads up to the graveyard.

A covey of birds rises suddenly from the tangle of bushes along one wall next to us. That—and the heat—get us moving back toward the front of the building, where we run unexpectedly into another couple. They are even more startled. Wary, the dark-haired young man rubs his arm nervously. "Hello! Do you know this place?" I nod. He goes on, as if we are owed an explanation for their presence. "The hair is standing up all over me. We moved to Canonsburg a year ago and have come out here several times . . . but no one will tell us anything about this place."

I answer, "I worked here as a kid. First job out of college . . . not a happy place."

"It's got a Gothic feel about it."

I pause. "Yes. It always seemed out of place with its surroundings."

"Do you come here often?" he asks.

"No, first time in forty years. I've been thinking about writing a book on it. It was a reform school in my time—the Morganza." I begin to tell them about the kids once sequestered there and the place's taint of anguish. As I talk, a brisk, cold wind suddenly rises. The leaves in the oaks above us rattle as the icy air swirls around us. Yet ten yards away the trees are eerily still.

"My god!" says the young man. "Where did the cold air come from? The hair is standing up on my arms again. We've stirred up something here."

"A number of kids died here. There is a graveyard up on the hill," I comment, just as a Canonsburg police wagon cruises past, circles the building slowly, and disappears down an unused orchard lane.

Unnerved by the police van, we trade business cards with the other couple and move back toward the cars, which are parked below in an abandoned cul-de-sac. My wife and I watch the other couple leave, heading back toward the golf course. Now that I've found the "Hill,"

I know my way around here and take a lane to the south, which runs down to the old arched stone bridge over Chartiers Creek, where Santa once picked up my three elves.

There, positioned next to the only exit from the farm an insider would use, sits the police wagon. The young cop inside sports a skin-head shave job and totally blacked-out glasses. The glasses and black electrician's tape covering his unit's number make it obvious he prefers anonymity.

His head turns slowly, cocked to one side, following us as we cross the old bridge and head uphill toward the interstate.

Every Gothic mystery seems to have its guardian centurion, I reflect, resisting a powerful impulse to turn my head and stare him down.

)|(

August 12, 2007, Albuquerque, New Mexico

Cruising the Internet, I find a brief webpage about the Morganza created by Norman J. Meinert of Allegheny County, Pennsylvania, in 2005. In it he cites a pamphlet titled "The Cemetery on the Hill at Morganza" by E. Irene Taylor and Dorothy Parry, who documented the existence of the graveyard after the Western Mental Hospital, which succeeded the Morganza, was closed altogether in 2000. I've never seen the pamphlet, but according to the authors cited there are now no remaining grave markers for Ella Douglass and Emma Ginton, who both died on November 2, 1897, ages eighteen and nineteen.

I still want to know what happened to them . . . and to the others. A suspicious number of girls aged fifteen to nineteen died between 1895 and 1902. Of the fifteen deaths for which there are ages at death, all either died at age thirteen or fourteen, or age eighteen or nineteen. Why no sixteen- or seventeen-year-olds? And why so many internments listed only as "No dates" or "Age unknown"? And why the later concrete crosses, erected without any identification?

As I read Mr. Meinert's webpage, every detail of the two-week-old scene and emotions of our last moments on the Morganza come back vividly. . . .

I glance at the cop as we cross Chartiers Creek, explaining to my wife,

"Not knowing what eventually happened to the Morganza's children—or to Billy, Curtis, and Country—still eats at me."

Like the Morganza itself, the fate of these children, the unexpected cop with taped-over ID, and the Hill's current state of desolation all imply that remembering, much less asking questions, is, as it was then, forbidden.

As we pass, my wife steals another look at the skinhead cop in his patrol wagon. "My god, this is creepy. They still don't want anyone around here, do they?"

—David E. Stuart
Flying Star Café
Central Avenue / Route 66
Albuquerque, NM